I0810138

IMAGES
of America

GRAND MARAIS

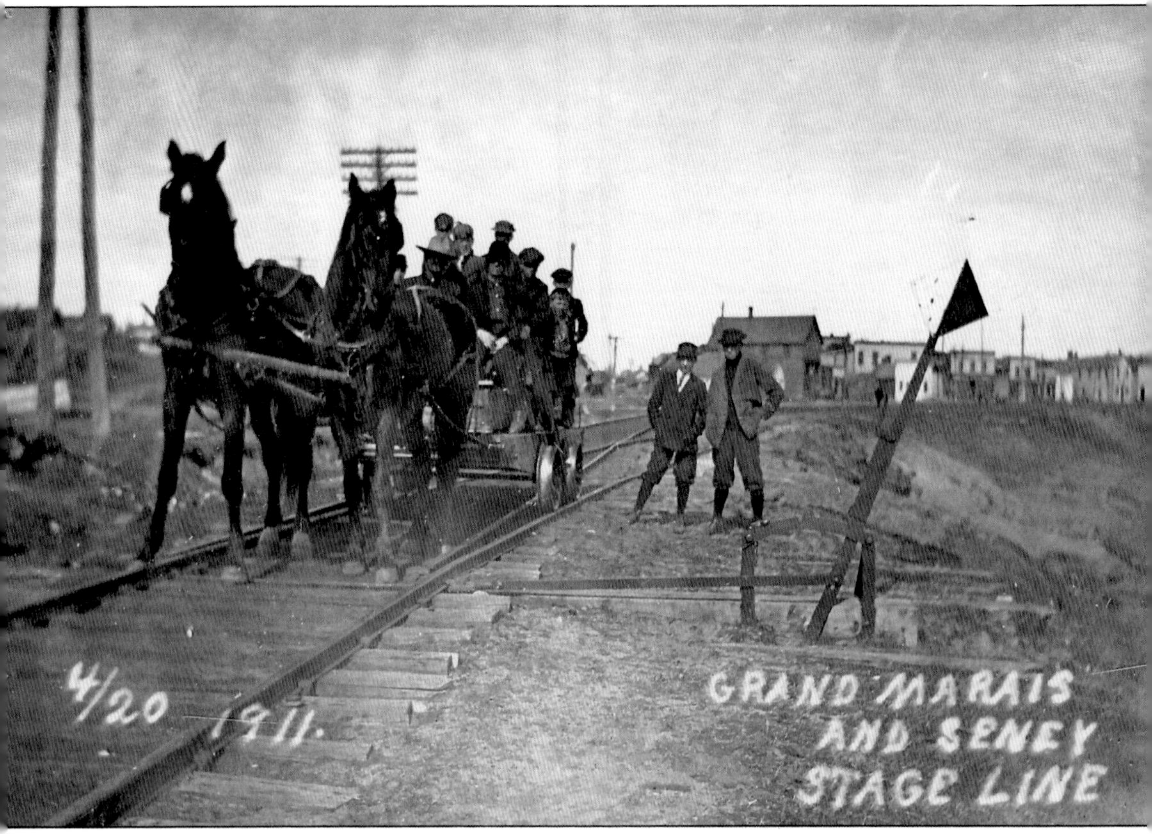

This 1911 photograph shows the rail stage leaving Grand Marais for the 32-mile trip over the rails to Seney, the nearest town. Taken after the Manistique Railway ceased operations but before the tracks were pulled up, the hand-built rail cart is a prime example of the ingenuity, resourcefulness, and cheerful determination that characterizes life in this remote northern village. Through boom times and lean years, Grand Marais survives. (Doris Krempa.)

On the cover: A lumber-loading crew poses for a photograph at the Marais Lumber Company loading docks around 1900. Finns, Swedes, French Canadians, and many others were drawn to Grand Marais during the boom years of 1893 to 1910. Names such as Abrahamson, Aho, Human, Kangas, Maki, Nyman, Olli, and Ylimaki attest to the men's various nationalities. Many of them chose to stay and live out their lives in Grand Marais. (Grand Marais Historical Society.)

IMAGES
of America

GRAND MARAIS

Grand Marais Historical Society

ARCADIA
PUBLISHING

ISBN 978-0-7385-6066-3

Published by Arcadia Publishing
Charleston, South Carolina

Printed in the United States of America

Library of Congress Control Number: 2008942606

For all general information contact Arcadia Publishing at:
Telephone 843-853-2070
Fax 843-853-0044
E-mail sales@arcadiapublishing.com
For customer service and orders:
Toll-Free 1-888-313-2665

Visit us on the Internet at www.arcadiapublishing.com

To all those who know and love Grand Marais
and to those who have yet to discover it

Contents

ACKNOWLEDGMENTS

This book would not have been possible without the support and encouragement of the many people who wish to see Grand Marais history preserved. The Grand Marais Historical Society offers special thanks to the following people for sharing their photographs and memories of Grand Marais: Louis Bailey, Isabelle Capogrossa, James Carter, Bryce Christoffersen, Charles Conn, Bruce Erickson, Mary Handrich, Mary Heacox, Patti Hughes, Doris Krempa, Bill LaCombe, Della Meldrum, Terry Pepper, Jack Peterman, Tom and Kathy Petitpren, Jana Robertson, Sheri Shafer, Brother Joel Soldenski, Marge Soldenski, Ted Soldenski, Argie Thorrington, David Tinder, Al Tornovish, Tudy Tornovish, Wilma Smith, and Evelyn Wood. We truly cannot thank you enough.

We also wish to express our deep appreciation to the following people and organizations for helping us in our search: Gregg Bruff, Pictured Rocks National Lakeshore; Mary Capogrossa, *Great Lakes Pilot and Pictured Rocks Review*; Mark Harvey and Julie Meyerle, Archives of Michigan; Laura Jacobs, University of Wisconsin–Superior; Rosemary Michelin, Marquette County History Museum; the National Archives; Victoria Petruske, Peoples State Bank; Sandy Schwan and Jeff Cottrell, Historical Society of Saginaw County; John Williams, Sucker River Club; and our history sisters at the Alger County Historical Society. You helped us gather scattered pieces of our history for everyone to enjoy.

All images in this book are used with permission and appear courtesy of the Alger County Historical Society (ACHS), the Grand Marais Historical Society (GMHS), the Historical Society of Saginaw County (HSSC), the Marquette County History Museum (MCHM), Pictured Rocks National Lakeshore (PRNL), and the David V. Tinder Collection, Clements Library, University of Michigan (DVTC) unless otherwise noted.

Finally, we wish to thank our editor, Anna Wilson, our publisher, John Pearson, and all the folks at Arcadia Publishing who believed in this book and helped us bring it to life.

Introduction

Drive north through the pine forests of Michigan's Upper Peninsula along State Highway 77, and the blue expanse of Lake Superior appears on the horizon. Soon the road curves down a steep hill, and there, spread out before you, is a delightful surprise: a sparkling natural harbor. Nestled around it is the village of Grand Marais, a historical gem waiting for you to discover it.

Grand Marais is one of the oldest locations of human habitation on the Great Lakes. Calling it Kitchi-bitobig or "Great Pond," the Ojibwa Indians located their villages here long before recorded history. The first visit by a European was recorded by Pierre-Esprit Radisson in his journal of 1658. He noted that the area was "most delightful and wondrous, for its nature that made it so pleasant to the eye and spirit."

The name Grand Marais, literally "great marsh," first appeared on the map "Carte des Lac du Canada" published in Paris in 1744. This was a misnomer, as there is no great marsh in the area. Historians now believe that the voyageurs described it as *le grand maré*, an old French term that translates roughly into "great pond." The two terms are identical in pronunciation, and *marais* was already a popular term on maps of the Great Lakes region, so cartographers of the day simply assumed there was a marsh here. After all, none but the Native Americans and the voyageurs had seen the area. To the voyageurs, a sheltered, pondlike body of water would have been invaluable during Lake Superior's sudden, fierce storms.

The reports of the early explorers led to the establishment of the Hudson's Bay Company in the 1670s. Although fur trading was lively in the area, no actual town site was established until 1853. In 1861, Peter Barbeau built a trading post on East Bay, forming the nucleus of a permanent settlement. Barbeau, a Sault Ste. Marie businessman, left the operation of the trading post to Angus MacDonald. One of MacDonald's early requests to Barbeau was for window glass, and he fashioned window frames from grooved siding scavenged off the shipwreck *Manhattan*, which was lying just outside the harbor.

In 1874, increased shipping traffic and subsequent losses on Lake Superior warranted the establishment of Au Sable Lighthouse, eight miles to the west. Grand Marais's importance as a harbor of refuge along this dangerous stretch of Lake Superior became apparent, especially as commercial fishing was beginning to take hold in the area. Conable and Sons established a fishery in the 1860s at the end of the long sand point on the north side of the harbor.

In 1871, an enterprising commercial fisherman from Sault Ste. Marie named Charles Endress located one of his operations in Grand Marais. His son, Emil Endress, decided to settle here and expanded the family businesses to include passenger and packet freight services for the south shore of Lake Superior. The year 1871 saw the advent of lumbering in the area. The earliest recorded lumberman was George Dawson, whose company cut pine in the area that is now known as Perry's Landing, named for his foreman Robert D. Perry.

In 1879, the Brazel brothers from Cheboygan built the first sawmill at the harbor on West Bay. Soon millionaire Saginaw lumberman Wellington Burt and his brother-in-law, Henry Gamble, established the narrow-gauge Burt and Gamble Railway, one of the state's first railroads dedicated to hauling logs. Congress appropriated funds for the construction of the harbor entrance and piers in 1881, opening the port to increased lake traffic. In 1882, Wellington Burt helped organize Burt Township and establish a post office for the growing community.

In 1883, Burt platted the new town site of West Grand Marais. At the same time, Philo Everett and Dan Ball platted the village of Grand Marais, which became known as East Town.

By 1885, a school had been built, packet freighters were making regular stops at the new harbor and town, and a stage service connected Grand Marais with Dollarville, Newberry, and the railroad. Logging operations had expanded both east and west of town, but Grand Marais remained a tiny logging community of only a few hundred people. The white pine in the immediate vicinity had been cut, and without a railroad to bring logs from farther away, the large mill closed and the population dwindled.

A series of events in 1893 began a new era of prosperity. The Manistique Lumbering Company purchased Burt's old sawmill, the Alger-Smith Company decided to mill its logs at Grand Marais, and the Manistique Railway extended its line all the way into town. By 1894, the population exceeded 1,000; by 1896, it was over 2,000. In 1898, the *Mining Journal* noted, "Grand Marais is probably the most prosperous small town in the Peninsula."

In the years between 1893 and 1910, no fewer than 29 saloons and a dozen hotels and boardinghouses were in business. The Bay View Hospital, dentists, lawyers, photographers, meat markets, clothiers, liveries, banks, and cigar factories soon followed. The United States Life-Saving Service established a station in Grand Marais in 1900, and the brave surfmen saved many lives along this stretch of Lake Superior's notorious "Shipwreck Coast."

The prosperity was not to last, and when the pine was gone, the businesses left too. The Alger-Smith Company closed its pine mill in 1909 and the Manistique Railway soon followed. The last train left in 1910, and with it, the town's link to the outside world was gone. With the economic collapse, people sold their homes and businesses for whatever they could get. Within weeks, the population shrank to only a few hundred people. Grand Marais struggled for survival. Transportation was limited to the Endress Company's *South Shore* packet freighter and a horse-drawn stage to Seney.

By 1920, commercial fishing had become the basis for the town's economy, supplemented by a fledgling tourism industry. When the state road from Grand Marais to Seney was completed in 1925, tourists were able to make their way north by automobile. Tourism grew steadily and a number of new businesses sprang up to offer services to visitors. A number of sport trolling operations opened in town, the campground was upgraded, and the summers brought visitors from downstate to enjoy the relaxed pace.

Meanwhile, the Great Lakes were devastated by the accidental introduction of the sea lamprey, and by 1962, commercial trout fishing was prohibited. The fisheries closed down one by one. Once more, Grand Marais refused to die. This time, the natural beauty of the area brought a new resident: the National Park Service. Pictured Rocks National Lakeshore was established in 1966, making Grand Marais the eastern gateway to 50 miles of unspoiled shoreline on Lake Superior. This encouraged even more people to visit the area. Today the Grand Marais economy is based on year-round tourism.

The Grand Marais Historical Society is pleased to present this photographic history of the town. Immerse yourself in our past, and then visit us in the present.

One

THE EARLY YEARS

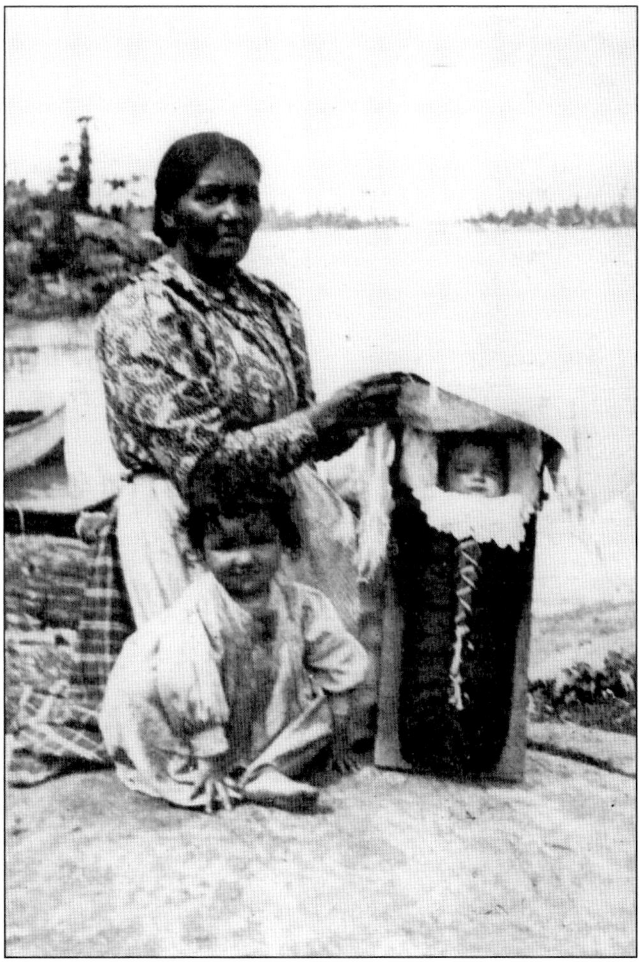

Native people fished and hunted in Grand Marais for centuries before European settlers arrived. Ojibwa Indians camped here annually and established a burial ground east of town near the present Rose Hill Cemetery. When a trading post was established at East Bay in 1861, the Ojibwas began trading furs for manufactured goods. This Ojibwa woman and her two children are shown on the shore of the bay. (MCHM.)

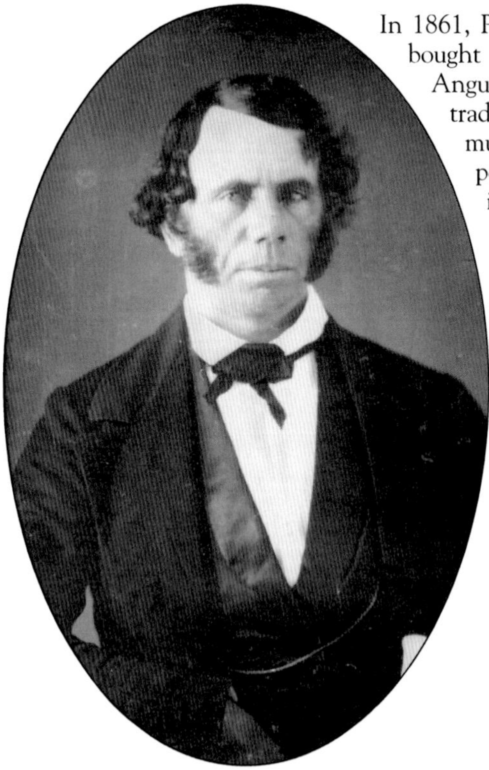

In 1861, Peter Barbeau, a Sault Ste. Marie businessman, bought land on the south shore of East Bay and sent Angus MacDonald to build and operate the area's first trading post. The post traded in pelts of lynx, mink, muskrat, and beaver. In 1864, Barbeau sold the post to Hiram Burt, who kept the post running into the early 1870s. The fur trade waned at that point. (MCHM.)

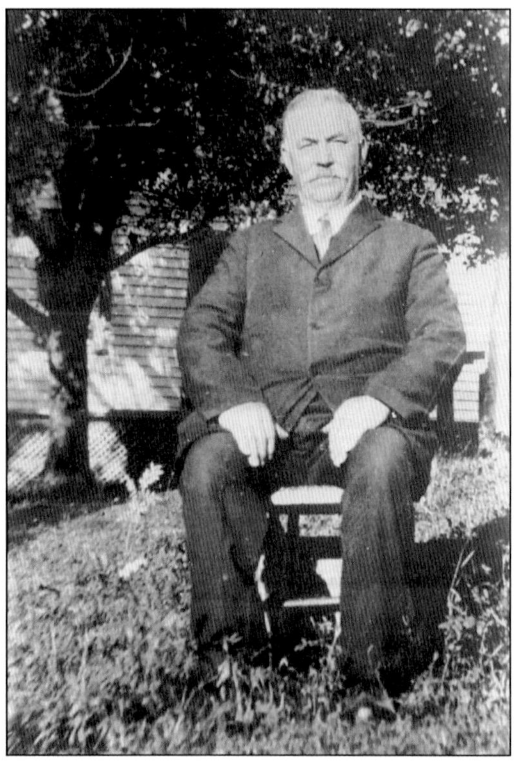

Early pioneer families began to settle in Grand Marais in the late 1870s as logging and commercial fishing caused the town to grow. These first settlers were Scots, Englishmen, French Canadians, and Swedes, coming to Grand Marais from many parts of the United States and Canada. One of the earliest settlers was John Masse, a lumberman who came to Grand Marais in 1878. (Della Meldrum.)

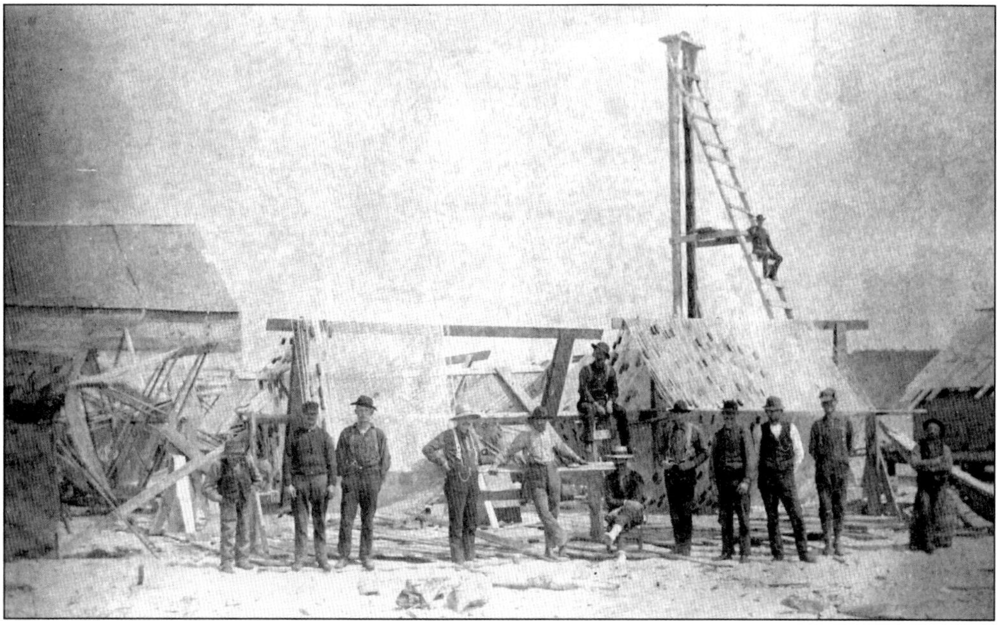

This early photograph shows a commercial fishing operation at the end of Coast Guard Point. This was one of the earliest locations for a fishery, as Conable and Sons established its operations here in the late 1860s. When the channel was built across the point, this location became an island. By the mid-1880s, when this photograph was taken, this was probably the S. H. Davis and Company fishery. (GMHS.)

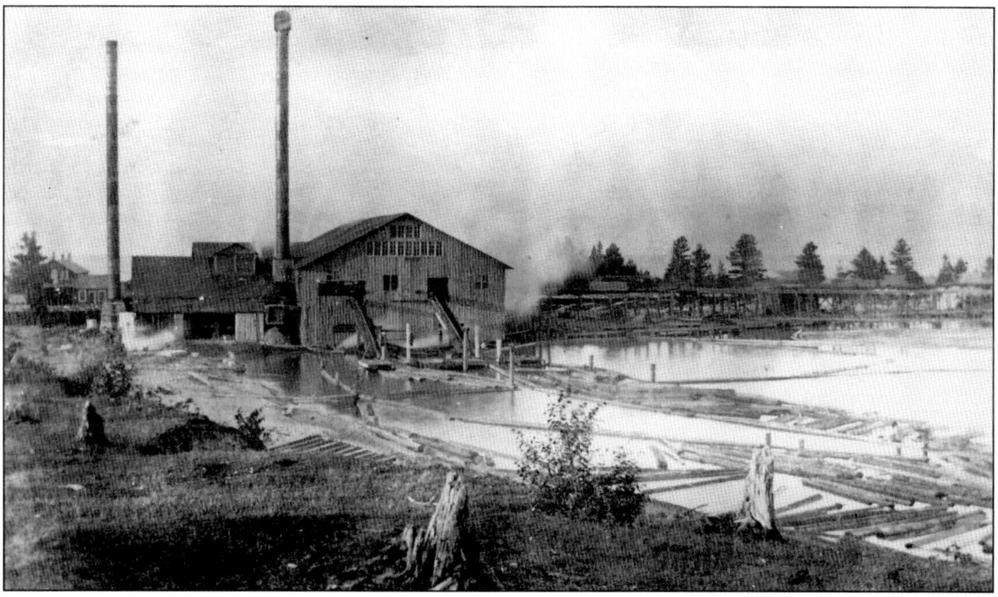

This mill, built by Peter and Michael Brazel in 1879, was the first sawmill built in Grand Marais. It was located where the marina now stands. Wellington Burt and Henry Gamble soon purchased the land, and the mill was jointly operated by the four men under the Brazel Brothers name. Burt and Gamble built the area's first logging railroad in 1879, a seven-mile-long narrow-gauge line. (GMHS.)

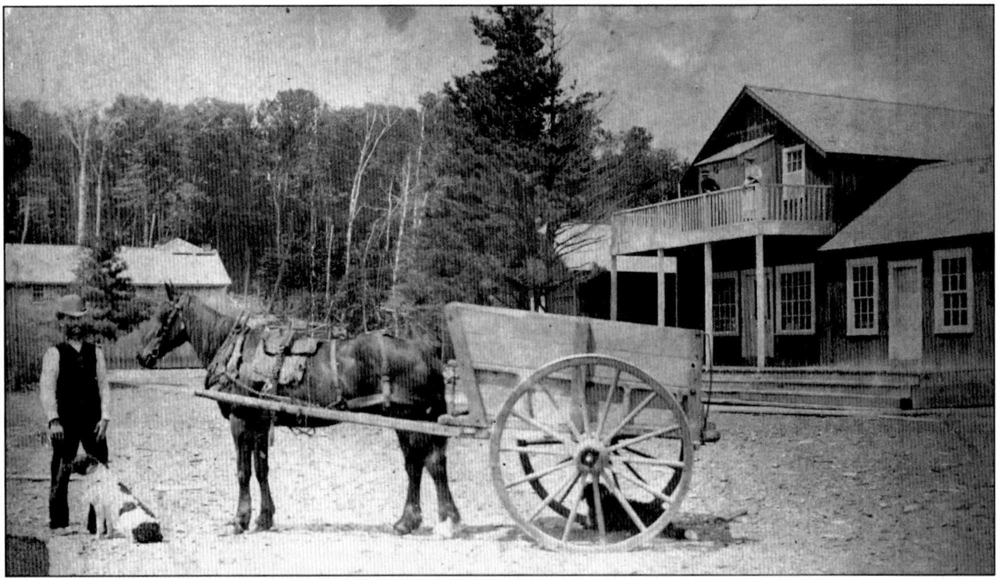

Peter Brazel and his brother Michael came from Cheboygan to Grand Marais in 1879 and started the first sawmill in the area. They built the Brazel House, possibly the town's first hotel, across the road from the sawmill. A Mr. Charlbrand operated it. There were few commercial establishments in Grand Marais at this time, and the hotel would have housed visiting businessmen and perhaps some of the mill workers. (GMHS.)

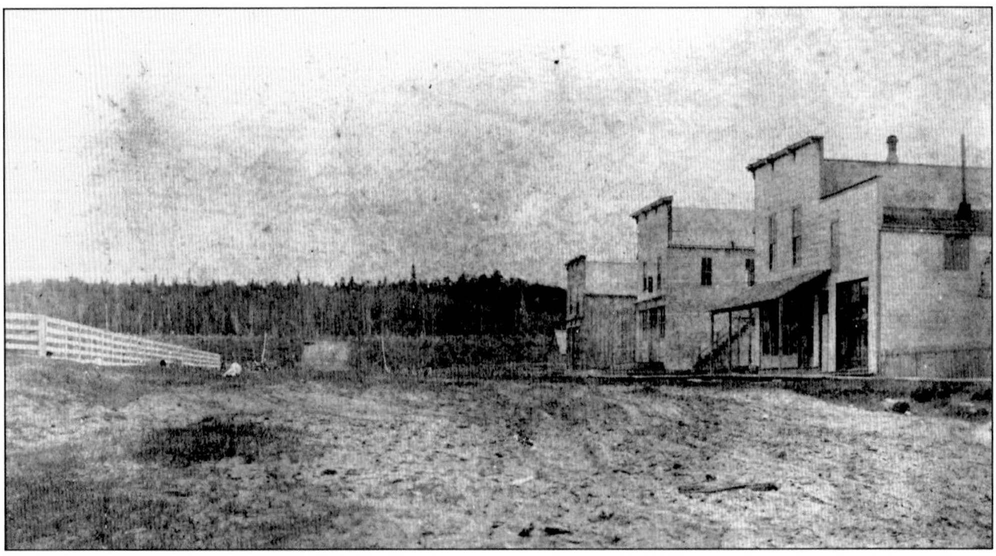

In this view looking south along Lake Avenue in the mid-1880s, only a few buildings have been erected. From left to right are a saloon, a second saloon and hotel, a third saloon, and a laundry. The building at left is the Duggan and Gamble Billiard Hall, built about 1885. Through the years it has been a variety of eating and drinking establishments, and today it is a brewpub. (GMHS.)

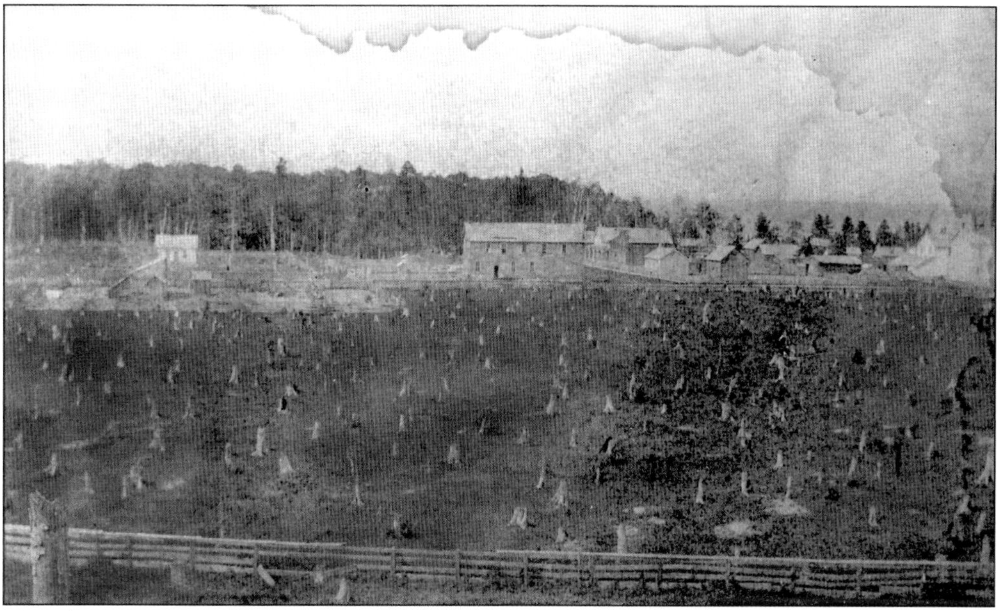

This photograph, taken about 1883, shows the western edge of the settlement. Trees have been cleared, but there are few buildings in town as of yet. The large building in the center is the Grand Marais Hotel, one of the first hotels in town. The view looks north; the stack of the sawmill is visible at the far right. Building slowed down until the railroad arrived in 1893. (GMHS.)

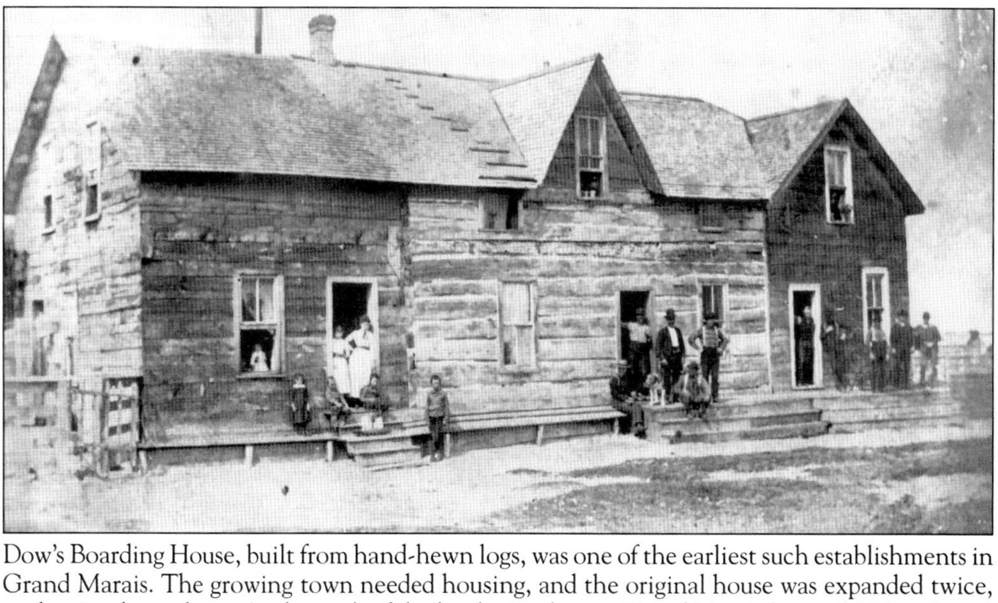

Dow's Boarding House, built from hand-hewn logs, was one of the earliest such establishments in Grand Marais. The growing town needed housing, and the original house was expanded twice, to the size shown here. At the peak of the lumbering boom, Grand Marais boasted 15 hotels and boardinghouses. This one was located on Carlson Street between McMillan Street and Alger Avenue. (GMHS.)

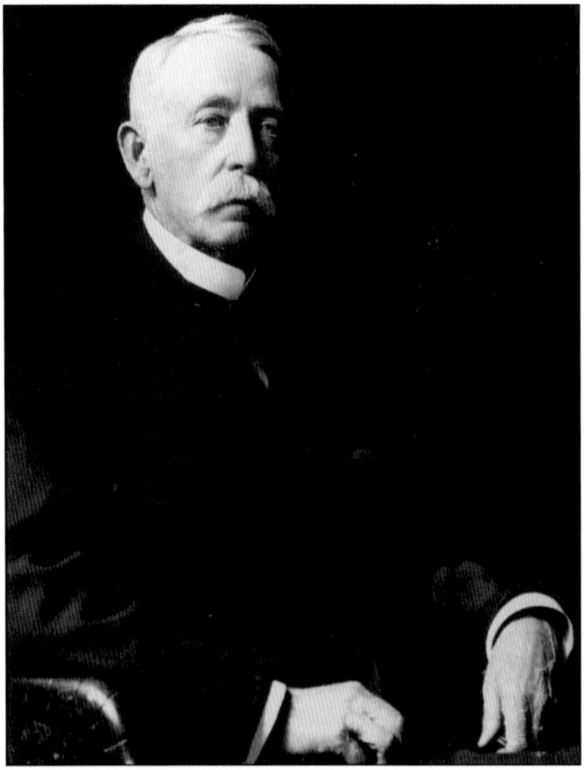

Wellington Burt of Saginaw was one of the wealthiest men in the state of Michigan. He made his fortune in lumbering and real estate and owned extensive timber holdings around Grand Marais. Due in part to his influence, Burt Township was formed in 1882 from land detached from Munising Township, thus giving Grand Marais its own local government. Burt platted the village of West Grand Marais in 1883. (Burt Township.)

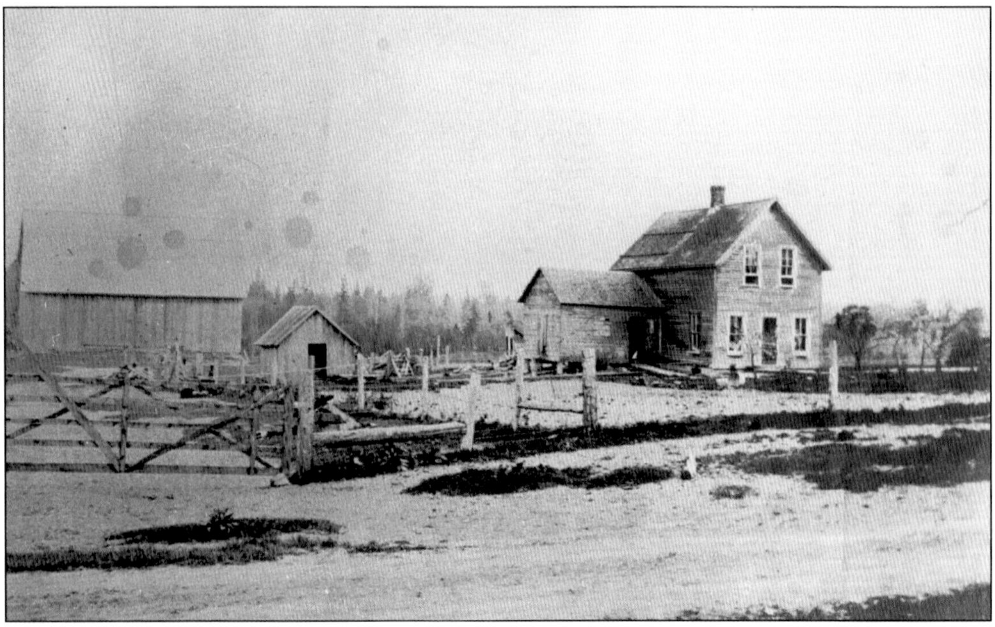

Small farms began to dot the landscape around Grand Marais in the early 1880s. Crops of potatoes, oats, rye, and wheat were grown, and orchards were planted. Many farmers raised herds of dairy cows. Farmers formed a cooperative, sharing threshing equipment, a gristmill, and a grain grinder. The lumber camps provided the largest market for farm products, and in the winter, many farmers worked in the local sawmills. (GMHS.)

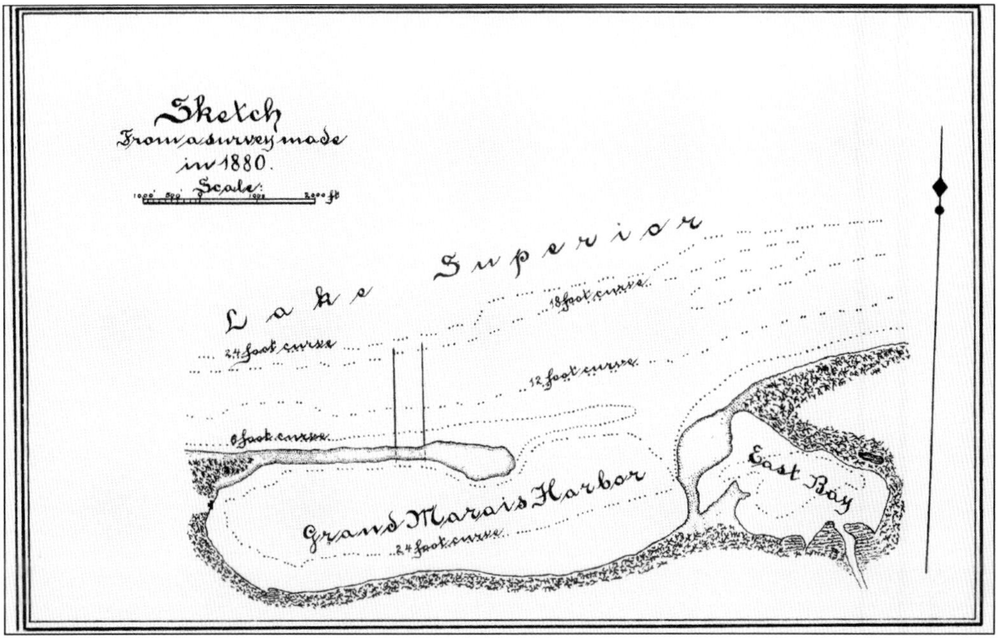

By 1870, the federal government began planning improvements to the harbor at Grand Marais. Several entrance channels existed, but the deepest was blocked by the remains of the *Manhattan*, a steamer that sank at the entrance in 1859. This sketch from 1880 shows the planned construction of a channel that would cut through the sand point on the northern side of the harbor. (GMHS.)

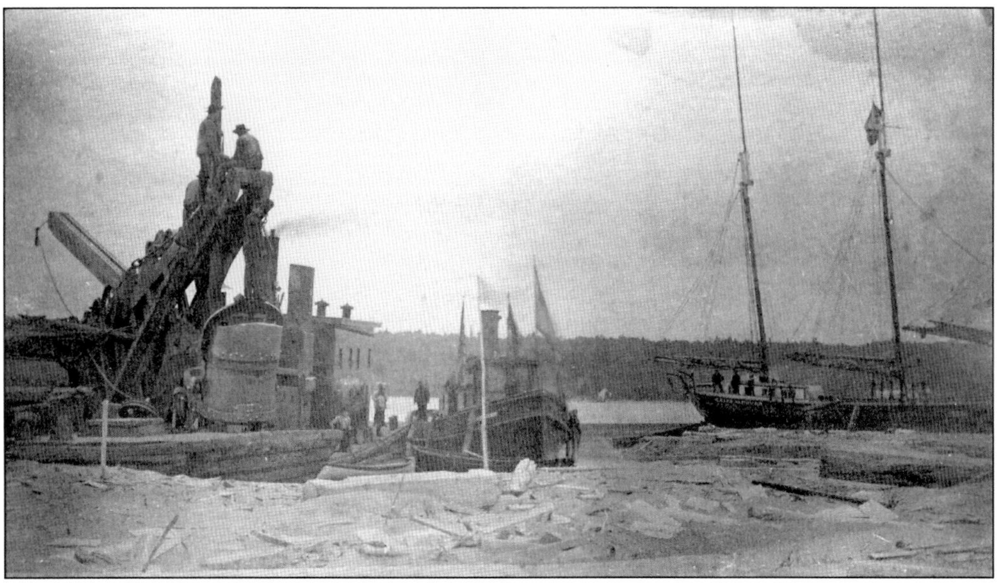

Once the channel was constructed, periodic dredging was needed to keep it open for navigation. This steam dredge is shown near the lumber-loading area in the early 1890s. The wooden three-masted schooner *Criss Grover* is shown at right. In 1899, the *Criss Grover* ran aground in fog and wrecked near Split Rock, Minnesota. It was loaded with dynamite, a cargo it often carried to mining camps. (GMHS.)

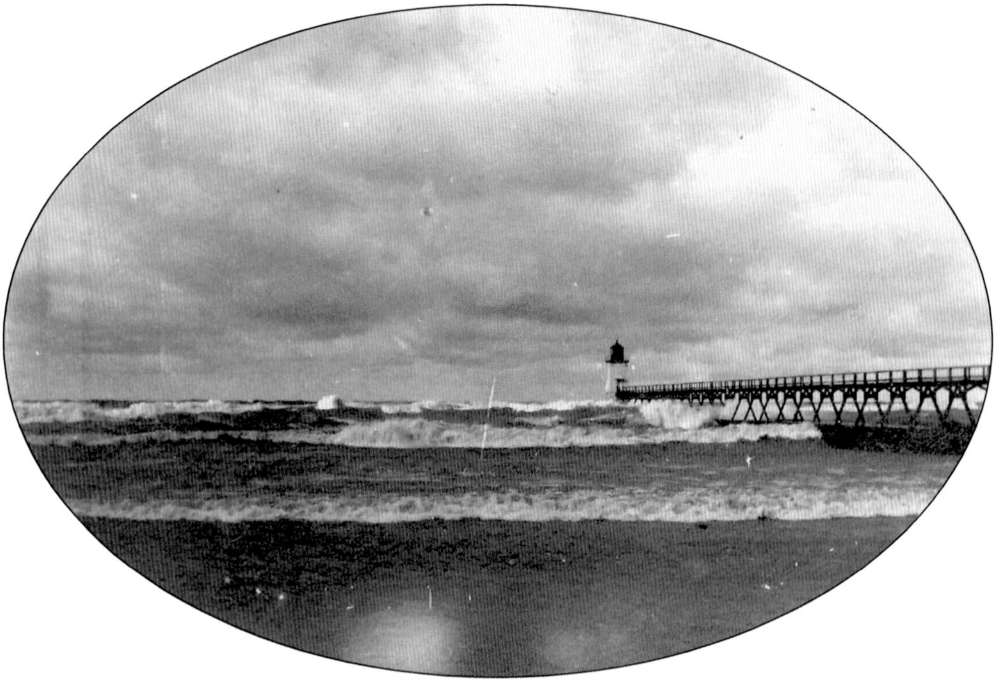

Following the construction of the harbor channel, light towers were erected in 1895 on the inner and outer ends of the west pier to help guide ships into the harbor. The pier was extended about 1903, and the outer light was moved farther out and connected with a 600-foot elevated walkway. In winter, storms pounded the pier and literally encased the light towers in ice. (ACHS.)

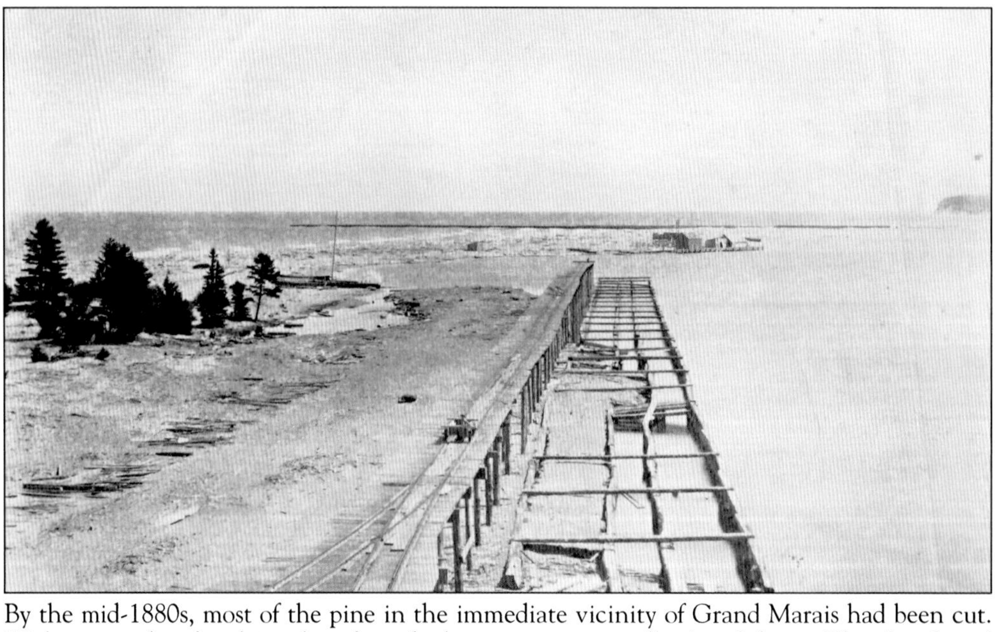

By the mid-1880s, most of the pine in the immediate vicinity of Grand Marais had been cut. Without a railroad to bring logs from farther away, many mills closed down. The abandoned lumber docks shown here sat empty until the Alger-Smith Company opened the Manistique Railway into Grand Marais in 1893. The town was poised for a comeback, and new docks would soon be built on this site. (GMHS.)

Two

TREES AND TRACKS

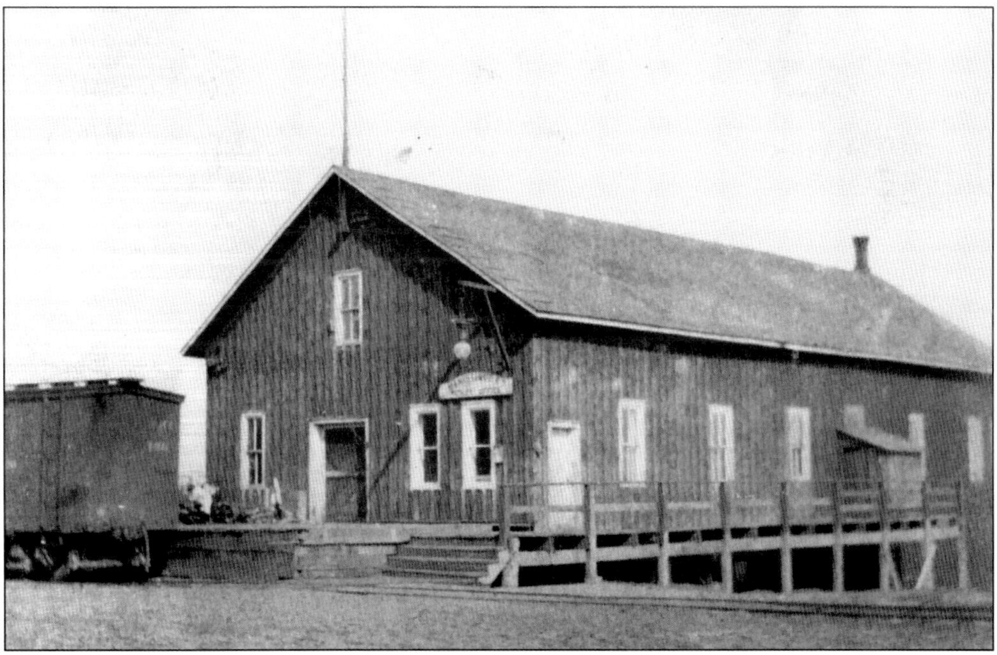

The Manistique Railway built this passenger depot on the harbor facing Grand Marais Avenue. The railroad opened for passenger traffic in October 1893, linking Grand Marais with the town of Seney, 25 miles to the south. From there, passengers could transfer to the Duluth, South Shore and Atlantic Railway for points east and west. A freight depot and roundhouse were located to the southeast on Ball Street. (Charles Conn.)

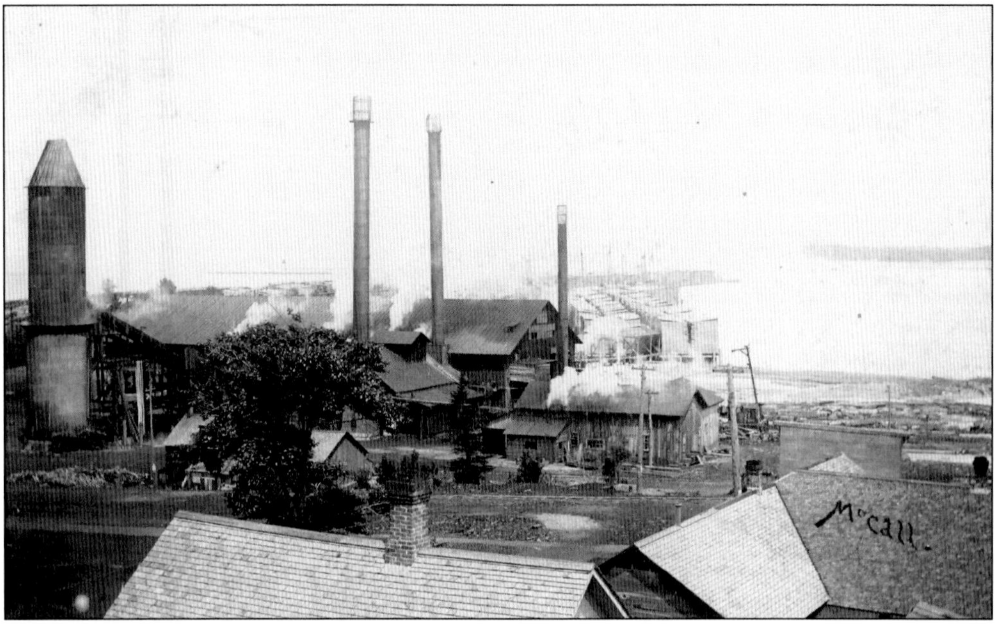

The Alger-Smith Company of Detroit bought the former Brazel Brothers mill in 1895, but it was too small to handle a large volume of timber. The company renamed it the Marais Lumber Company, enlarged the mill, and refurbished it with better machinery that could cut 150,000 feet of lumber in a single day. This mill burned down on February 28, 1903, in a spectacular fire but was immediately replaced. (ACHS.)

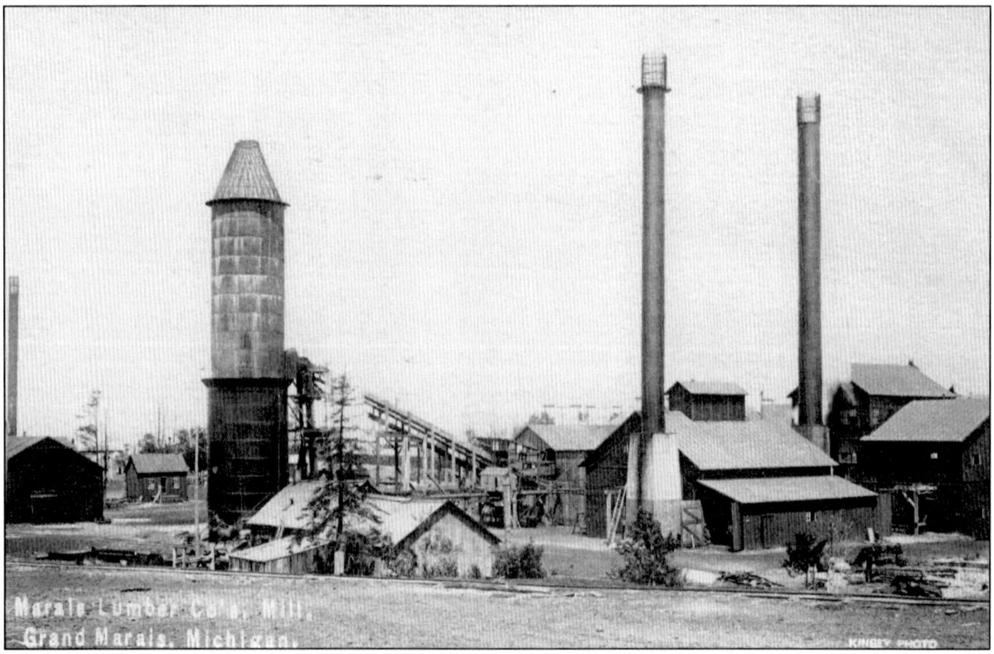

After the fire destroyed the Marais Lumber Company mill, causing a $50,000 loss, the Alger-Smith Company shipped a sawmill up from Cheboygan and assembled it on the same spot where the old mill had stood. The power plant, far left, supplied the mill and town with electricity. This mill continued to operate, running two shifts a day, until 1909. (GMHS.)

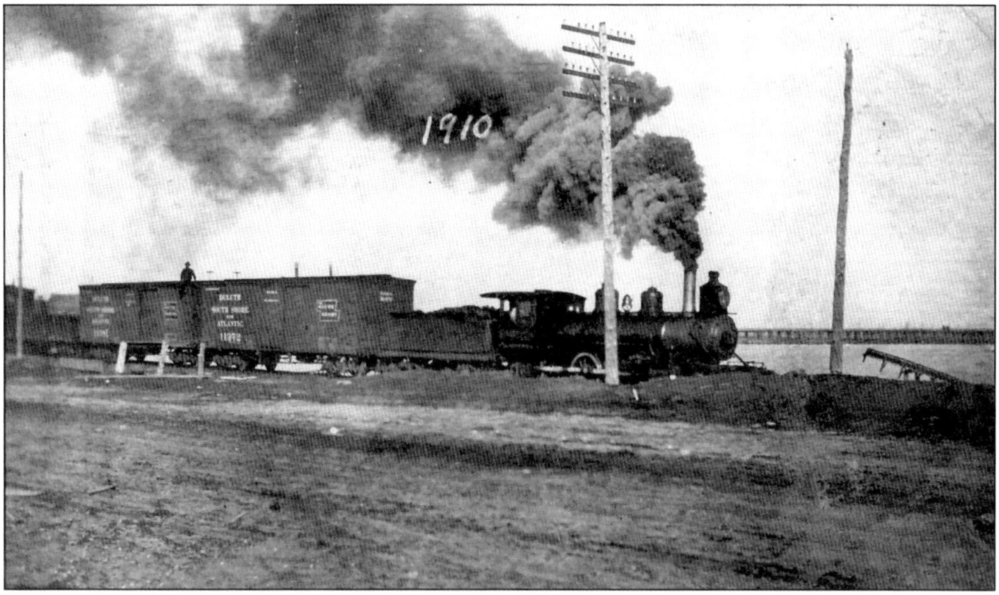

The Alger-Smith Company also owned the Manistique Railway. It was built to service the company's logging operations, but as the population of Grand Marais grew, it became a carrier of passengers and freight as well. As the lumber boom ended in Seney, 25 miles to the south, even stores and houses were shipped north to Grand Marais. This 1910 photograph was taken shortly before the railroad shut down. (GMHS.)

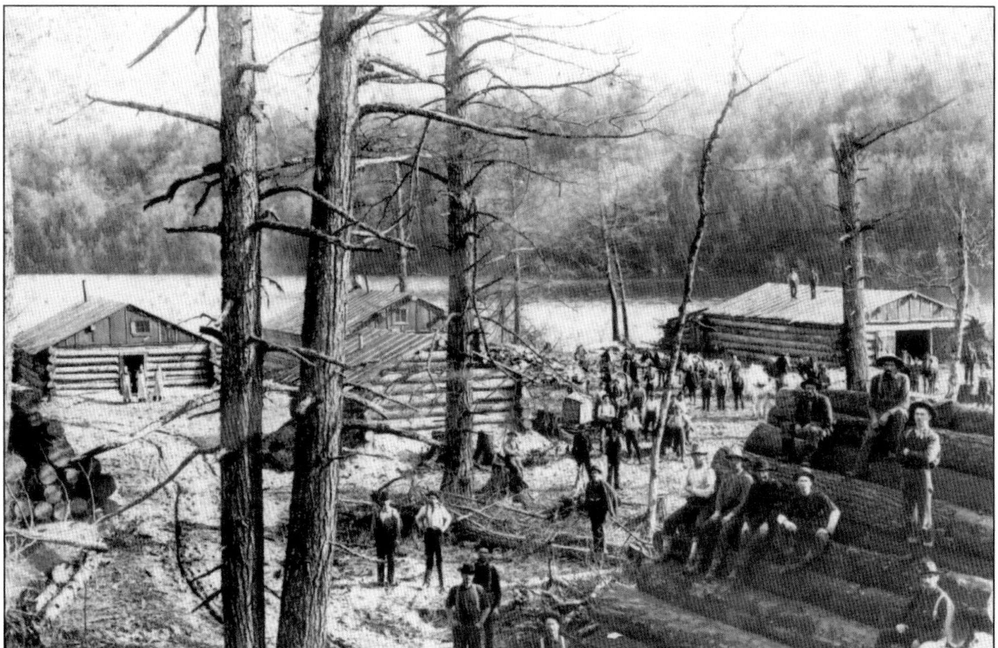

Lumber camps were hastily constructed, fairly primitive, and meant to last only as long as the timber that was being cut. This 1890s photograph of a camp near Grand Marais shows the cook shack at left, the barn at right, and the bunkhouse and camp office in the center. Note the size of the logs on which the lumberjacks sit. (GMHS.)

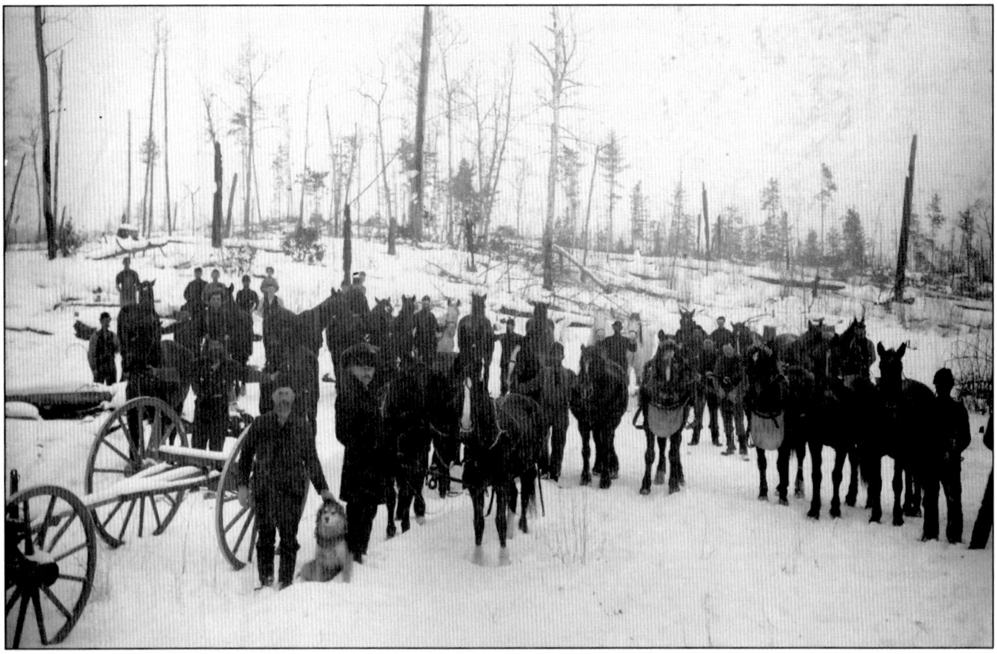

In the lumber camps, good horses were even more valuable than the lumberjacks. This photograph shows the high regard held for the four-legged members of the crew, placing them front and center. Note the logging that has already taken place in the background. This was one of many crews operating in the Grand Marais area near the start of the 20th century. (ACHS.)

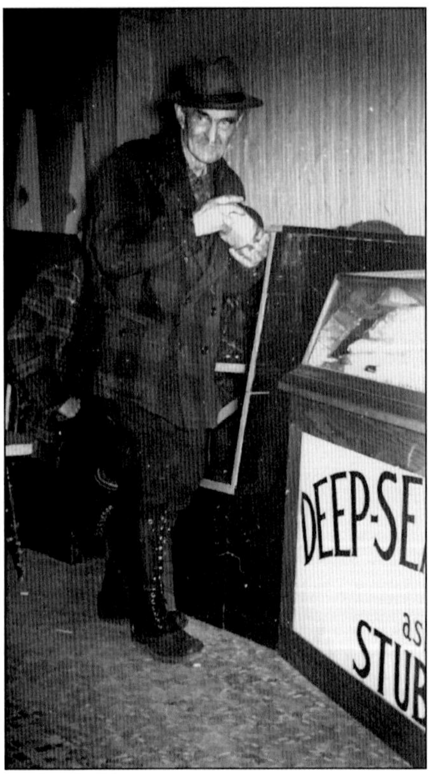

Lumber camps often turned to local hunters for help in supplying the camp cook with fresh meat. Charlie Goodman, shown here about 1941 when he was 80 years old, was a crack shot who could single-handedly keep a logging camp in venison. Goodman came to Michigan from Pennsylvania and worked his way north via the logging camps. Once in Grand Marais, he stayed for life. (Ted and Marge Soldenski.)

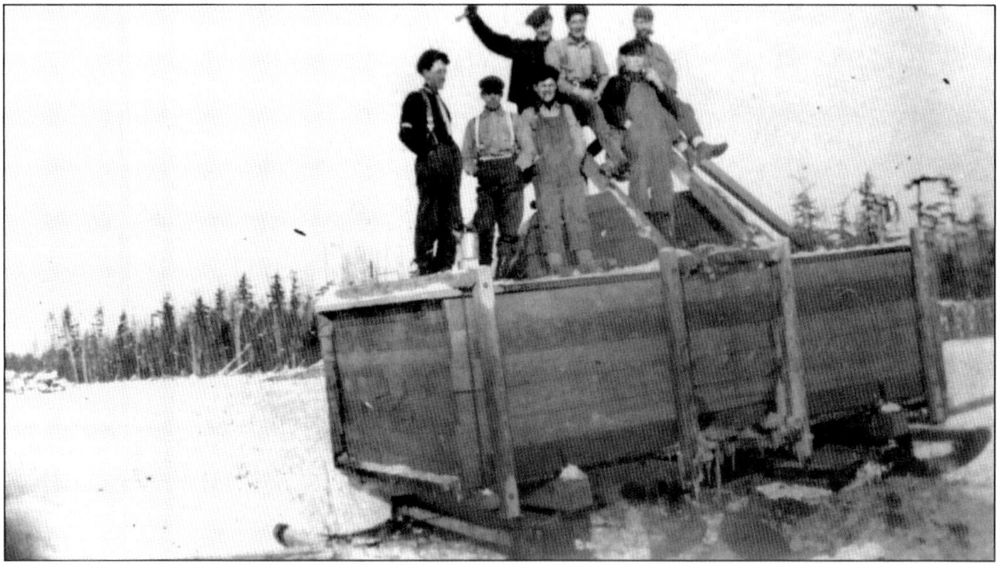

Lumbering took place primarily in the winter, when the frozen logging trails were solidly packed with snow and ice. This allowed teams of horses to pull their heavy loads more easily, with less friction underneath the heavily laden sledges. This sledge was filled with water and used to ice down the trails for the logging crews. (GMHS.)

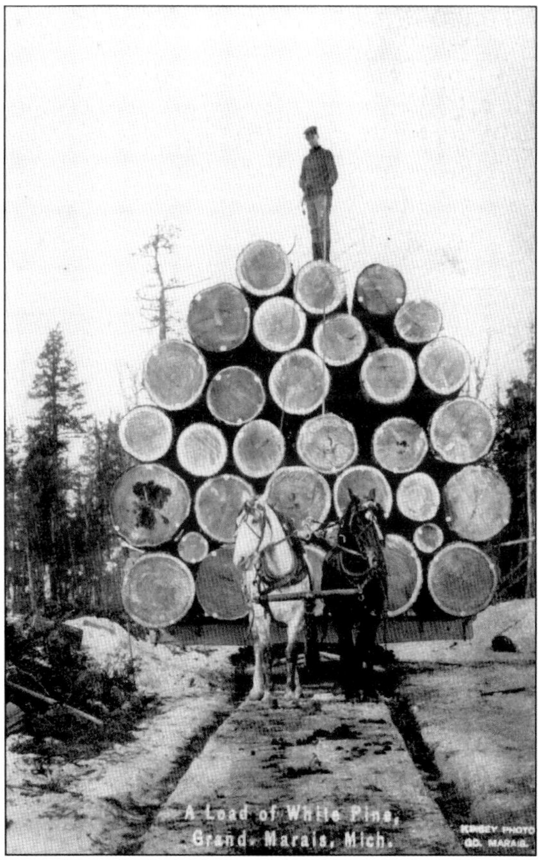

Enormous loads of huge logs could be moved by a single team of horses if the roads were well iced. "World champion" loads were a common sight on postcards of the time. This load of giant virgin white pine was photographed near Grand Marais about 1906. One such load of Michigan white pine was a featured exhibit at Chicago's World's Columbian Exposition in 1893. (Doris Krempa.)

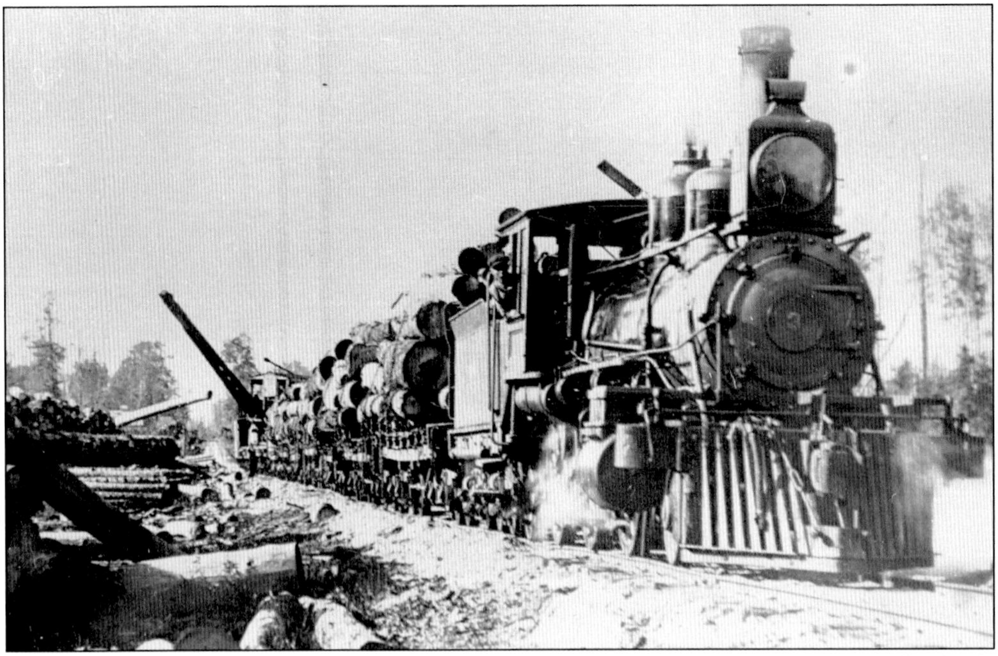

Engine No. 3 was one of the workhorses of the Manistique Railway, making regular hauls from the outlying lumber camps to Grand Marais. In 1905, four engines were hauling up to 300,000 feet of lumber a day to the busy mills. Shown here at camp No. 8, the crane is lifting a log onto the railcar as the engineer looks out from his cab. (GMHS.)

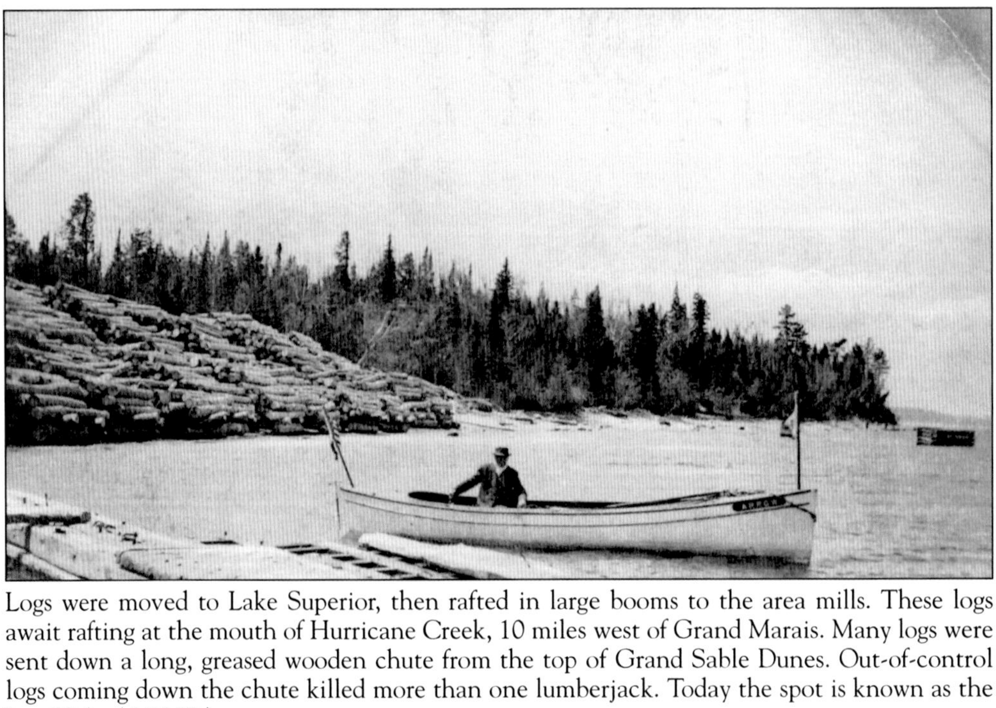

Logs were moved to Lake Superior, then rafted in large booms to the area mills. These logs await rafting at the mouth of Hurricane Creek, 10 miles west of Grand Marais. Many logs were sent down a long, greased wooden chute from the top of Grand Sable Dunes. Out-of-control logs coming down the chute killed more than one lumberjack. Today the spot is known as the Log Slide. (ACHS.)

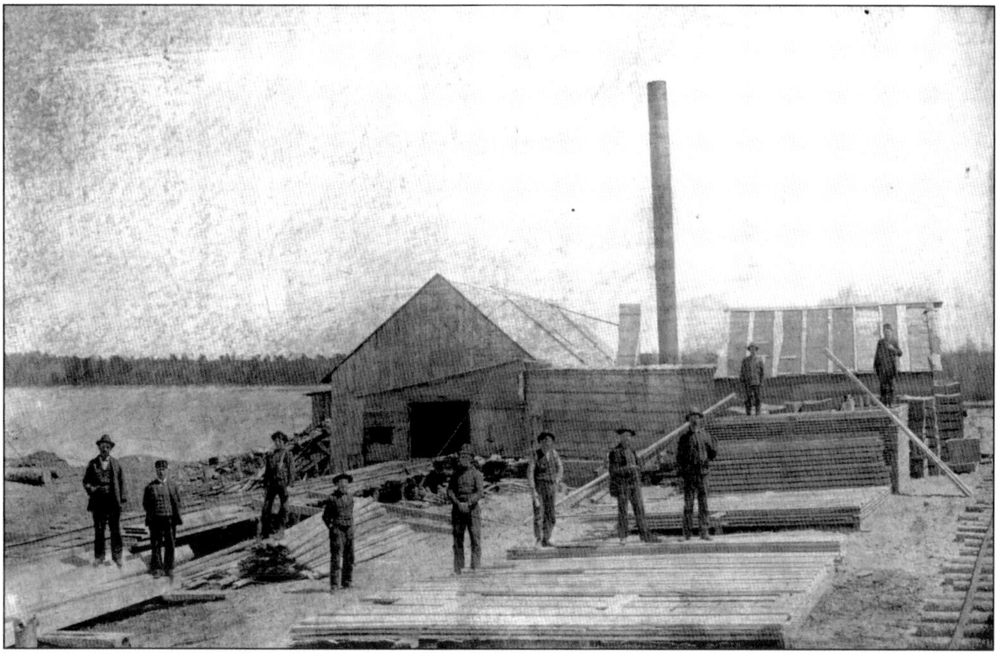

This sawmill on East Bay was originally built by Charles Coon in the mid-1890s. Coon sold it to Charles Stone in 1898; later it was sold to Colin Doig and William Leighton. The mill produced plank lumber and shingles. A spur line off the main Manistique Railway line served the mill. This photograph was taken around the dawn of the 20th century. (GMHS.)

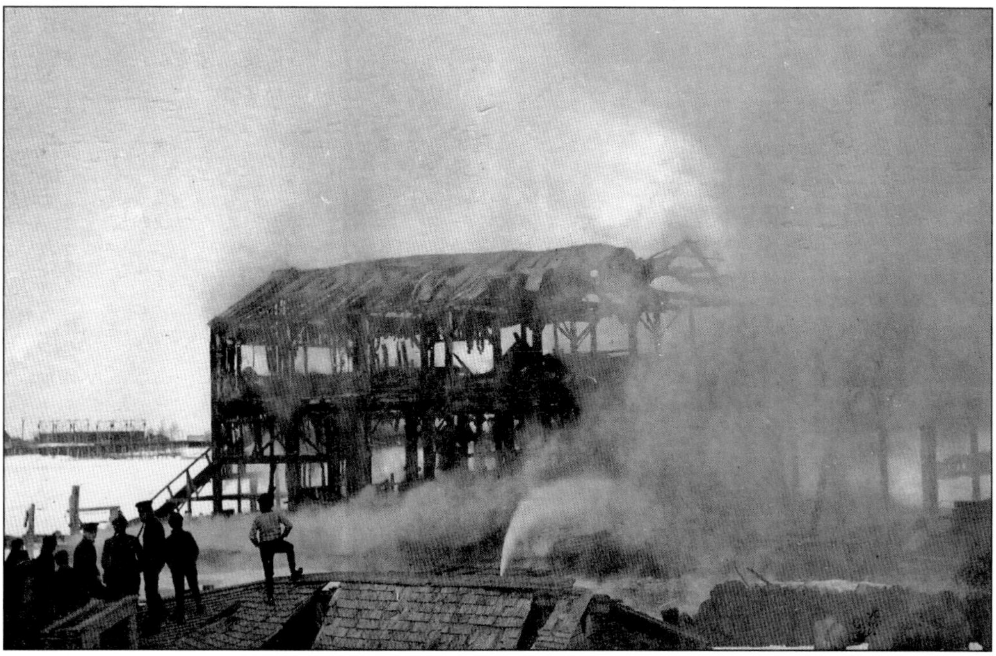

Fire was always the greatest threat to any lumber mill, and the mills in Grand Marais were vulnerable. This early photograph shows the devastating effects of a mill fire on the south shore of the bay. Even though it is winter, the building is a total loss. Fortunately, disasters such as this were few, and most of the mills in town never faced this situation. (GMHS.)

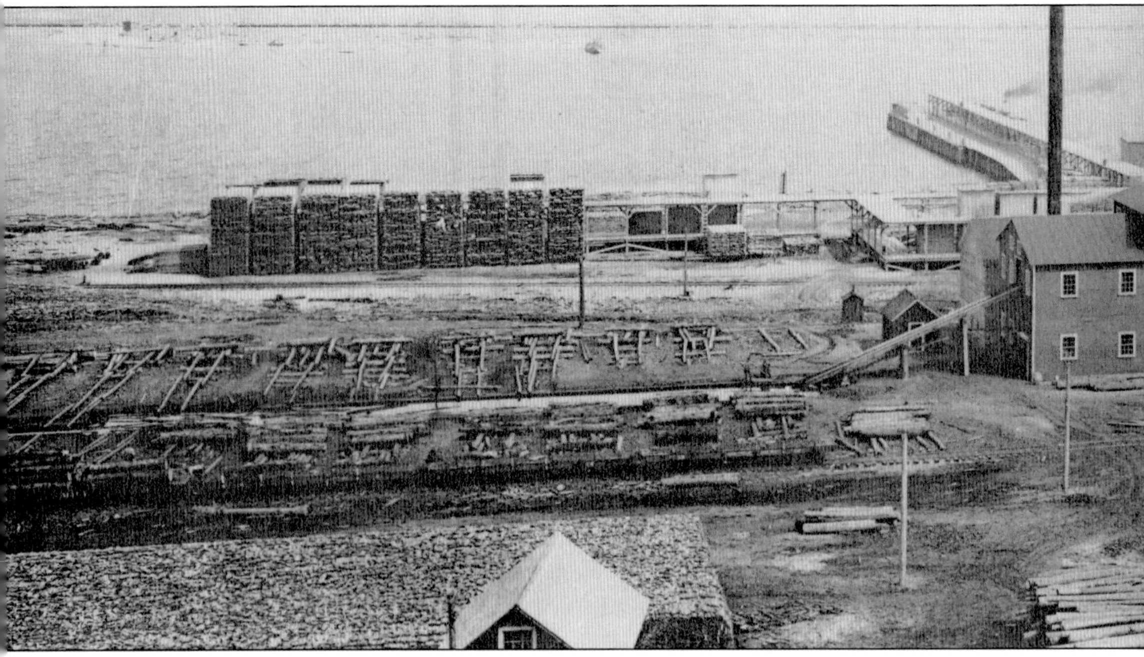

The Cook, Curtis and Miller sawmill was located on the south shore of the bay about one mile east of town. While most of the mills in the area were interested in white pine, Cook, Curtis and Miller specialized in hardwoods. This panoramic view shows the entire operation. Logs were brought in by rail and were piled in huge stacks, shown at bottom. The logs were rolled into a

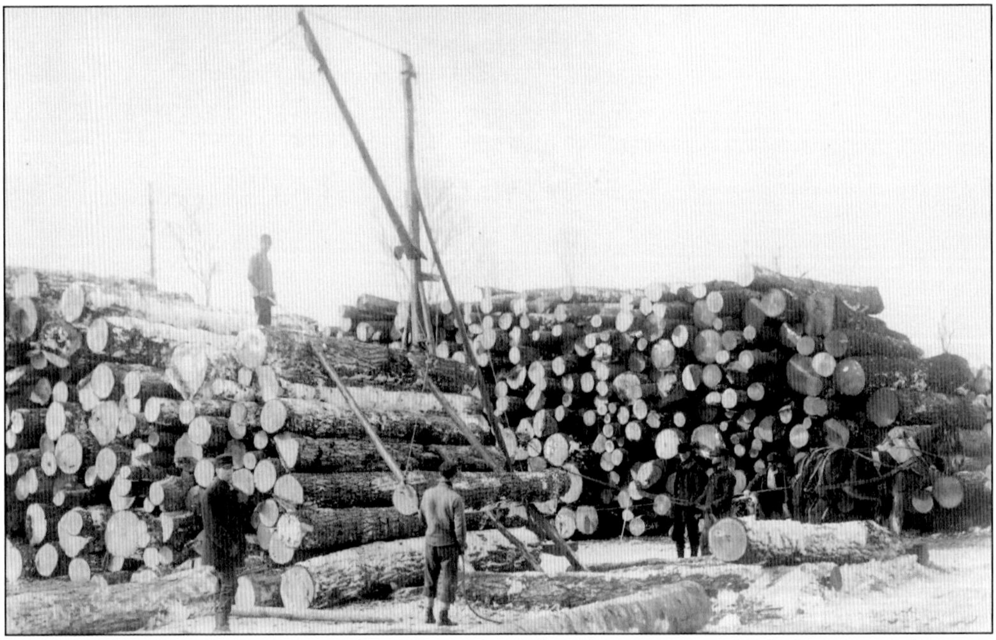

This crew of the Cook, Curtis and Miller hardwood mill is using a makeshift crane and a team of horses to slide a heavy log up a set of poles. From there it would be stacked on the top of the pile. This was a dangerous job as the logs could shift and give way without warning. Note the men and horses positioned well off to the side. (MCHM.)

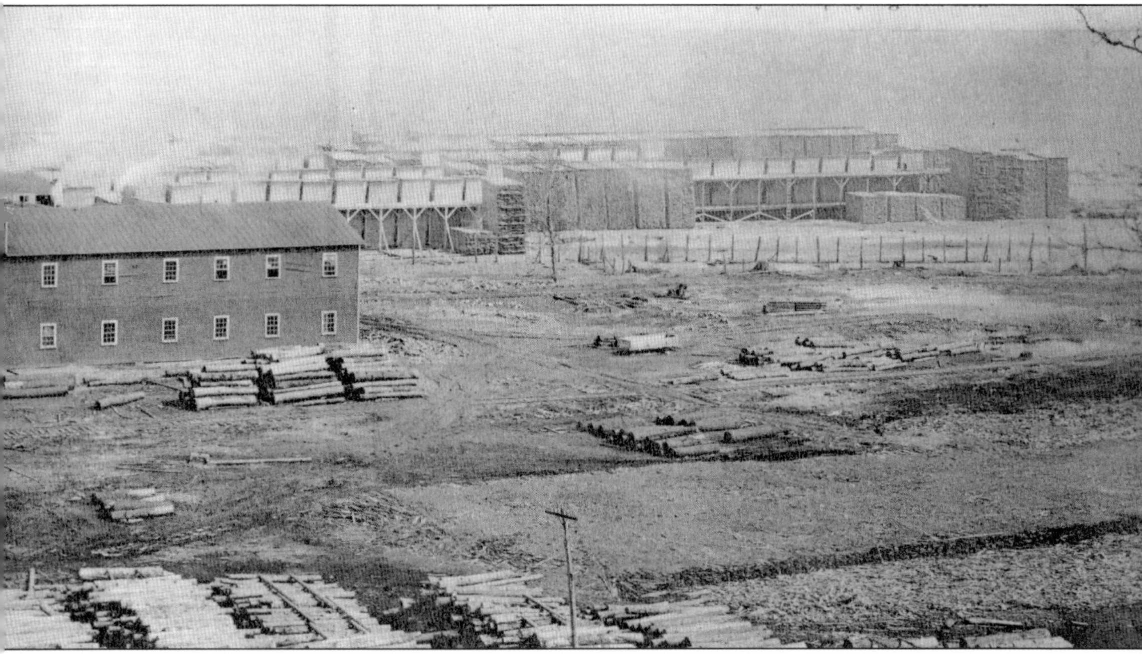

pond, center left, and then were pulled up a conveyor device into the mill itself. Cut lumber was stacked on the loading docks for shipment. The hardwood milled here was also used to power the town's electric plant. Note the long docks stretching out into the harbor. This mill was one of the last to close after the white pine was gone. (Bill LaCombe.)

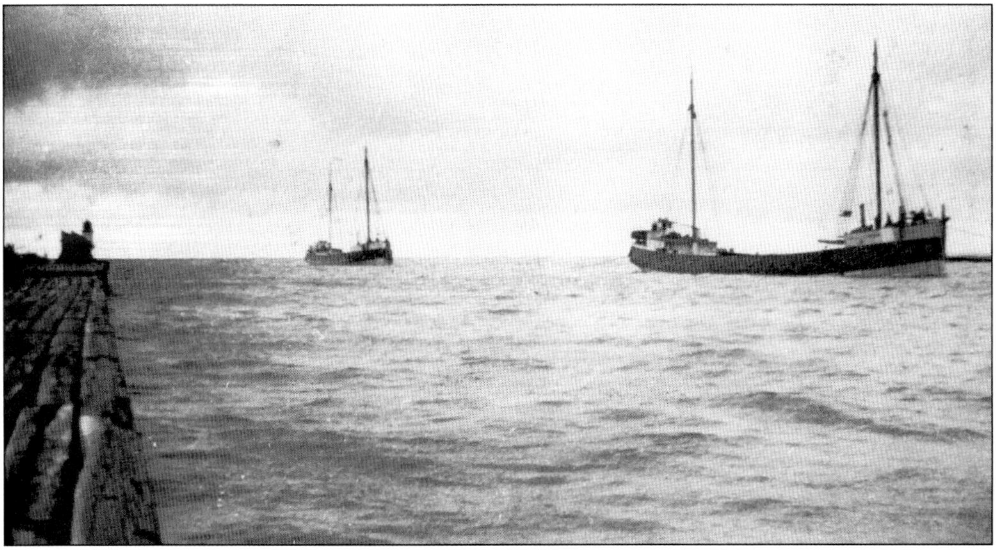

Lumber schooners were twin-masted, shallow-draft vessels ideal for navigating the unimproved harbors of northern Michigan's lumber towns. By the 1880s, many aging Civil War–era schooners were being recaulked for use as lumber barges. A single steam-powered ship would tow as many as four barges behind it. These two lumber schooners are entering the channel at Grand Marais, towed by an unseen boat to the right. (GMHS.)

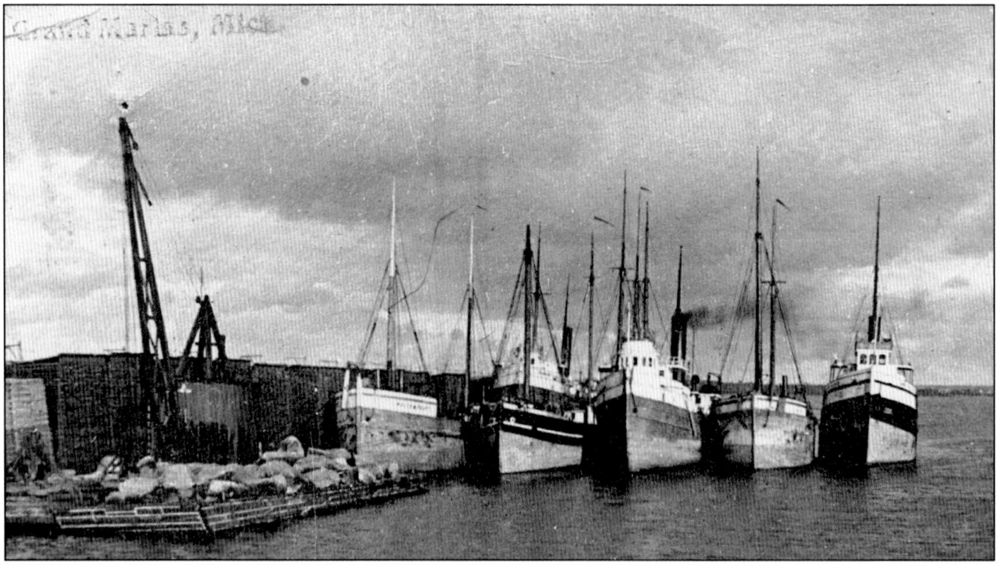

These five lumber schooner-barges await their turn to be loaded at the Grand Marais docks. Most schooner-barges were sail powered, with only a small steam engine. A larger vessel towed these barges once they were loaded with their cargo. Note the smokestacks of a lumber freighter in the background behind the barges. Towing barges was dangerous, and many barges went down in storms. (GMHS.)

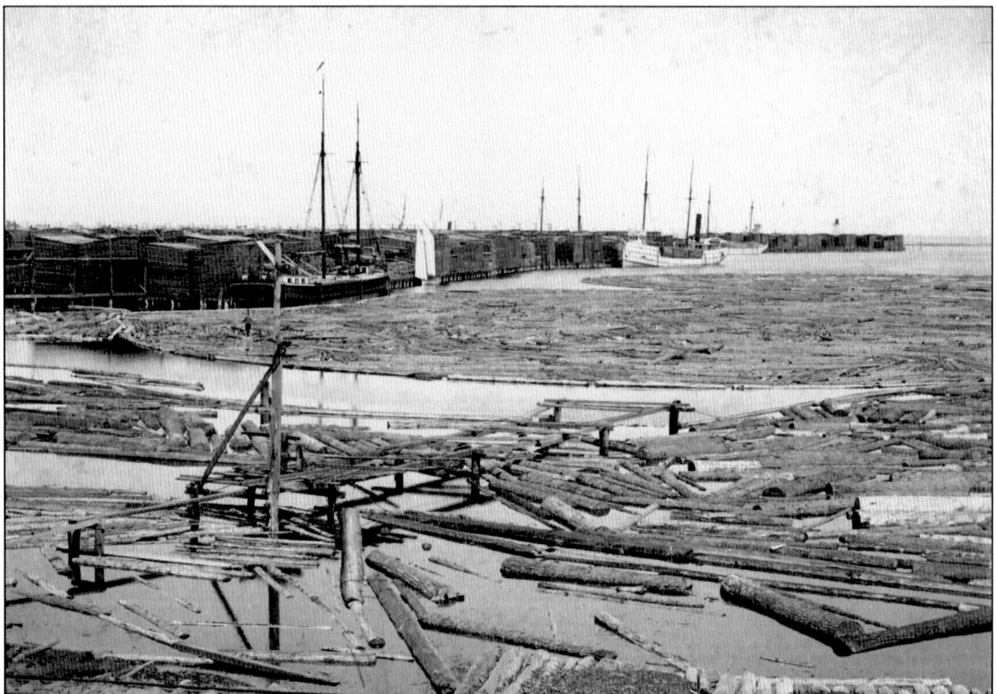

Logs were corralled in the harbor in large booms, waiting to be milled into boards. The cut lumber was then stacked on the loading docks and eventually loaded onto lumber barges and schooners for transport to distant cities. This *c.* 1905 photograph shows the massive amount of lumber that could be stacked on the docks at one time. (Bill LaCombe.)

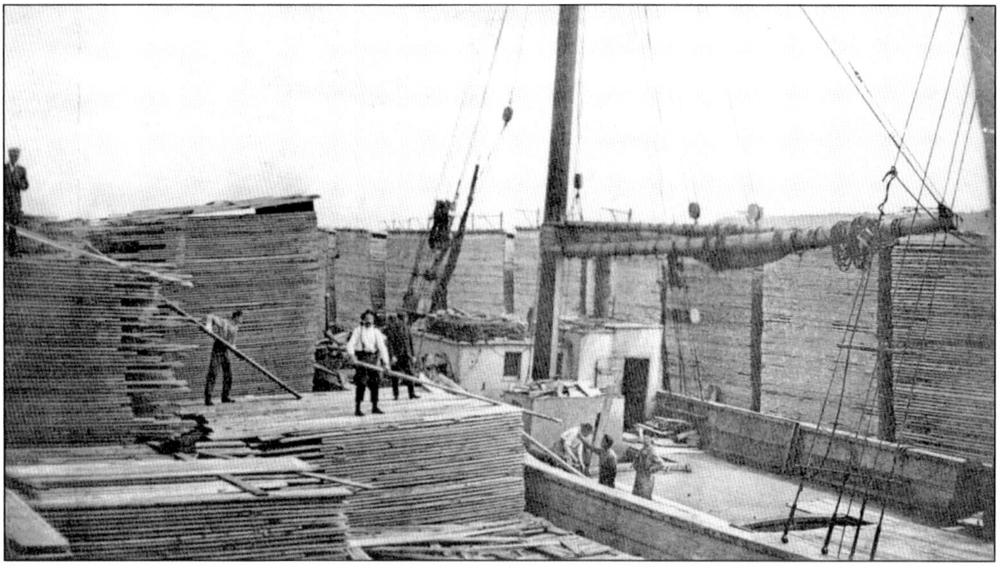

Stacking the cut lumber on the barges and schooners was mostly accomplished by hand. This crew prepares to load a lumber schooner, which is moored between two loading docks. This is a basic, no-frills cargo ship, likely towed by a larger freighter. By the time the crew finished, not only would the hold be full of lumber, it would be piled high on the decks as well. (GMHS.)

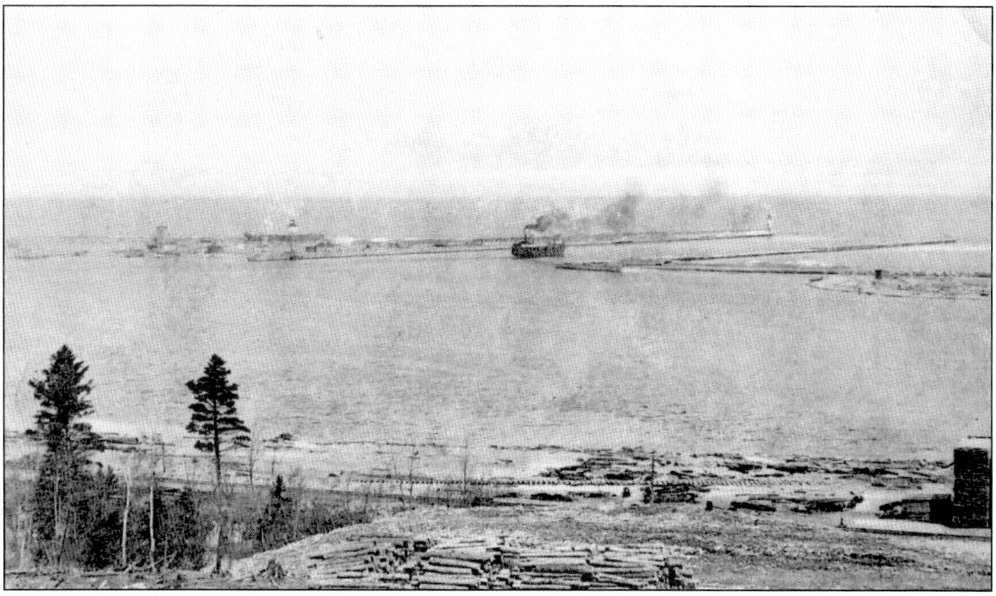

The area lumber mills anxiously waited for the spring ice breakup, when shipments of cut lumber could resume. This *c.* 1907 photograph is labeled "First Boat Out." No doubt it was a welcome sight to the lumbermen. Here a loaded freighter heads out of the channel from Grand Marais Harbor. This view also shows the western end of the Cook, Curtis and Miller hardwood mill yard. (GMHS.)

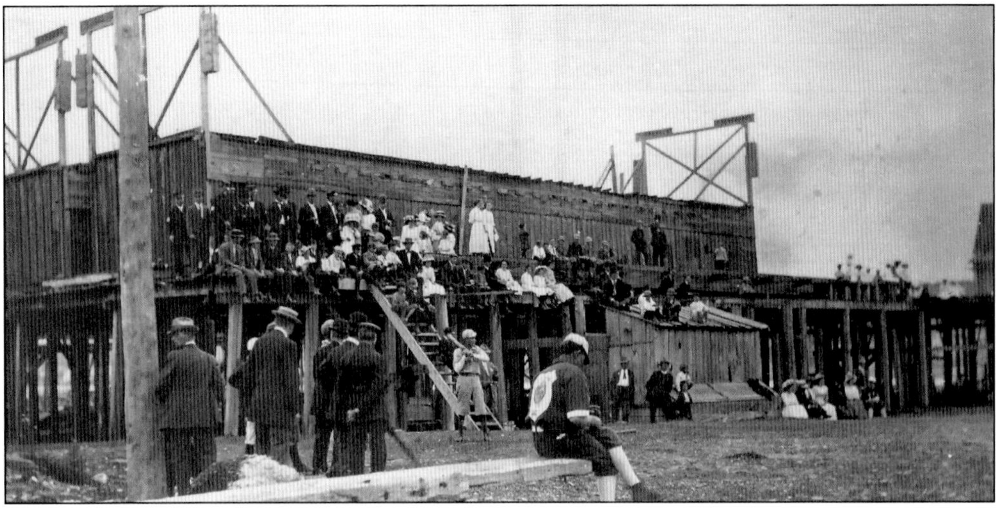

The lumber docks and tramways provided an excellent viewing platform for one of the town's favorite pastimes, a baseball game featuring the Grand Marais team. This 1890s photograph captures a moment during an afternoon game. This was also a social outing; note the well-dressed ladies and gentlemen at the top of the steps. Children sat on the shed roofs to enjoy the view. (GMHS.)

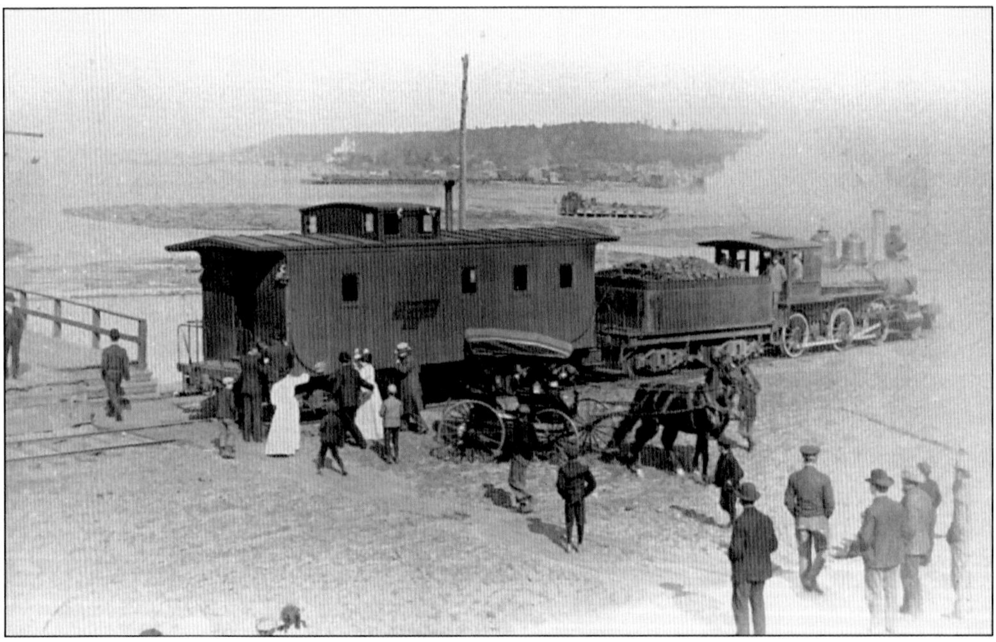

Not all trains hauled lumber. Newlywed couples who had the means could hire a special "wedding train" to take them 25 miles south to Seney, where they could transfer to a train on the Duluth, South Shore and Atlantic Railway and embark on their honeymoon. A wedding train was considered to be quite a status symbol. Here a young couple prepares to board while townsfolk look on. (GMHS.)

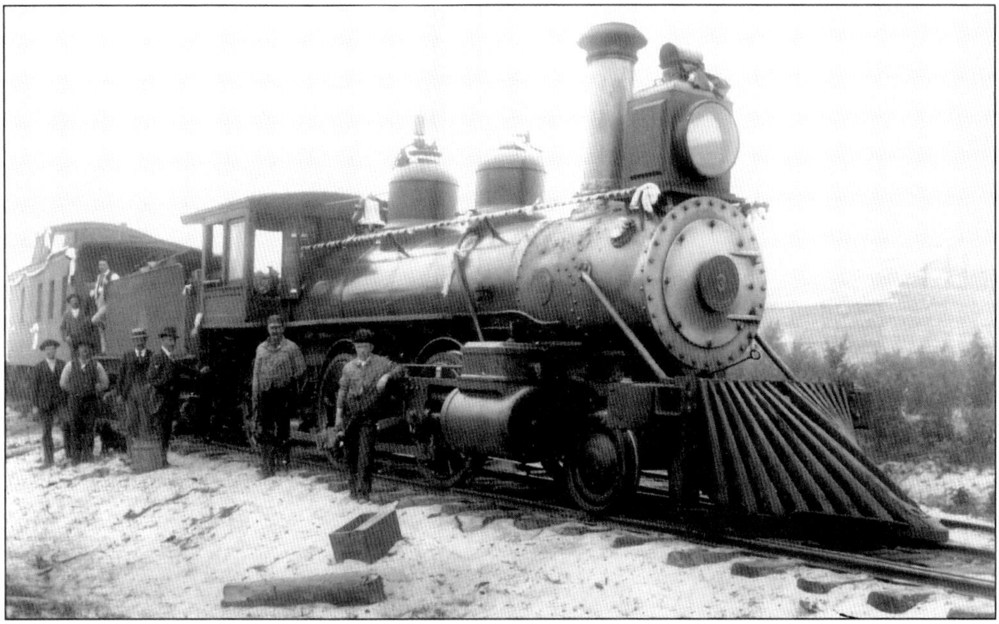

Railroads were expensive to maintain, and the Manistique Railway depended on a small amount of rolling stock to keep its operations going. Engine No. 3, shown here between Grand Marais and Seney, was a workhorse and made regular runs to Grand Marais. The bunting on the caboose suggests this was a ceremonial occasion of some sort, perhaps a wedding train. (Archives of Michigan.)

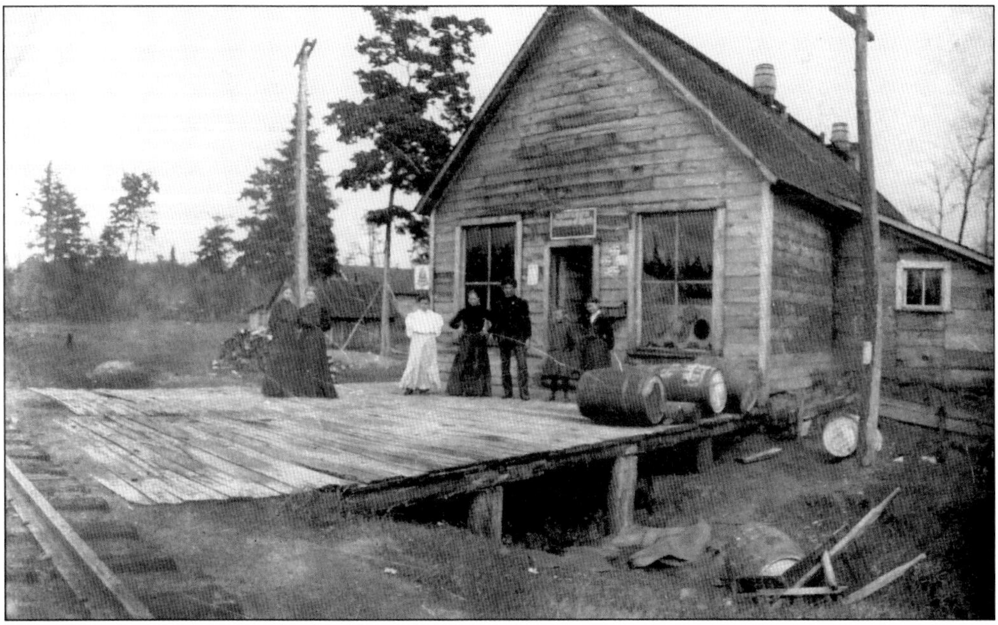

This photograph, possibly taken between Grand Marais and Seney, is representative of the small whistle-stop stations along the logging railway lines. The stations were often manned by an agent and his family, and supplies for lumber camps and area settlers could be unloaded here. Note the water barrels on the roof, a reminder of the constant fire danger. (Della Meldrum.)

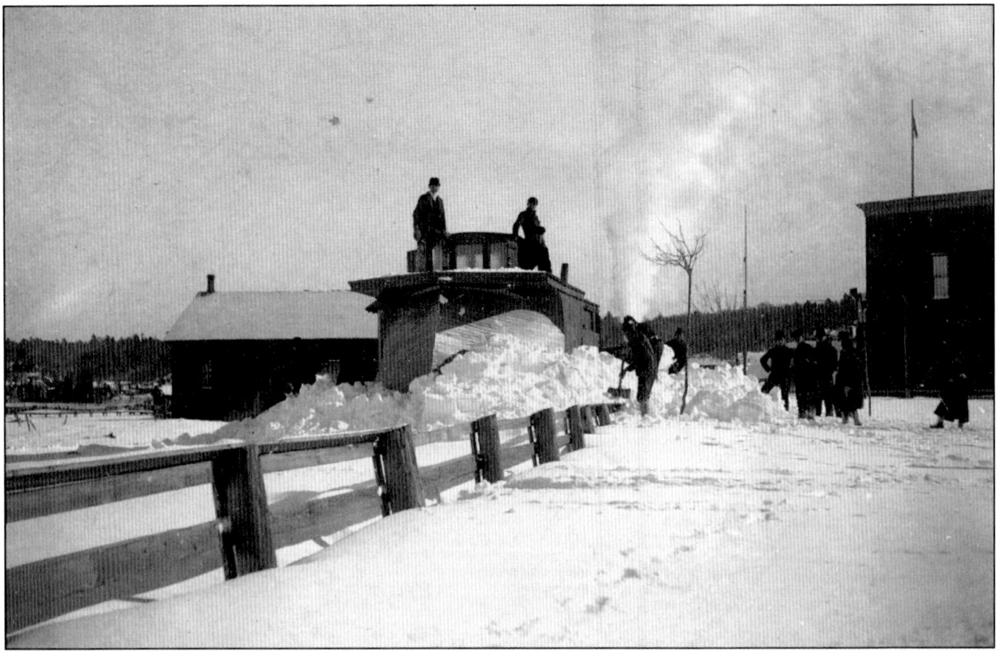

Keeping the railroad tracks clear was a constant problem, especially in winter. If the tracks were impassable, Grand Marais was virtually isolated. The railroad invested in huge plow equipment to deal with the snow, but occasionally even the plow train needed some help. Note the man with a shovel clearing snow by the fence. The railroad depot is at the left. (GMHS.)

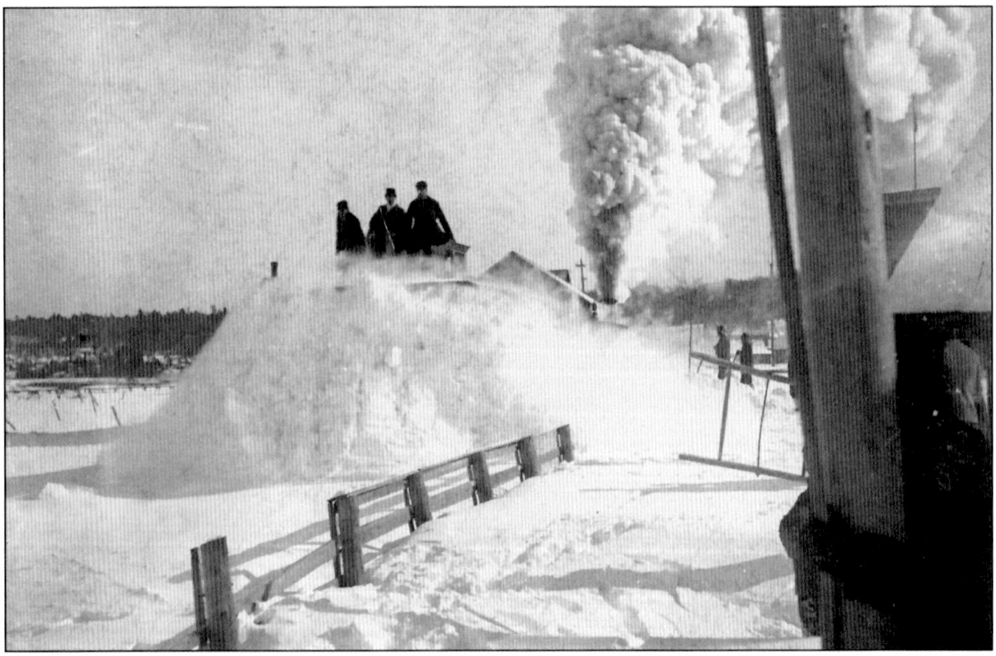

Here the plow train clears deep snow off the tracks along the bay in Grand Marais. This photograph was taken shortly after the previous photograph; the engine is at the rear, pushing the plow and bellowing out smoke from its smokestack. The depot chimney is just visible to the left of the train. (Ted and Marge Soldenski.)

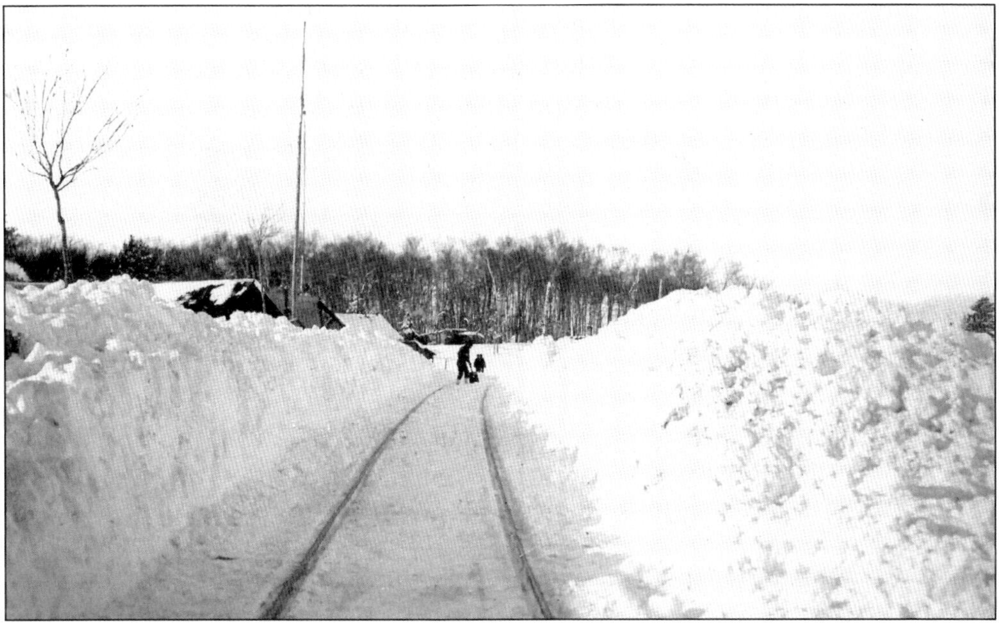

The tracks are finally cleared after the heavy snow. The pole and structure on the left are visible in the previous photograph. This was the end of the line, looking north-northwest toward Lake Superior. The man at the far end is still shoveling out the end of the tracks. Since the tracks ran along the bay and were exposed to the wind, huge drifts were common. (Ted and Marge Soldenski.)

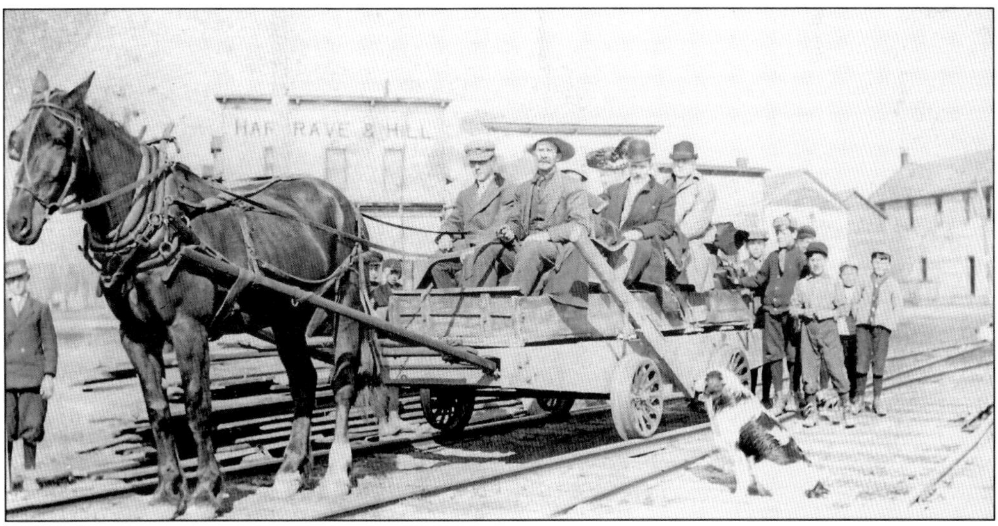

When the railroad left in 1910, the only way to get to Seney was via a horse-drawn wagon with railroad axles and wheels attached. The 32-mile trip over the rails took all day, with a change of horses halfway, and the railcar could only operate in good weather. The railroad tracks were pulled up in 1911, and the town was virtually isolated in the winter. (Della Meldrum.)

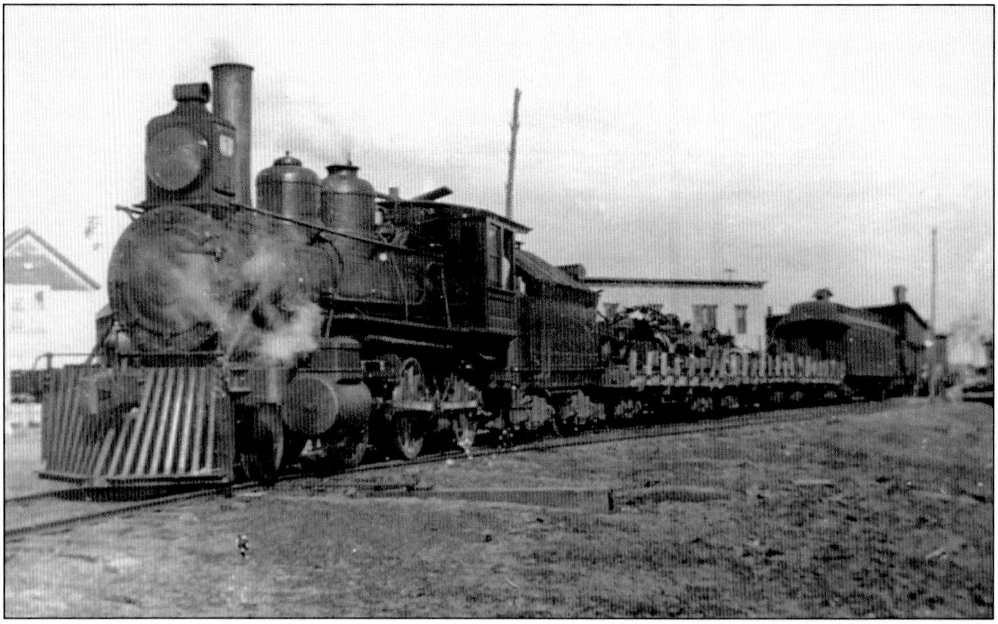

On what was surely a sad day for Grand Marais citizens, the Manistique Railway returned in 1911 to start pulling up the railroad tracks. The flatcars here are loaded with scrap iron and rails. Soon the railroad was gone for good, leaving the town virtually isolated except for the small fishing fleet and a few horse-drawn conveyances that hauled people to Seney, 25 miles to the south. (GMHS.)

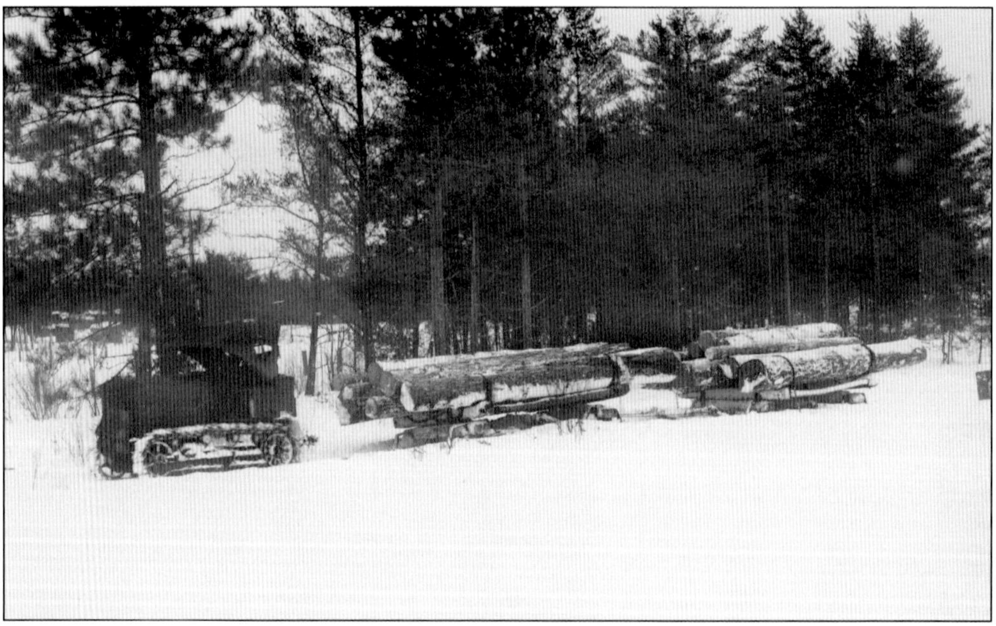

Lumbering continued on a small scale in Grand Marais for many years. Although the large mills were gone, loggers still found ways to bring cut logs to small mills in the area. Here an early tractor is pulling two sledges loaded with large logs. The tractor might have been built by hand from various vehicles and parts. Loggers were ingenious at creating the equipment they needed. (GMHS.)

Three

Grand Marais Booms

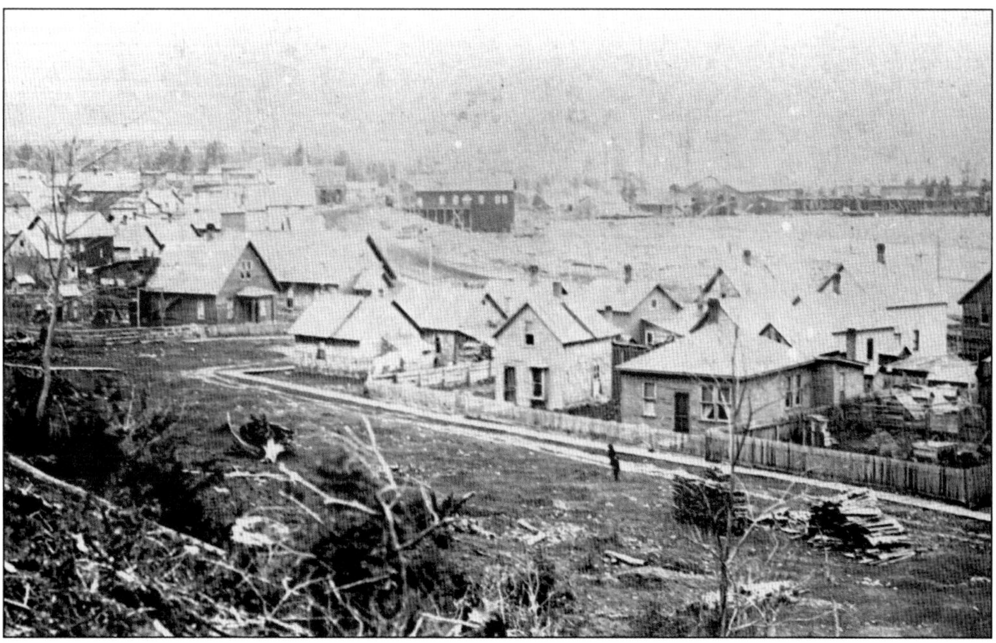

When the Alger-Smith Company brought the railroad to town in 1893 and opened its large mill, it did not take long for people to pour into the area. Houses seemingly sprang up overnight. Some were knocked down in Seney, 25 miles to the south, and reassembled in Grand Marais. This view shows the town in the 1890s. Note the railroad depot, center, and the lumber docks in the background. (GMHS.)

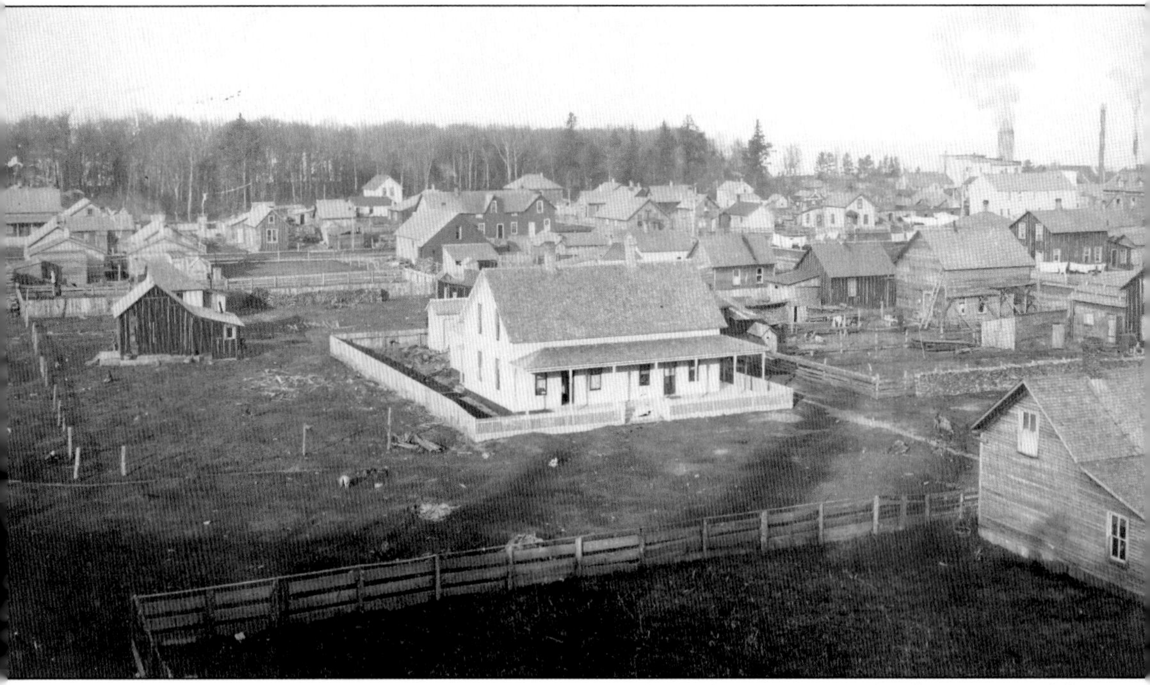

A photographer set up his equipment on a steep hillside about 1895 to take this picture of the rapidly growing part of town known as West Grand Marais. The smokestacks of the Marais Lumber Company in the background show it operating at full steam, running two shifts a day by this time. It is wash day, for many houses have clotheslines filled with laundry hanging out to dry. Fences around the homes kept out wandering cows, which roamed freely. The cows

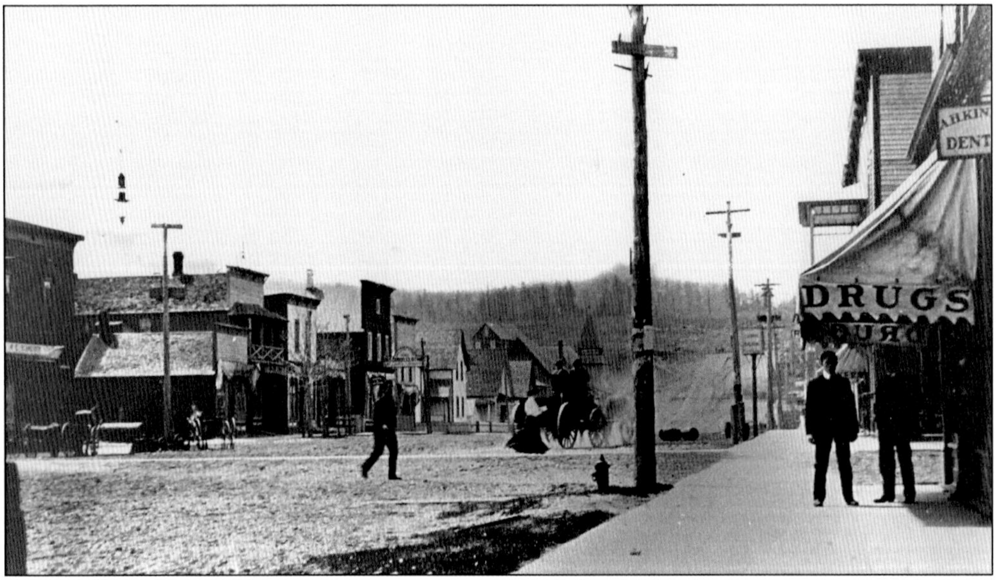

By the late 1890s, Grand Marais was prospering. Businesses, many of them saloons, lined both sides of Lake Avenue. This view looks south on Lake Avenue from just north of Carlson Street. Note the fire hydrants and electricity poles, the cement sidewalks, and the walkway where the lady is crossing the street. A number of these buildings still stand today. (GMHS.)

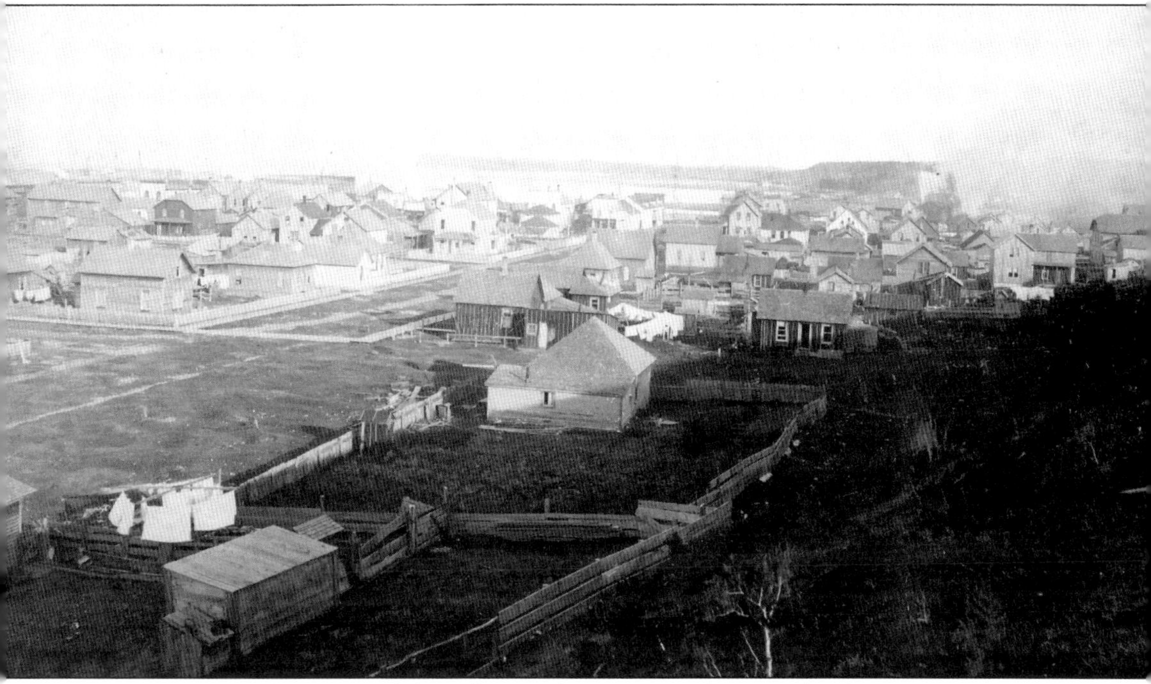

continued to share the streets of the village with cars and pedestrians for almost 40 years. Not until the 1930s did the newly formed women's club sponsor an ordinance restricting the cows, and even then, some villagers complained. The cows, they said, took care of the need to mow grass in the public areas of town. (GMHS.)

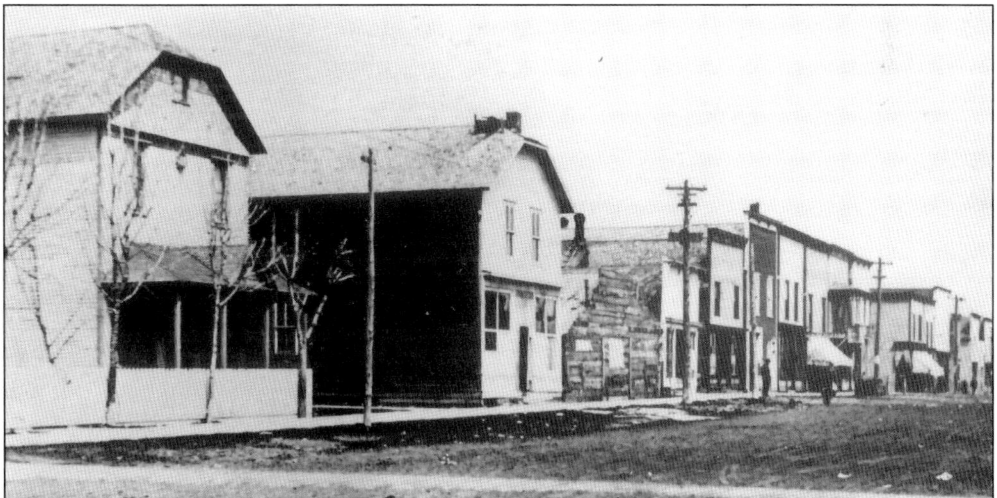

In the 1890s, business was booming on Lake Avenue. In this view looking north, the west side of the street is lined with restaurants, a livery stable, and at least seven saloons. The large building in the center is O'Brien's Hall, owned by Dr. Stephen J. O'Brien. The building at left served as the Green Shingles Tavern and later as an adult rest home; it is now a private residence. (GMHS.)

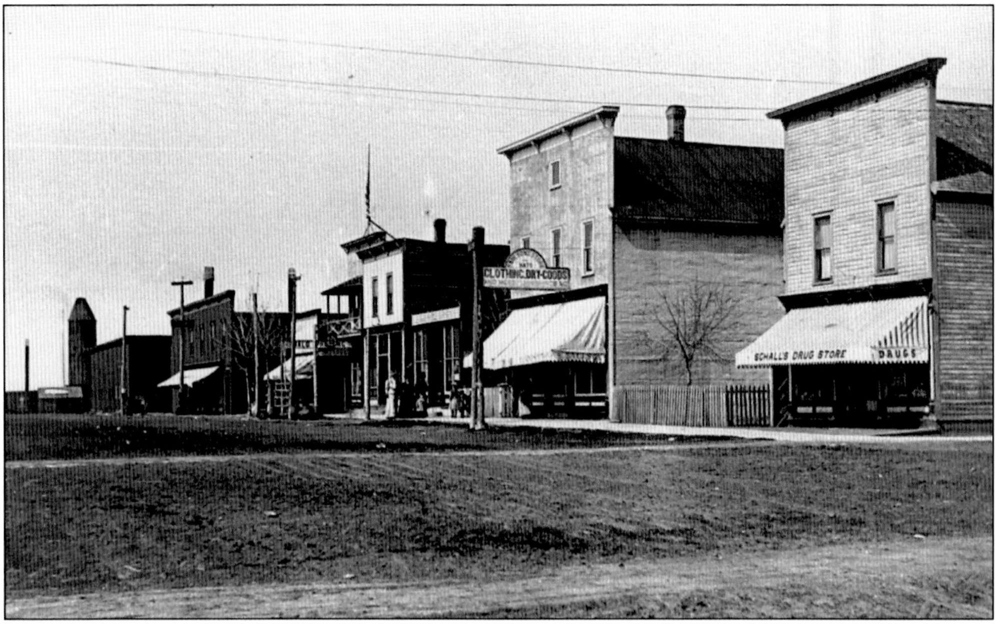

Schall's Drug Store, right, was a popular fixture in Grand Marais in the 1890s. Next door to it is the Saulson and Company Dry Goods store, which nearly burned down in 1904 when the Morse and Schneider store (at far left with awning) caught fire. A spark blew down the block and set the dry goods store ablaze, causing $10,000 in damage. That building was saved but the Schneider store was a total loss. (GMHS.)

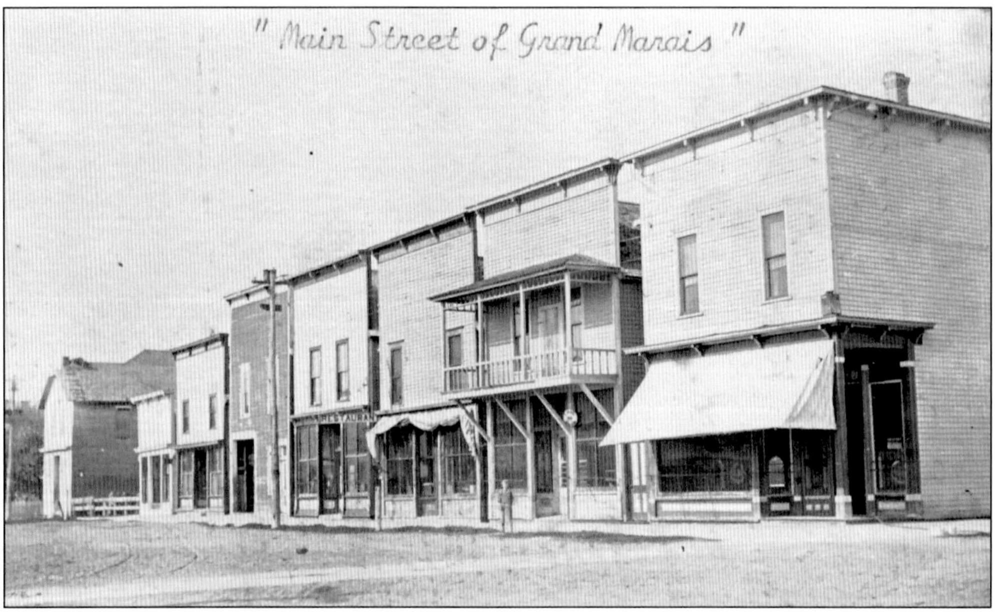

This photograph shows Lake Avenue in the 1890s, looking south. From left to right are O'Brien's Hall, the office of Dr. Stephen J. O'Brien, the Dave Thomas Saloon, the Beaulieu Livery, the Dewey Saloon and Music Hall, the Alhambra Restaurant, the Warren Kipp Saloon, and Hugh Logan's Superior Sample Room. Note the little boy in the center of the photograph. (GMHS.)

J. Verne Kinsey was a noted photographer who took many pictures of people and places around Grand Marais. He also photographed schoolchildren for their school pictures, and newspapers of the time note that he worked as far south as the Grand Rapids area. Many of Kinsey's photographs were used on postcards, including double-wide panoramic shots. His photographs provide a valuable record of early Grand Marais. (Della Meldrum.)

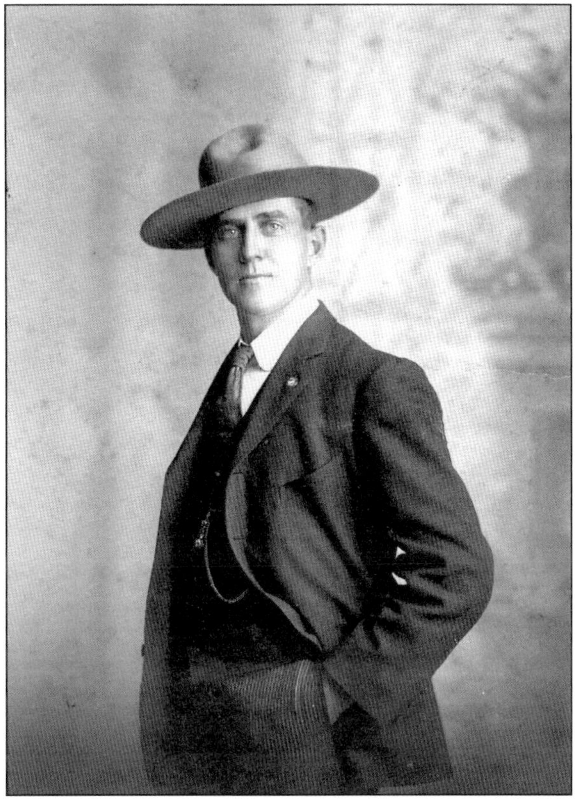

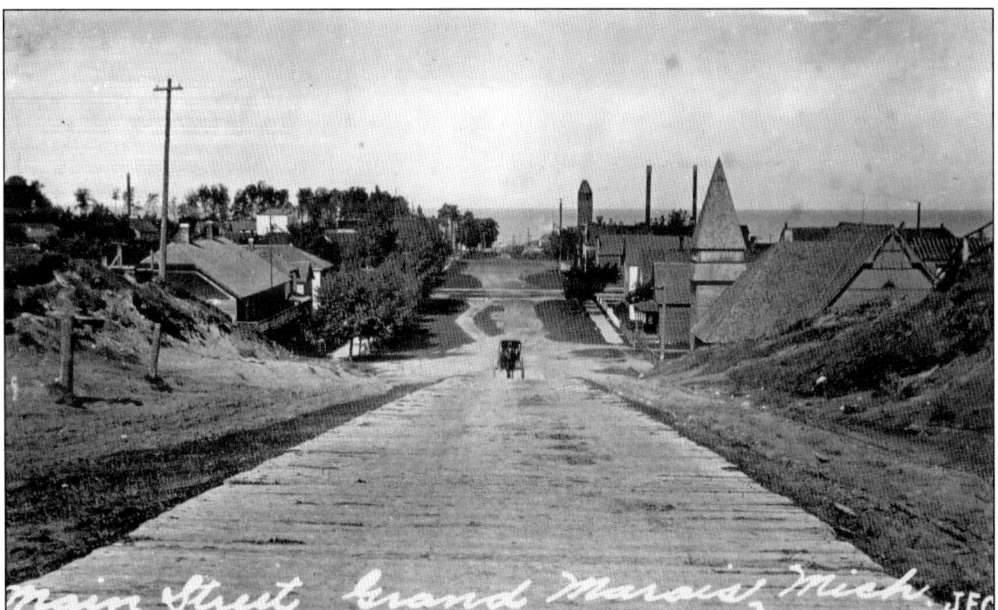

This photograph, looking north down the hill leading into Grand Marais, shows the plank road formed by wooden planks laid crosswise. This prevented the road from turning into a sea of mud in the rain and gave some traction to the buggies and wagons. The Bay View Hospital is at left, the Methodist church is at right, and the mill is in the distance. (GMHS.)

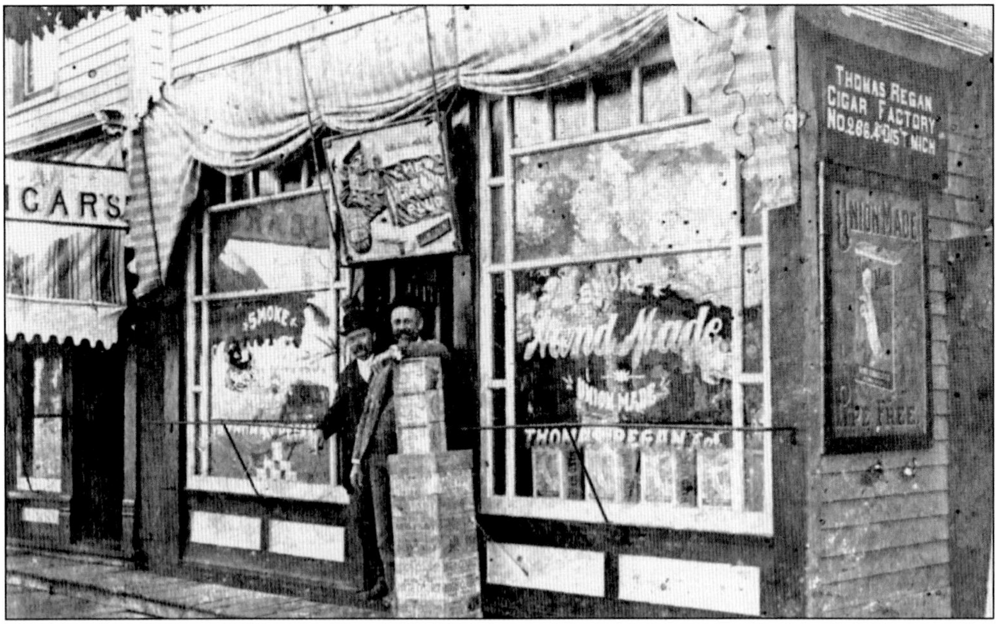

Thomas Regan operated one of several cigar stores in Grand Marais during the boom years. Cigars in those days were rolled by hand. Note the emphasis on union-made cigars, such as the Nerve Navy and High Court Navy tobacco brands labeled on the crates. Regan's shop was located on Lake Avenue next to the Saulson and Company Dry Goods store. Today it is the site of the local bank. (GMHS.)

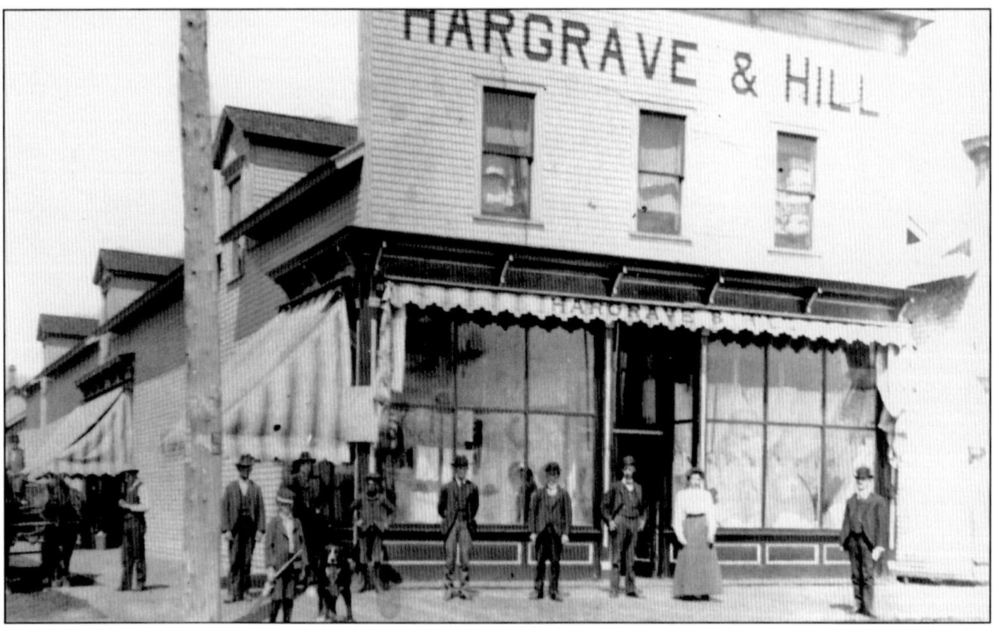

Wilkes W. Hargrave and Roy C. Hill owned a successful business in Seney, and when that town went bust, they moved to Grand Marais and opened one of the town's leading department stores. The store faced the bay and was located on Grand Marais Avenue. This photograph was taken in the 1890s. Note the well-dressed clientele in front of the store, including the young boy and his dog. (GMHS.)

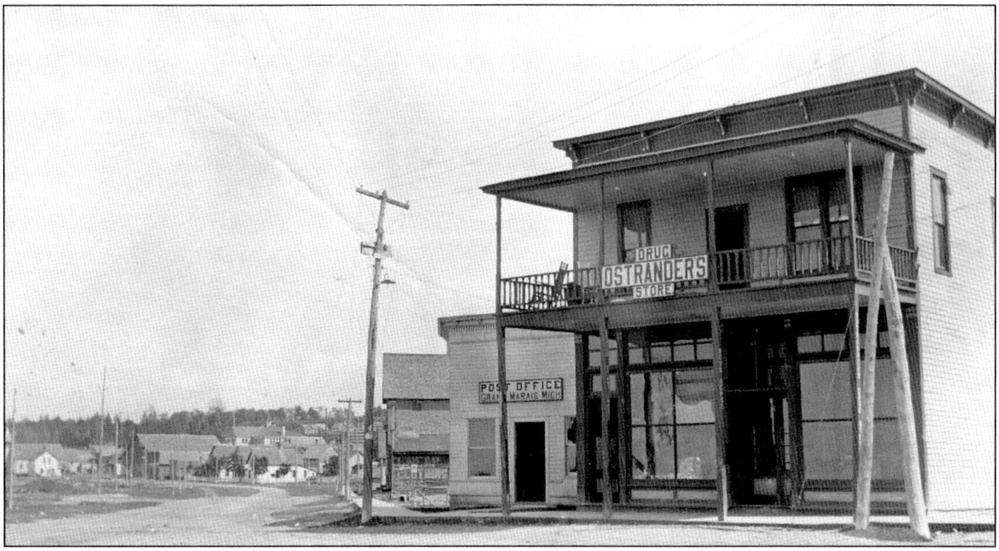

The Ostrander brothers opened one of the earliest drugstores in the county in 1896. Their business was originally located on Lake Avenue, but they moved into the former Grand Central Saloon building, shown here, in 1909. The Ostrander family remained in business here for over 60 years and established several other drugstores in cities around the Upper Peninsula. This view looks west along Grand Marais Avenue. (GMHS.)

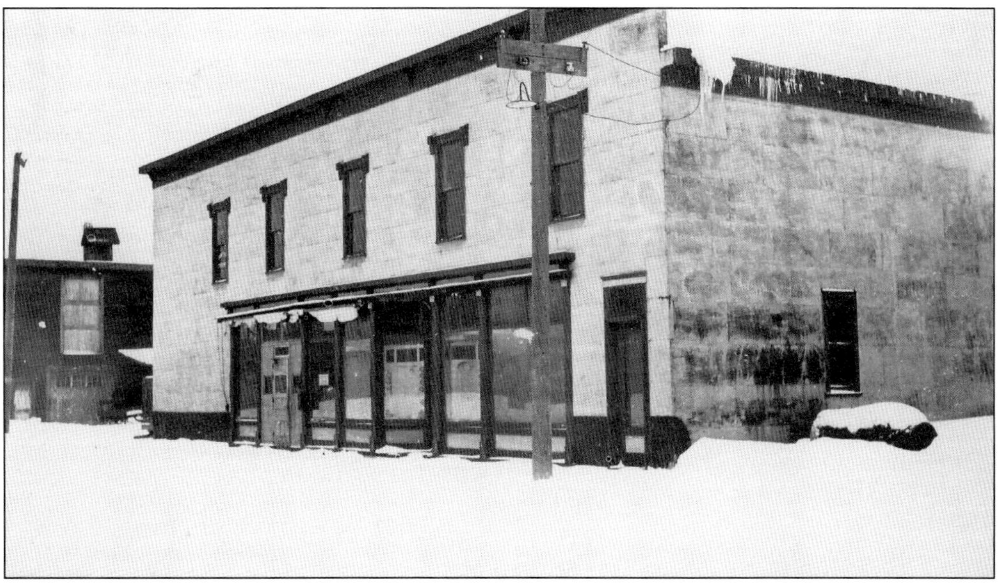

Rudolph E. Schneider and Edwin Morse moved their successful business from Seney in the mid-1890s and established a large department store in Grand Marais. Several doctors and lawyers had offices on the second floor, and the Grand Marais Savings Bank was housed on the ground floor. The original building burned down in 1904 and was rebuilt with a larger store. The building in the background was the store's warehouse. (GMHS.)

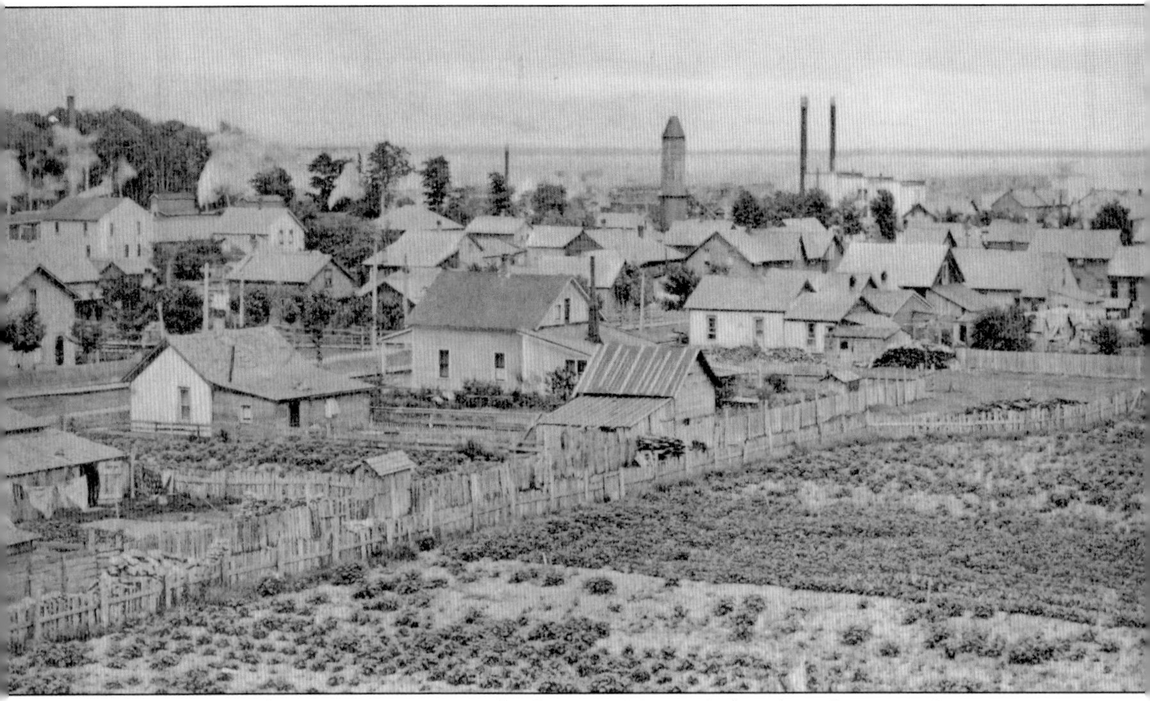

By 1906, Grand Marais was at its peak. Over 2,000 people lived in the town, businesses were prospering, and the mill continued to run at capacity. This photograph of West Grand Marais shows how the village has matured. Houses are outlined with fences, there are sidewalks, and garden plots are laid out neatly. True to the time, every house has a privy out back. At this point,

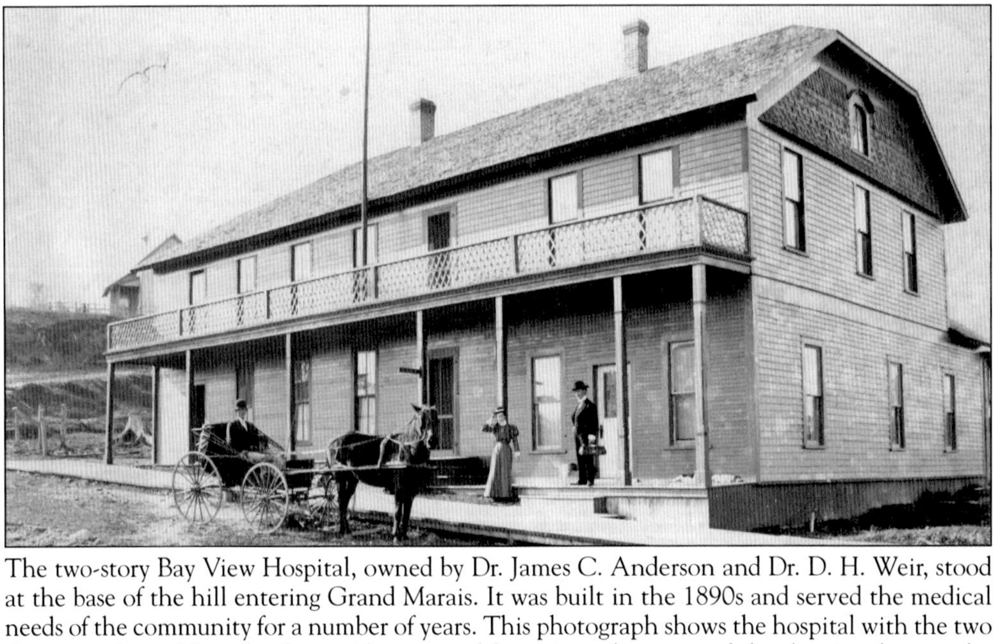

The two-story Bay View Hospital, owned by Dr. James C. Anderson and Dr. D. H. Weir, stood at the base of the hill entering Grand Marais. It was built in the 1890s and served the medical needs of the community for a number of years. This photograph shows the hospital with the two doctors in front. Note the doctors' buggy, used for visits to homes, and the sleeping dogs on the porch. (Jana Robertson.)

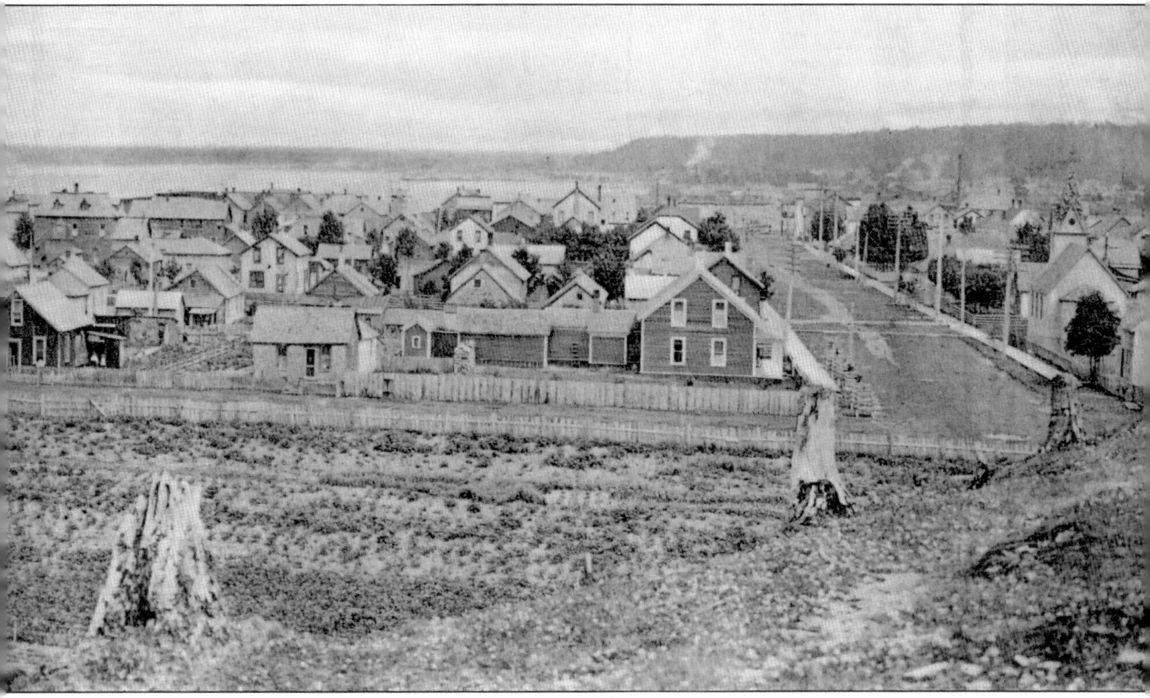

Grand Marais boasted no fewer than 15 hotels and boardinghouses and 29 saloons. The town also had a number of churches, and the Swedish Lutheran church with its tall steeple is at the far right. Many of the houses in this photograph still stand and are maintained as private residences. This view looks east down Randolph Street at the corner of Alger Avenue. (GMHS.)

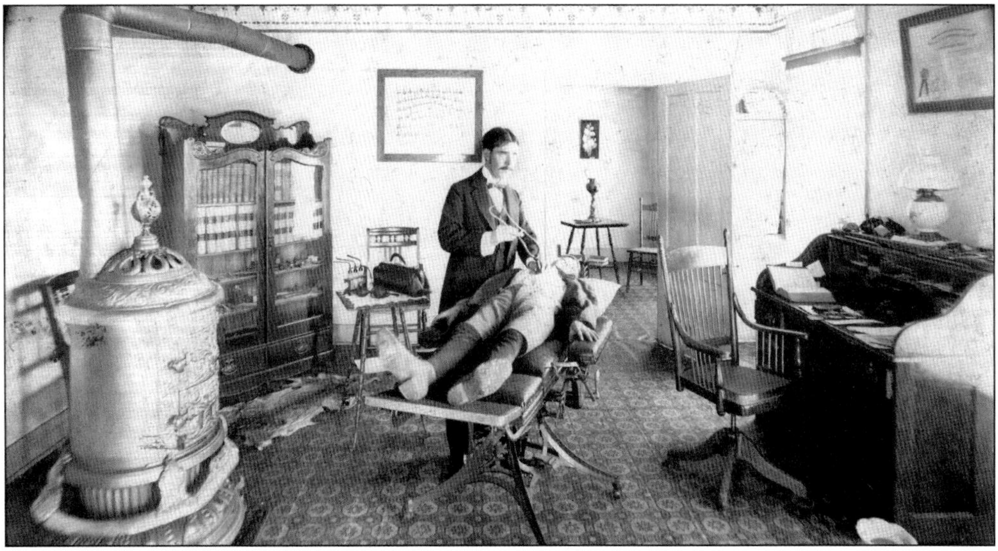

Dr. James C. Anderson not only co-owned the Bay View Hospital, he also ran a busy office practice on the corner of Randolph and Campbell Streets. In this posed portrait, the doctor "listens" to a patient with his stethoscope. Note the large parlor stove and rolltop office desk, also the cabinet full of medical texts and the typical doctor's black bag on the chair. (Jana Robertson.)

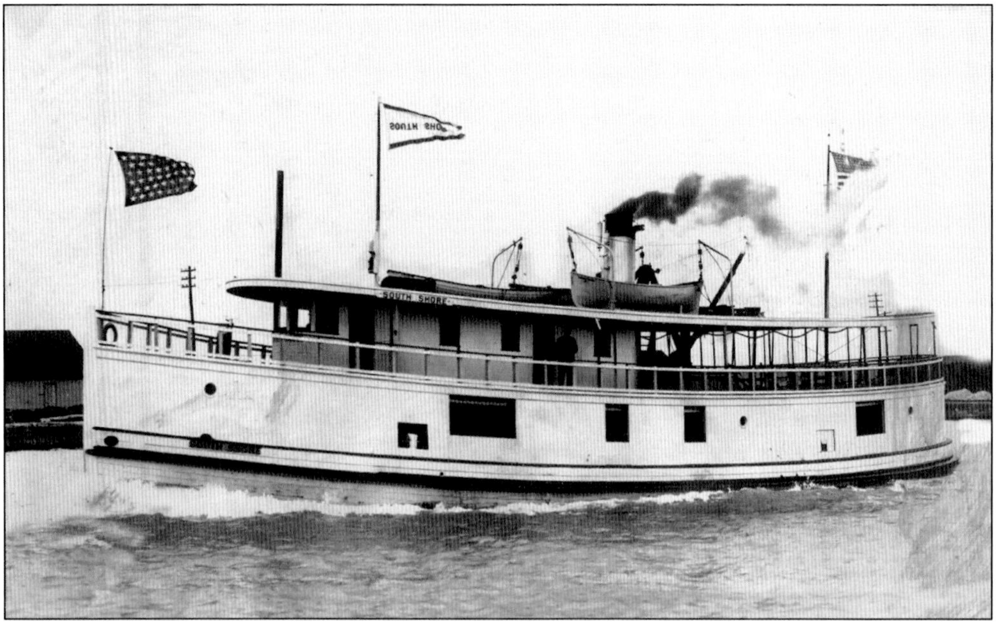

The *South Shore* was a packet freighter owned by the Endress Company. It made weekly passenger and cargo runs between Grand Marais and Sault Ste. Marie, with stops at the lifesaving stations along the way. The *South Shore* sank in a storm in 1912, seven miles west of the Grand Marais pier. The Grand Marais Life-Saving Station crew rescued the nine crewmen and four passengers. (GMHS.)

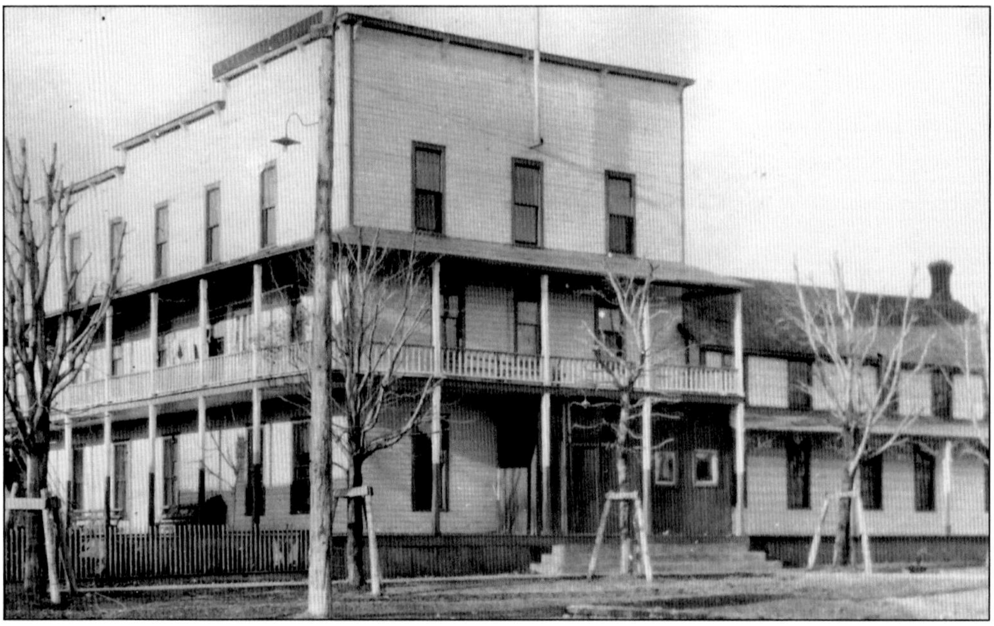

The Wabash House Hotel was one of the earliest hotels built in Grand Marais. The original structure was a log building, shown at right. The three-story addition was added later. The owners named it after the recent shipwreck of the steamer *Wabash*, which foundered west of Grand Marais near Pictured Rocks in 1883. The hotel was located on the south side of Brazel Street just west of Lake Avenue. (GMHS.)

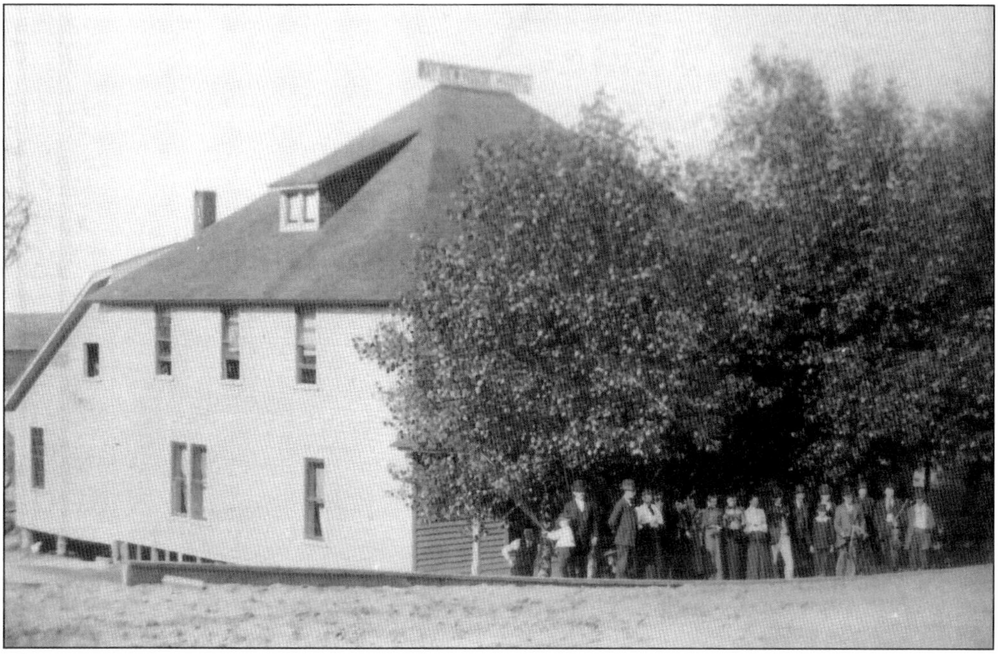

The Bay View House in East Town was located on Everett Avenue. This unidentified group photograph in front of the hotel features a man with a bicycle, a man holding a violin, and a young boy spraying water from a hose. Since there was only one train in and out of town each day, visitors who needed lodging kept the local hotels busy. (GMHS.)

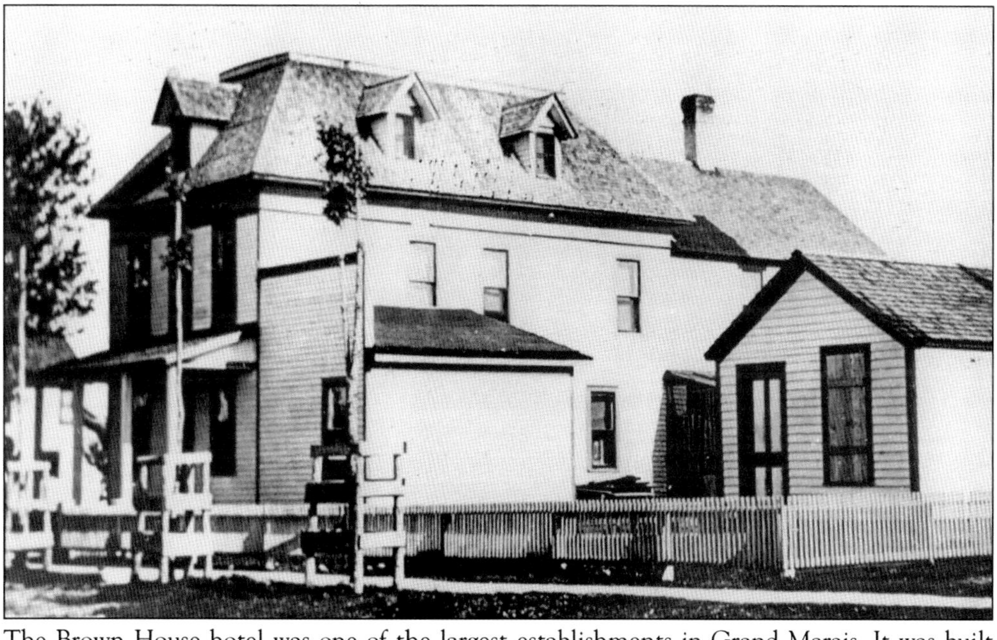

The Brown House hotel was one of the largest establishments in Grand Marais. It was built about 1885. L. W. Nettleton purchased the building about 1903 and changed the name to the Nettleton Hotel. This 1895 photograph shows the building with newly planted maple trees in front, caged in wooden cribs to prevent damage from wagons and cows. The building at right is a bathhouse. (GMHS.)

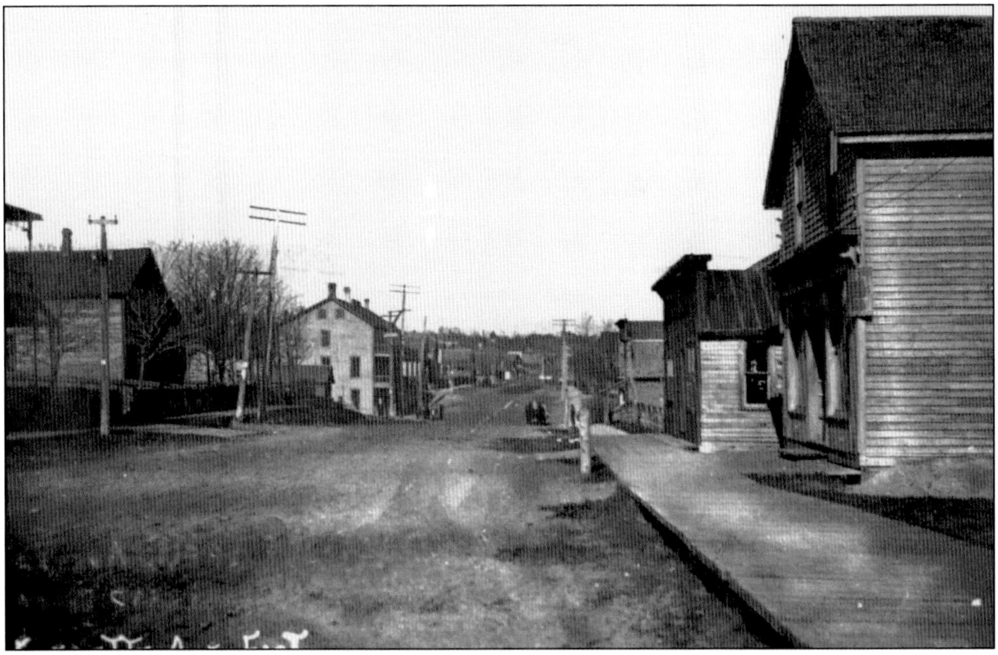

This 1910 view looking west toward Grand Marais shows Everett Avenue and East Town. At the far left, the awnings of the Swanson House hotel are just visible at the edge of the photograph. The large three-story building in the center is the Carpenter House hotel, built next to what is now Carpenter Creek. Across from the Carpenter House stood the notorious Bucket of Blood Saloon. (GMHS.)

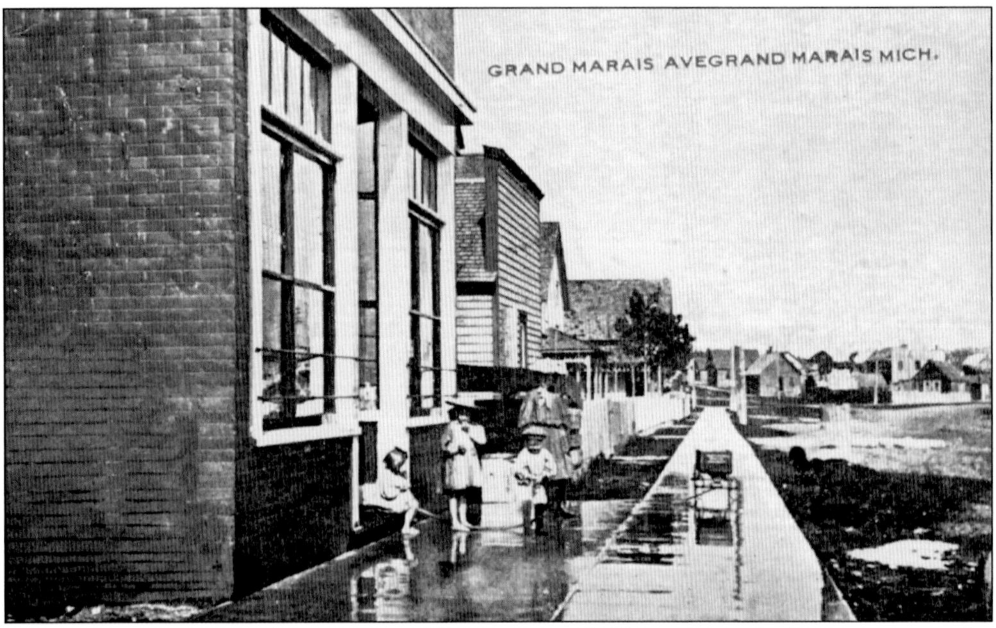

This early-1900s postcard shows part of East Town. Children play with their wagon on the sidewalks on a rainy day in front of the Norkowski store. Although the roads were a muddy mess in the spring, the sidewalks were made of poured concrete, keeping everyone's shoes a bit cleaner. This view looks west toward town. (GMHS.)

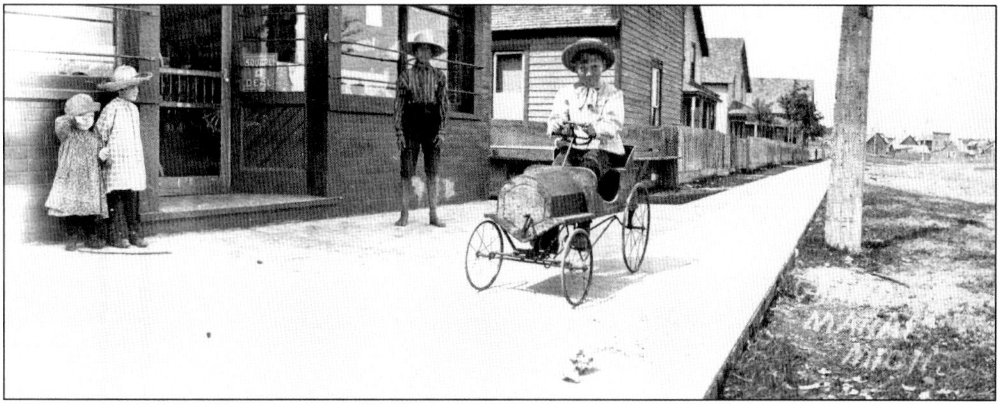

Grand Marais was divided into two de facto sections: West Town, which was mostly Lutheran Swedes and Finns, and East Town, which was mostly Catholic. The kids from East Town had their rivalries with those from West Town. Here a boy rides a pedal car in front of the Norkowski store, which was located on Everett Avenue in East Town. This photograph was taken about 1908. (ACHS.)

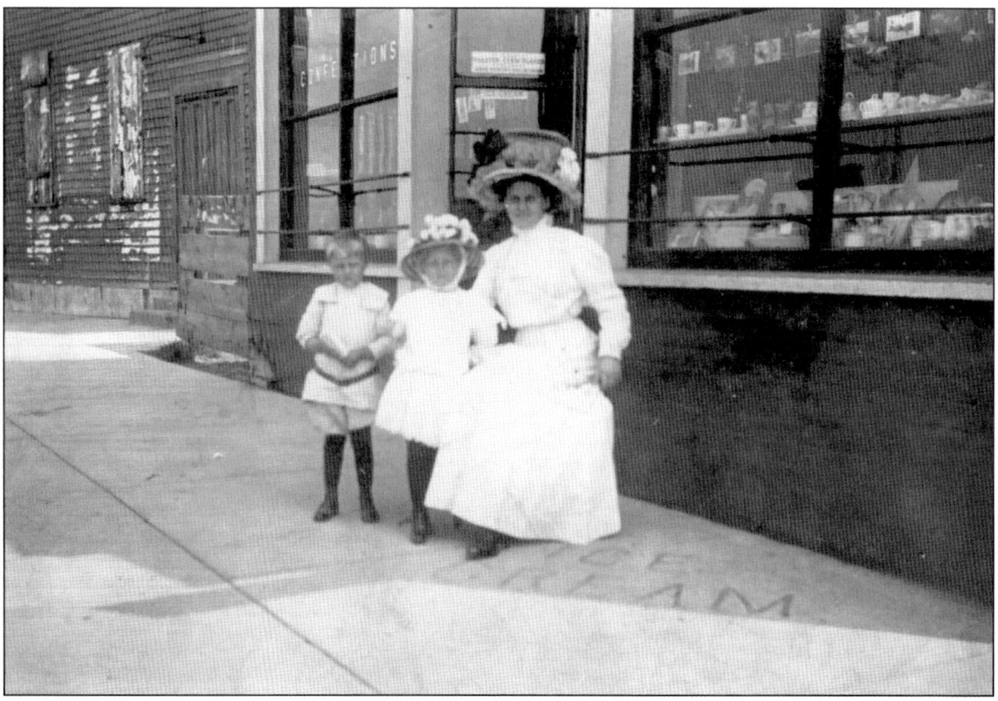

The Norkowski store was a popular East Town destination for candy and sweets. Here Mrs. Norkowski poses with her two children in front of the store. Note the word *ice cream* written on the sidewalk. The building in the background is the Grand Marais Opera House, a large hall for movies, dances, and even roller-skating. It was torn down about 1950. (ACHS.)

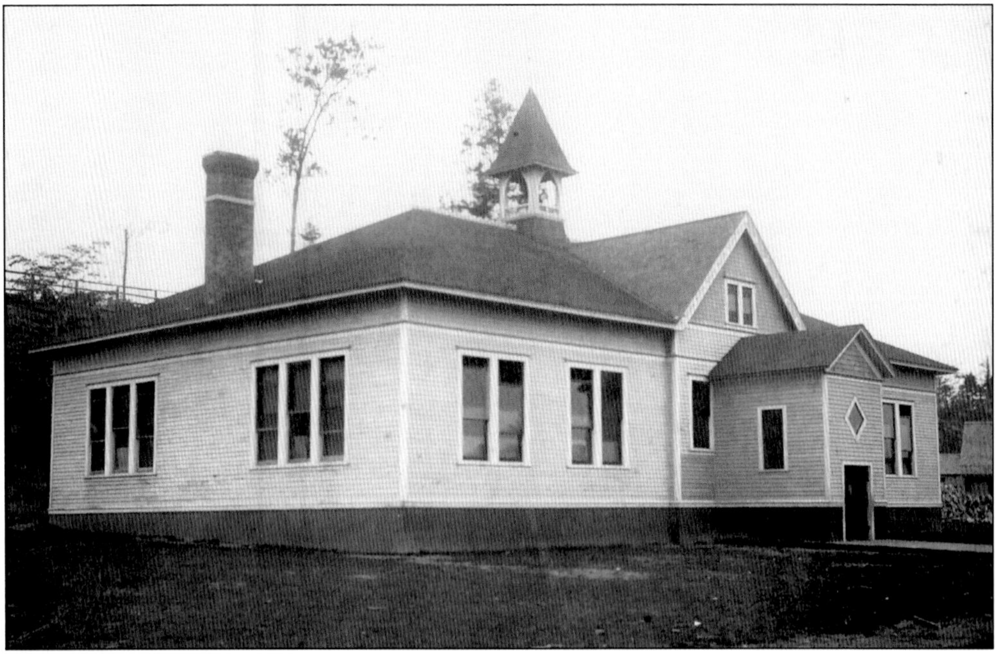

This one-room school was built in 1885 at Grand Marais Avenue and Colwell Street. The beginning enrollment was 50 pupils, and when Grand Marais began to grow in the early 1890s, the school quickly became too small for the number of students. Several other schools were built in other areas of town, and this building was extensively remodeled. (GMHS.)

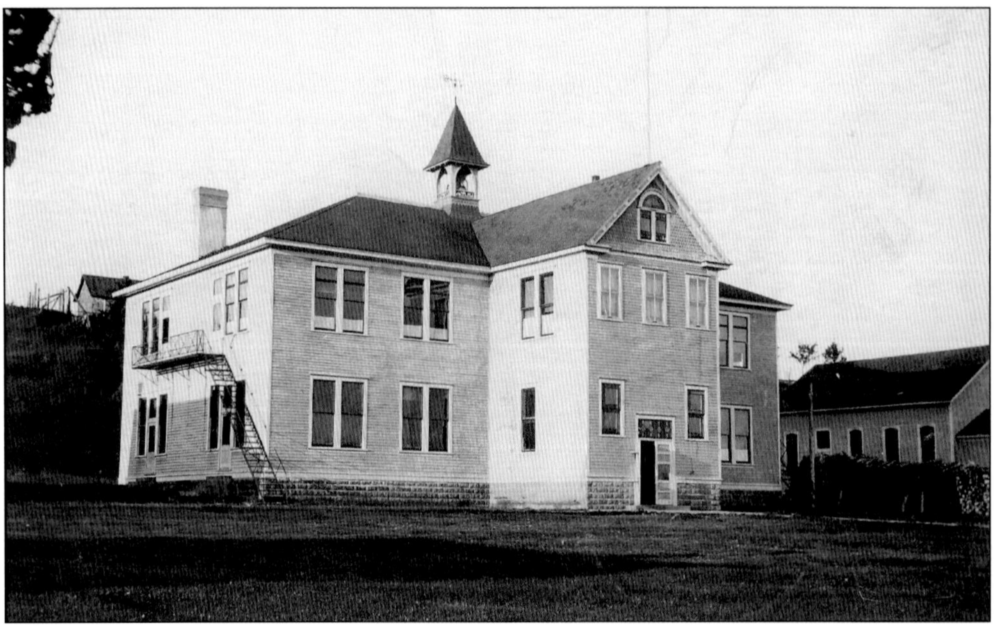

As the school enrollment strained the available space, the original one-room school was redesigned and a second story was added around 1895. The renovated school could now hold 400 students and 12 teachers. The building at the far right was a gymnasium. Note the stacked wood and the modern fire escapes. This building was used until the 1920s, when the present school was built. (GMHS.)

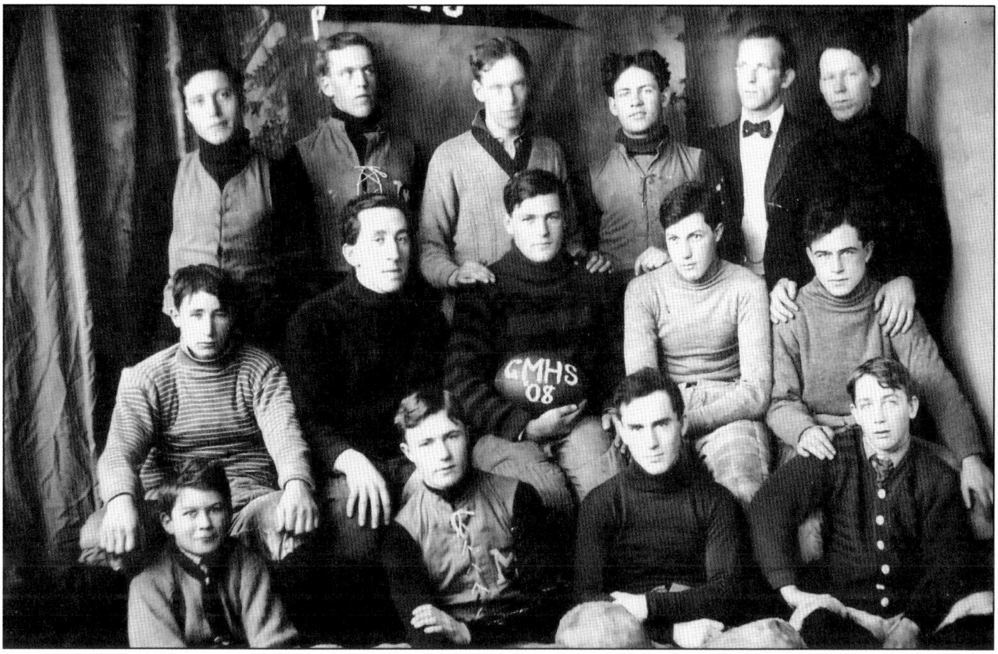

Grand Marais High School boasted this varsity football team in 1908. The man in the bow tie, top right, is Emil Lederle, the school superintendent. Players' ages ranged from early teens (bottom left) to late teens, and with only 14 players in the photograph, it might have been hard to field a team. (Bill LaCombe.)

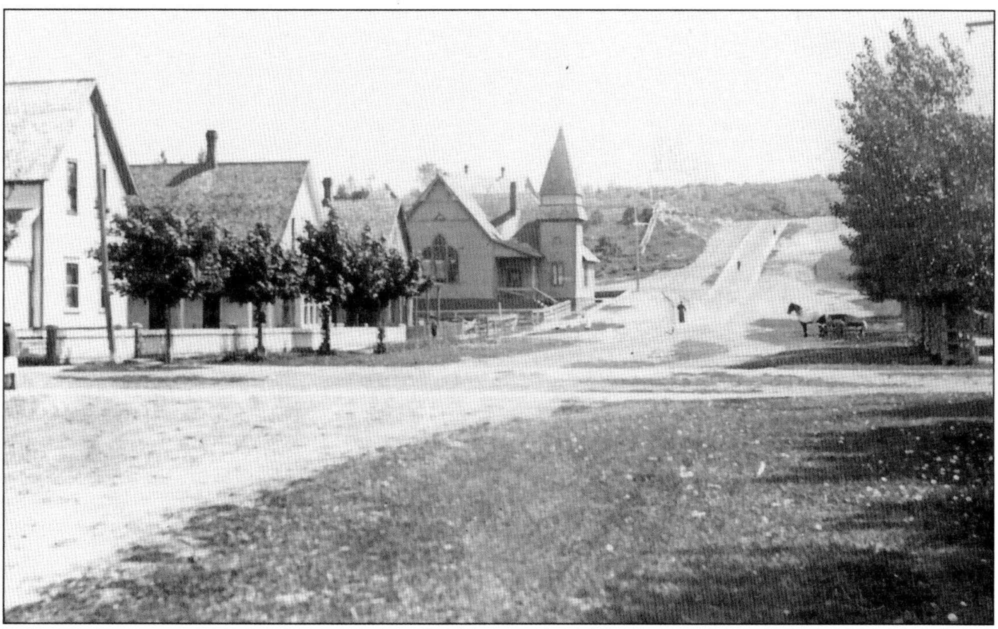

By the early part of the 20th century, Grand Marais was a tidy, prosperous town. This view, looking south on Lake Avenue, shows the new Methodist church and a number of neat homes, all with picket fences. Trees were planted along the main streets in the 1890s and were protected with wooden cribbing, shown at right. Planks covered the hill leading out of town and provided traction for wagons. (GMHS.)

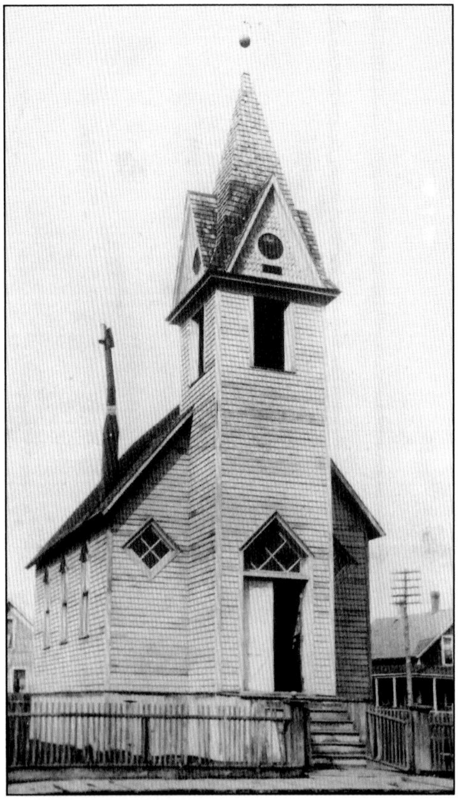

The Swedish Lutheran church stood on the southwest corner of Randolph and McMillan Streets. The lumber boom of Michigan's Upper Peninsula attracted many Scandinavian immigrants, a number of whom came from Sweden. The church was built in 1900. In 1907, the Finnish Lutherans built their own church, which is still in use today. (GMHS.)

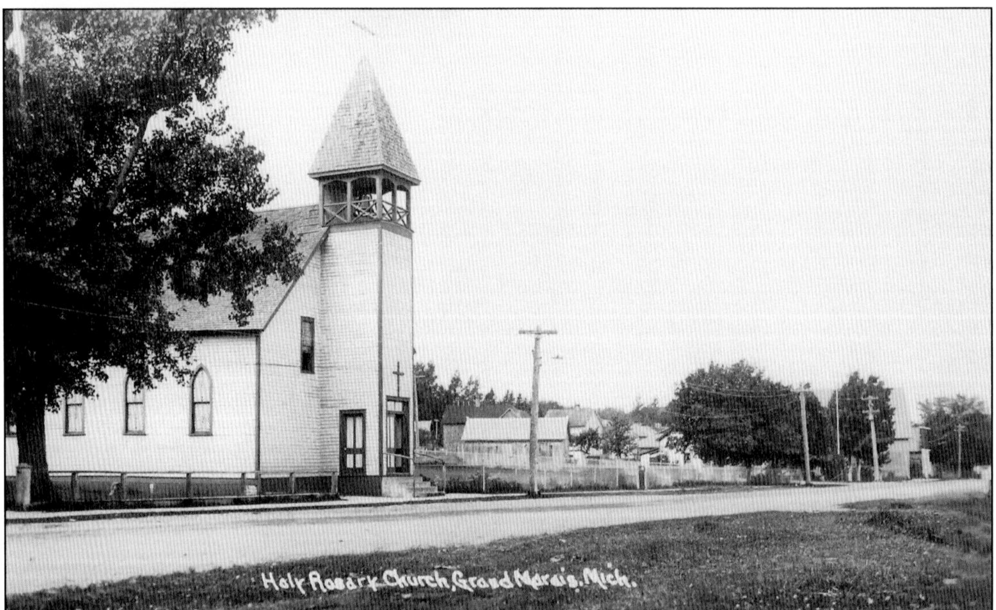

The Catholic residents of Grand Marais held religious services in a storefront building until 1895, when the parish seat was transferred from Seney to Grand Marais. Holy Rosary Catholic Church was built soon after on Grand Marais Avenue. It burned down in 1935, and the present church was rebuilt on the same spot. This photograph shows the church around 1930. (GMHS.)

This church, located on the corner of Lake Avenue and Veteran Street, was built in 1898 and originally was home to the Presbyterian congregation. The original Methodist Episcopalian church stood one block away. The Methodist congregation later moved to this building, renaming it the First Methodist Church. It is still an active house of worship for the Methodist congregation. (GMHS.)

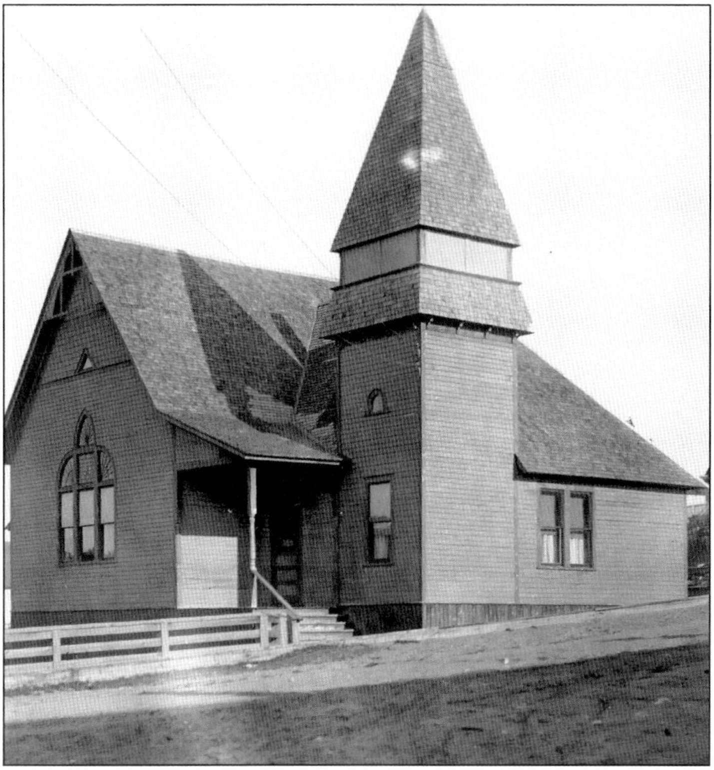

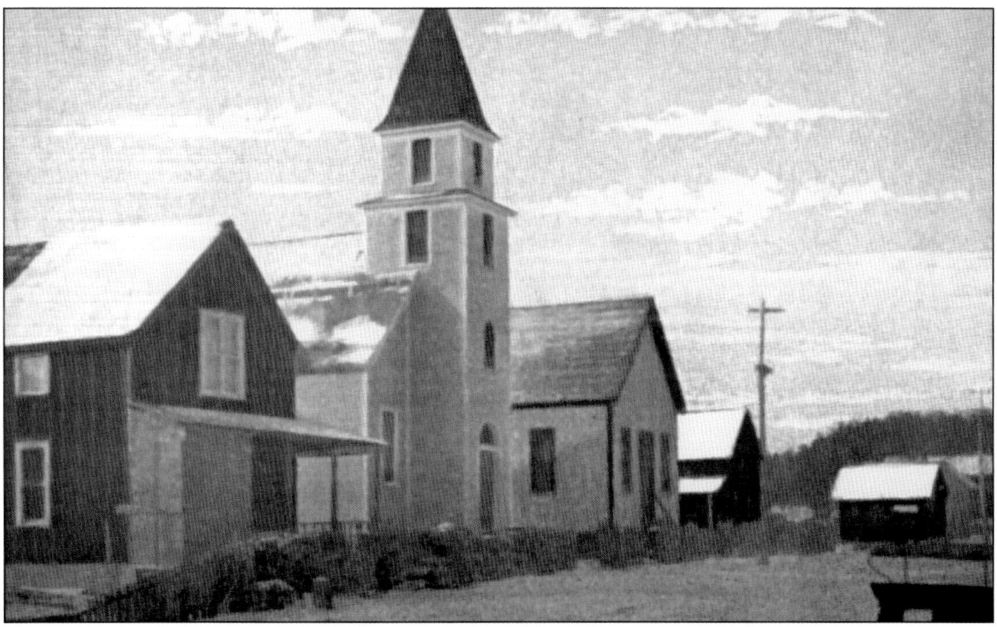

This artist's drawing shows the Finnish Lutheran church, which was finished in 1907. Pastor Jacob Hoikka was the first Finn to be ordained in America. The altar painting depicts Jesus teaching from a boat along the lakeshore, appropriate for a church on the shore of Lake Superior. Now called the First Lutheran Church, it is located on Brazel Street across from Woodland Park. (Doris Krempa.)

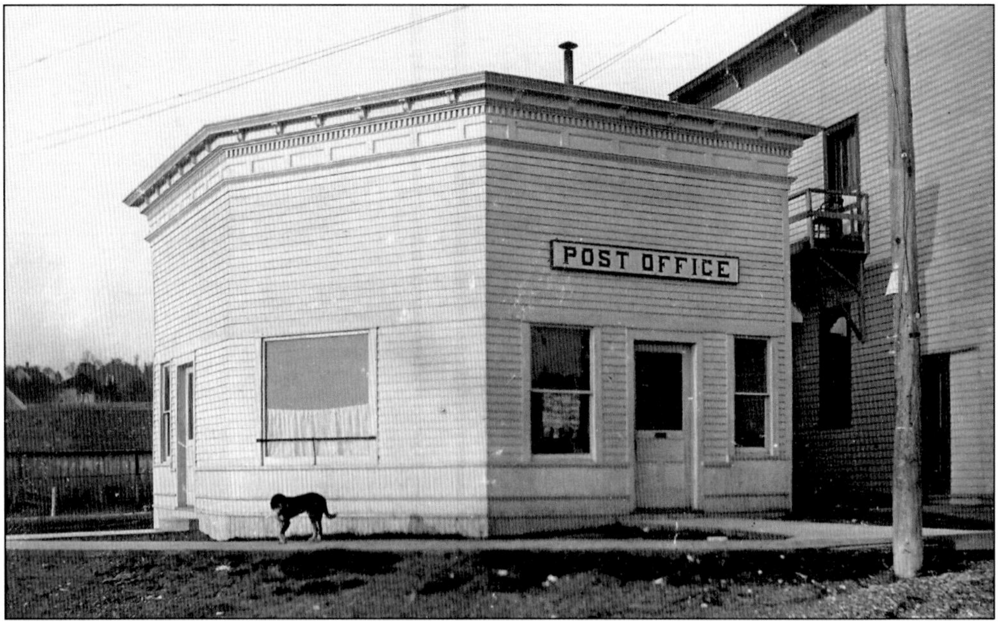

The post office was established in Grand Marais in 1882 and was housed in various buildings until 1907, when it moved into the former Fred Card jewelry store. A new front was added to the rectangular building to give it this unique five-sided shape. The post office remained in this building until 1978. Today the building is the Old Post Office Museum and showcases Grand Marais history. (GMHS.)

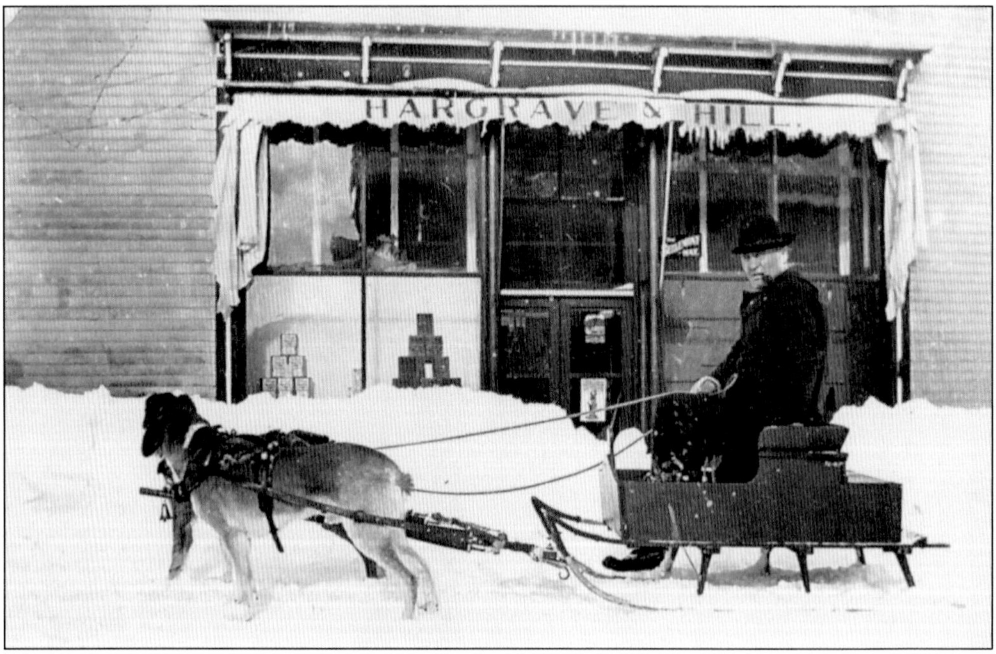

Even after the railroad came to town, the mail was carried to nearby Seney and back by dogsled. These hardy carriers fought giving up their contract with the post office, and men like Buff Jones, pictured here, made the trip on small lightweight sleds. It was not until about 1895 that the mail contract was switched to the railroad. (GMHS.)

Four

PULLING UP STAKES

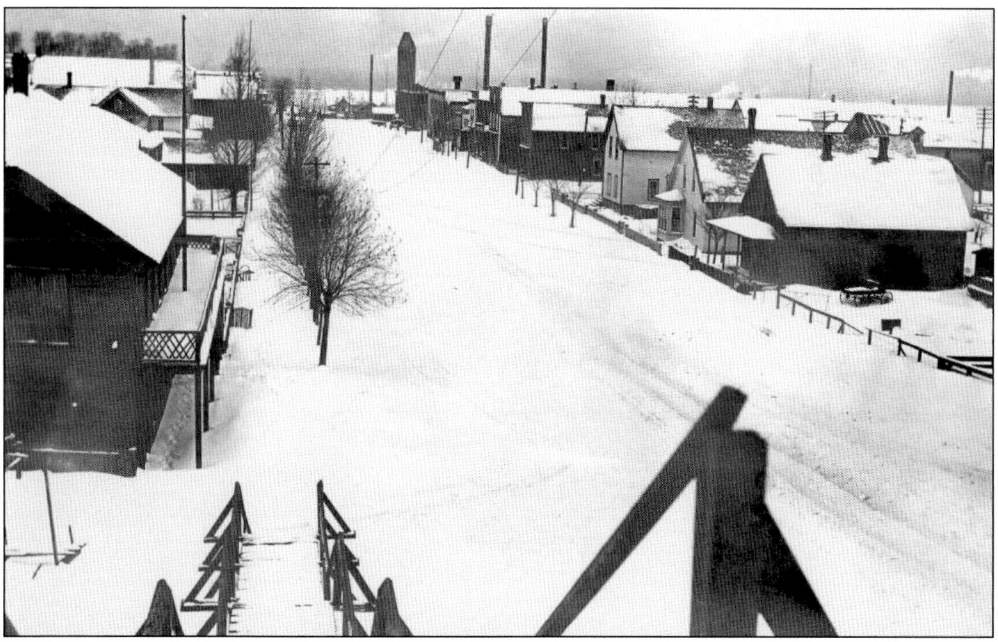

With the loss of the mill and the railroad, Grand Marais became a quiet town of just a few hundred residents. Many businesses closed, their owners having pulled up stakes. This photograph, taken about 1914, shows how still the town was in winter. The state road into town had not been completed and Grand Marais was quite isolated. The winter stage was a lifeline to the residents. (Della Meldrum.)

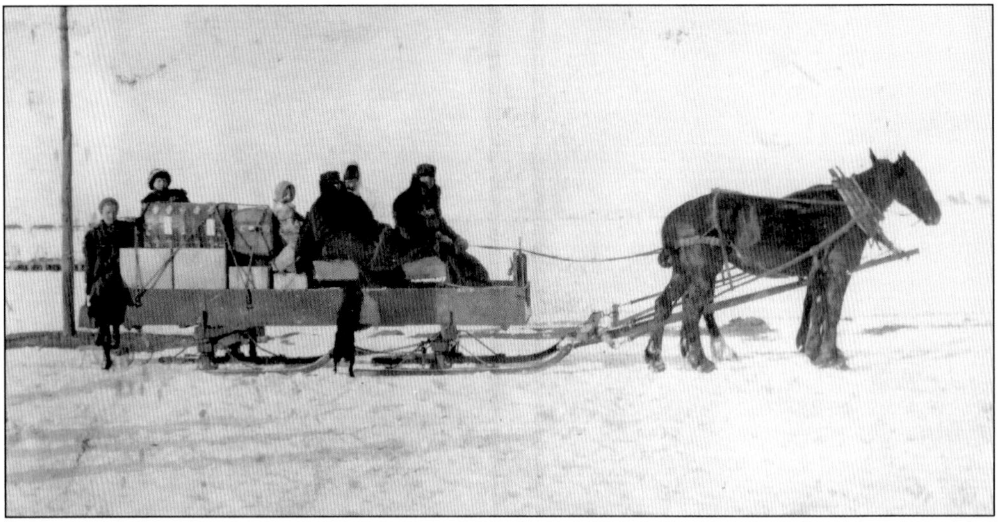

Passengers and light freight traveled to Seney in a horse-drawn sleigh during the winter months. It was surely a cold trip and not very comfortable. This view with the bay in the background shows a mix of people and packages, securely tied down against the bumpiness of the trail. The driver would also carry mail back and forth. (GMHS.)

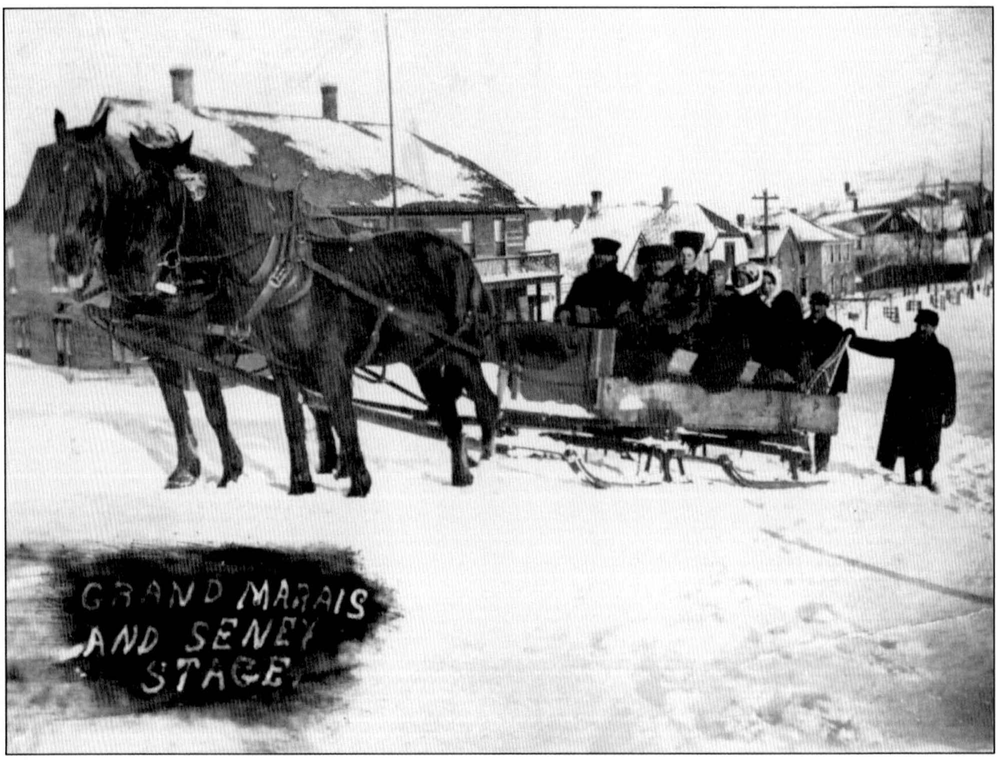

The winter stage could carry 10 to 12 people at a time. This was a cold, arduous trip under the best of circumstances, and considering Michigan's fickle winter weather, anything could happen on the daylong journey. Note the snowshoes being packed into the stage just in case they were needed. Passengers on the stage could catch a train in Seney to points east and west. (Della Meldrum.)

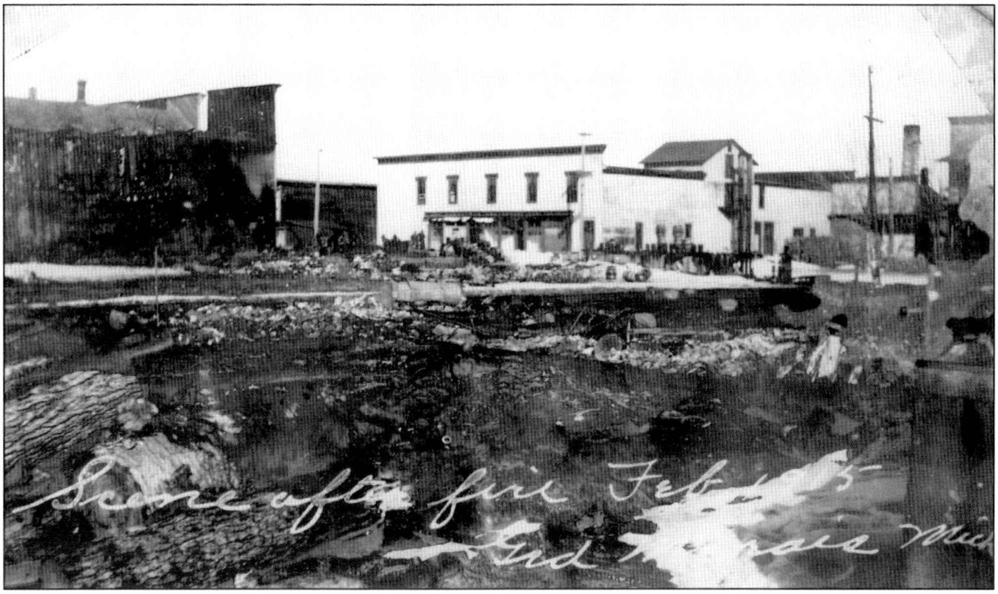

The year 1915 was especially tough on those people left in Grand Marais. In April, a fire burned a number of buildings on the western side of Lake Avenue, leaving several businesses in ashes. This photograph, taken shortly after the fire, looks northeast across the charred, empty lots. The white building is a department store on the east side of Lake Avenue. The lots stood empty for years. (Argie Thorrington.)

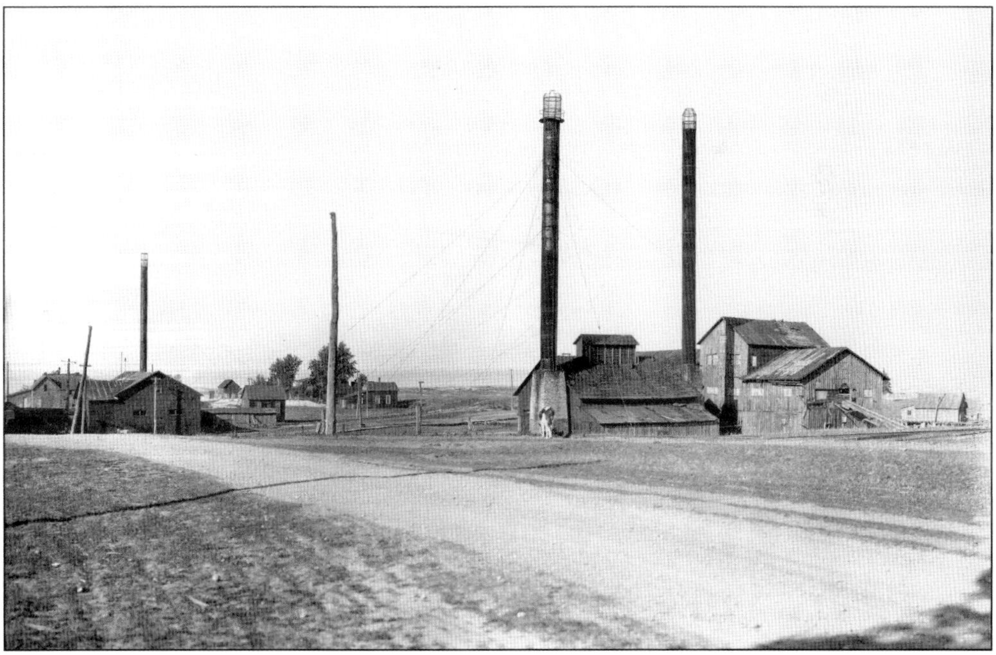

The Marais Mill Company's big sawmill stood empty and decaying by the 1920s. Look closely and a cow can be spotted in the center of this 1924 photograph. Local cows roamed the streets, and residents often awoke in the morning to the sound of cowbells under their windows. It was said that the Grand Marais Women's Club was formed partly to get the cows off the streets. (HSSC.)

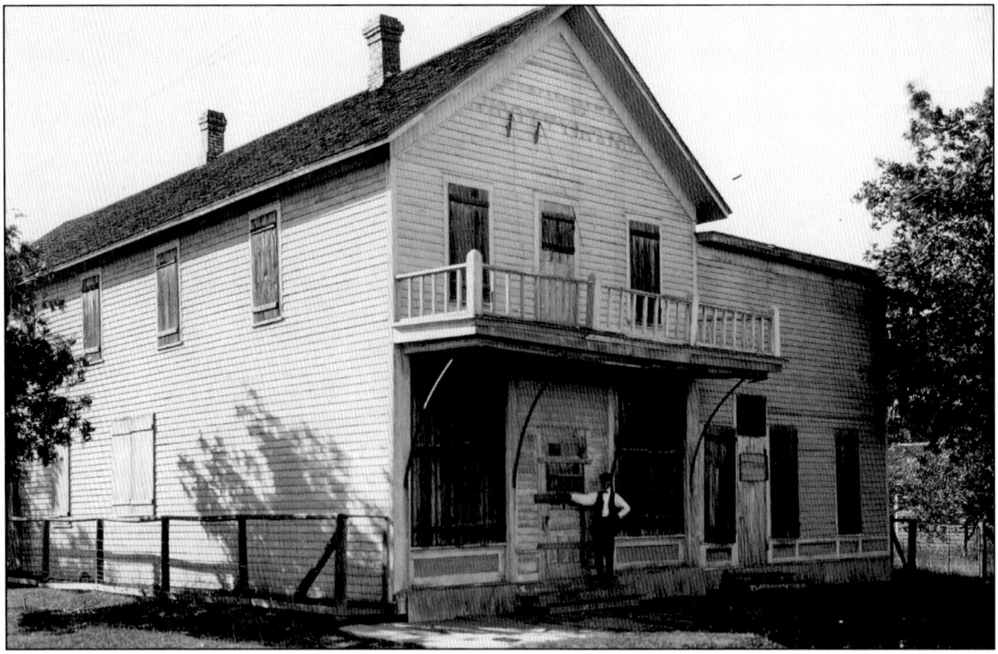

The Grand Marais Hotel, built in 1883, was probably the earliest commercial building in town. Nicknamed the "Black Diamond" for its covering of tar paper and silver nail discs, it originally housed a general store, then a meat market. Henry Gamble purchased it in the early 1890s and turned it into a hotel. Although empty in this 1924 photograph, from 1928 to 1972 it served as the Masonic lodge. (HSSC.)

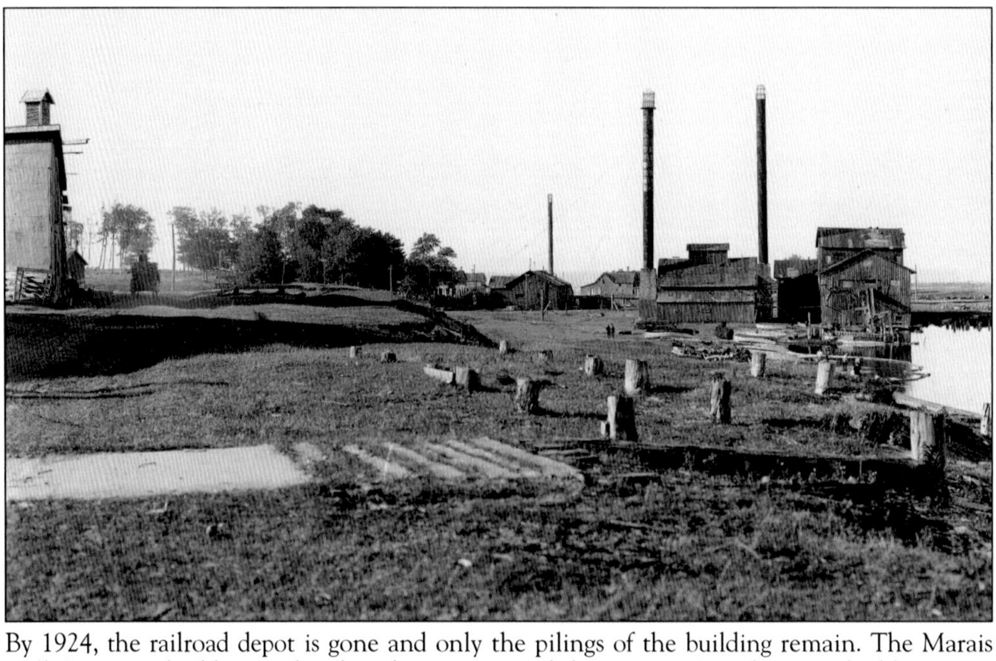

By 1924, the railroad depot is gone and only the pilings of the building remain. The Marais Mill Company building is abandoned, its main stack long gone. Grand Marais had become a small fishing village with little to bring people to the area. All that was soon to change with the completion of a new state road into town from the south. (HSSC.)

Five

The Lifesavers

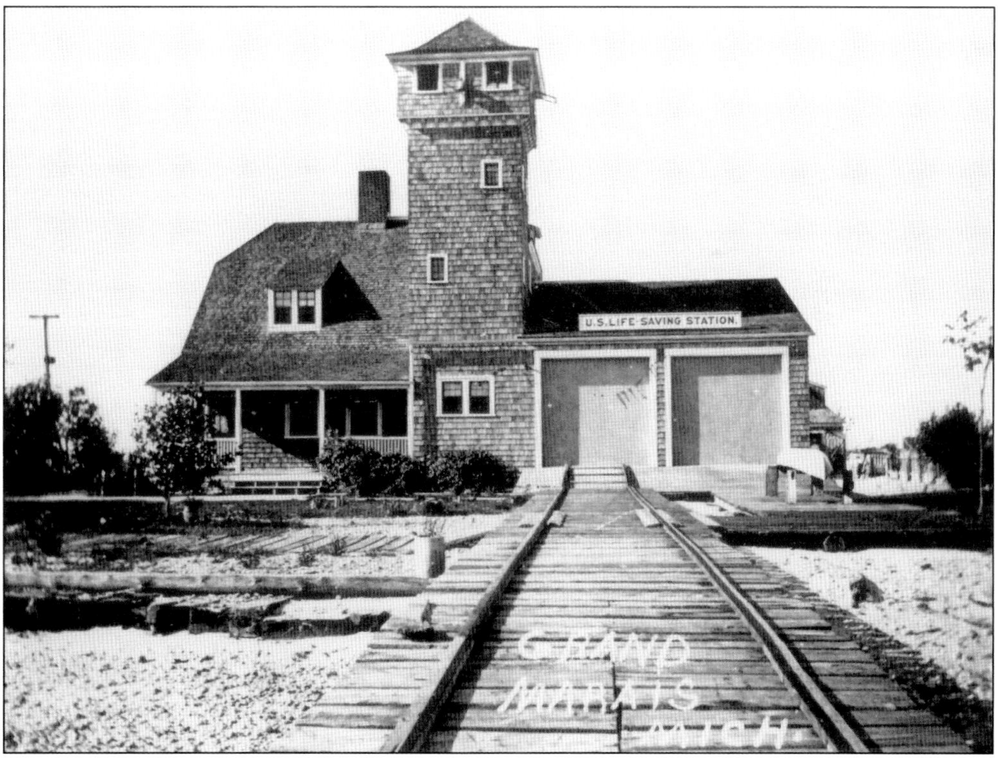

By the 1870s, the need for a series of lifesaving stations on Lake Superior's coast from Whitefish Point to Munising had become critical. Stations were built at Whitefish Point, Crisp's Point, the Two-Hearted River, and Deer Park in 1877, but it was not until 1898 that construction began on a station at Grand Marais. It opened in 1900, and a new era of rescue began. (Archives of Michigan.)

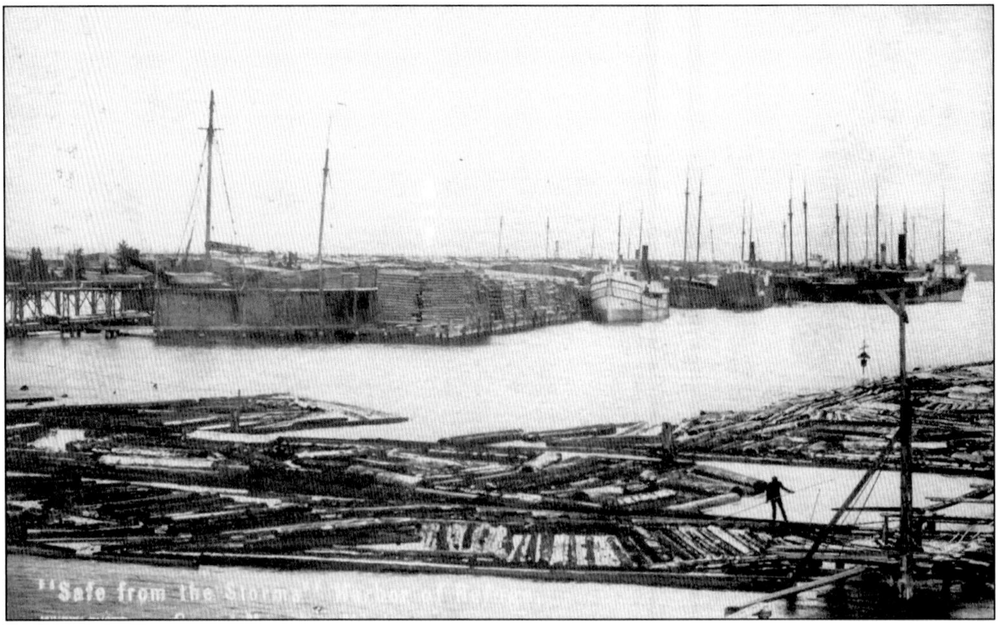

With the advent of the lumber boom, shipping increased dramatically in Grand Marais. At the peak of the boom, over 400 ships per year registered at the harbor. Most ships on the lakes were still wooden, and wrecks were common. This 1907 J. V. Kinsey photograph shows at least eight boats at the lumber docks, with the masts of several more visible at the pier. (Doris Krempa.)

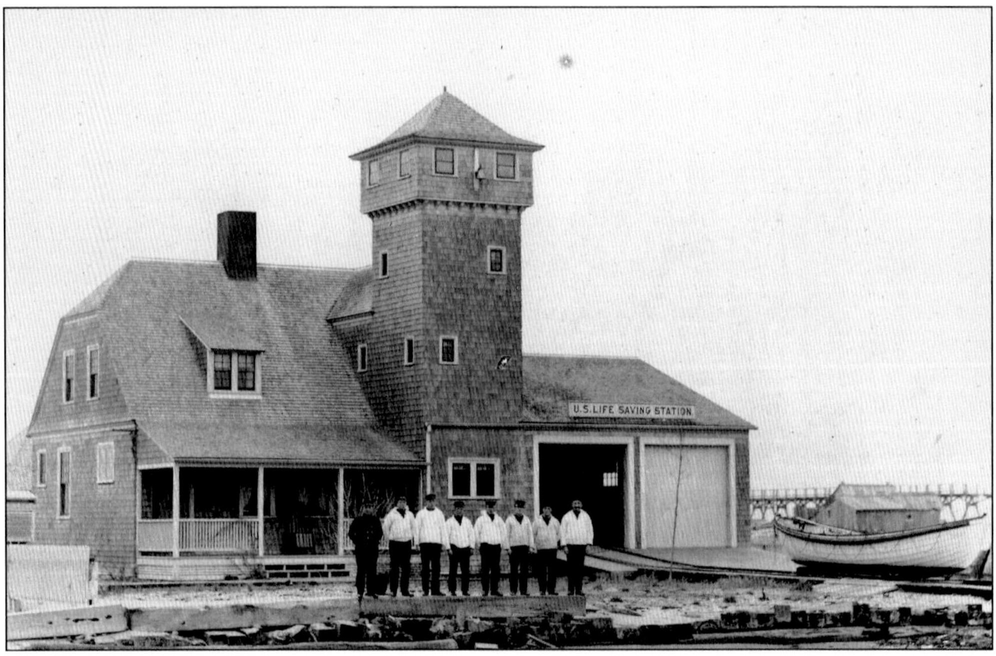

A captain and a six- to eight-man crew usually manned a lifesaving station. The crewmen were seasonal employees, only working during the typical April–November navigation season. They had to find other employment in winter and turnover was high. The low pay and harsh physical work meant that some stations hired a brand-new crew every spring. Shown here are Capt. Benjamin Trudell and his crew shortly after the station opened. (GMHS.)

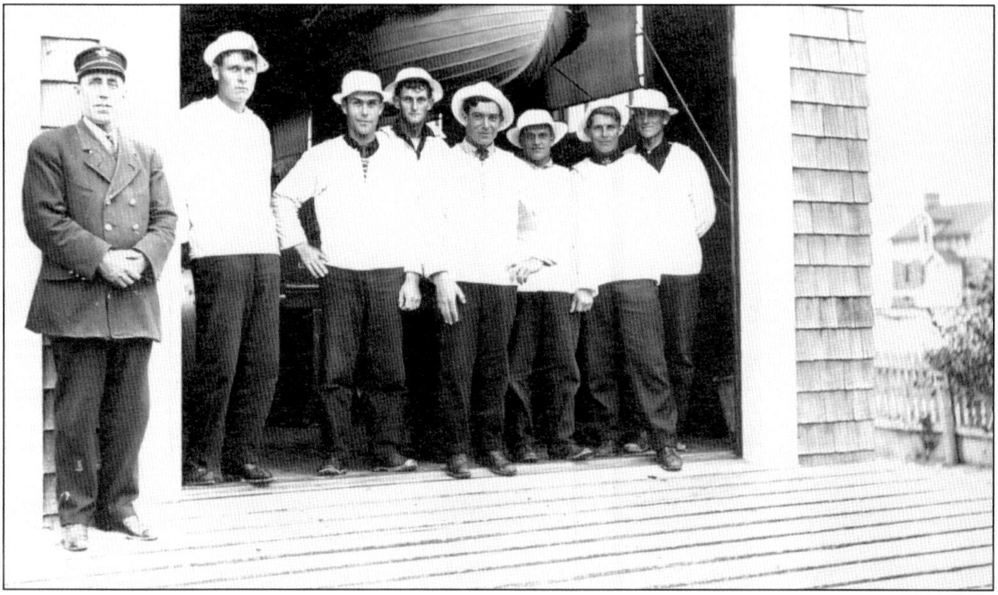

Capt. Benjamin Trudell was much admired in the U.S. Life-Saving Service. He ran the Grand Marais station from 1900 to 1923 and was known for his well-trained crews. In November 1919, the steamer *H. E. Runnels* ran aground in a terrifying storm. The lifesavers and several local men rescued all of the crew and later received the Life-Saving Gold Medal for their heroic actions. (Della Meldrum.)

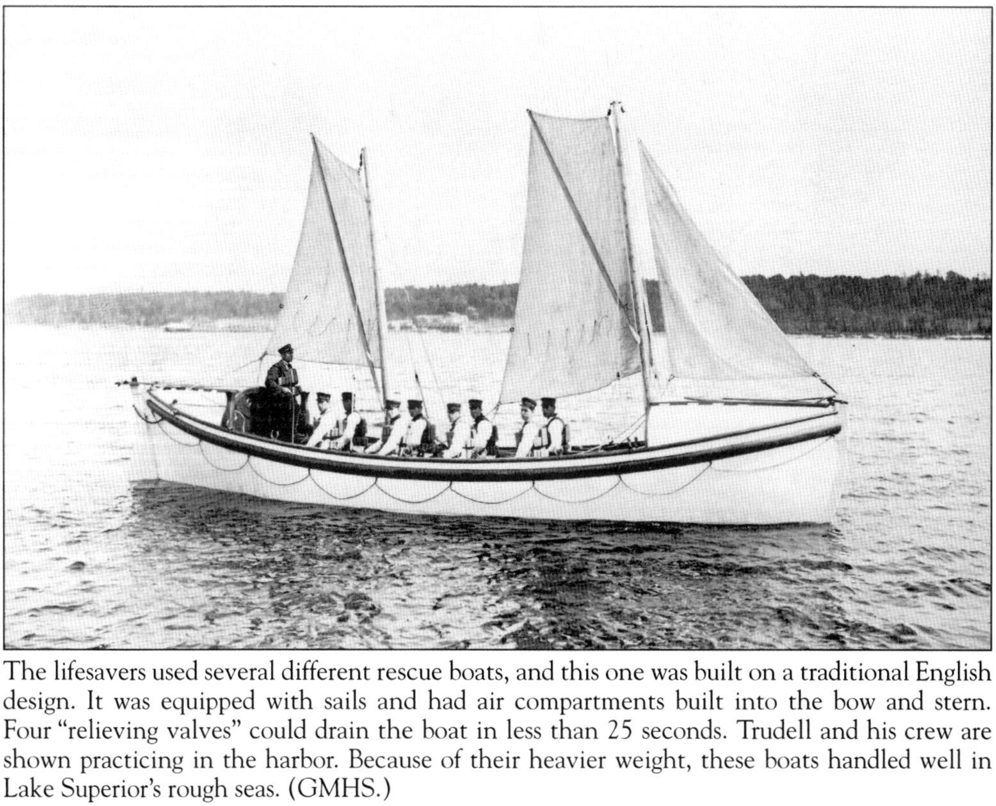

The lifesavers used several different rescue boats, and this one was built on a traditional English design. It was equipped with sails and had air compartments built into the bow and stern. Four "relieving valves" could drain the boat in less than 25 seconds. Trudell and his crew are shown practicing in the harbor. Because of their heavier weight, these boats handled well in Lake Superior's rough seas. (GMHS.)

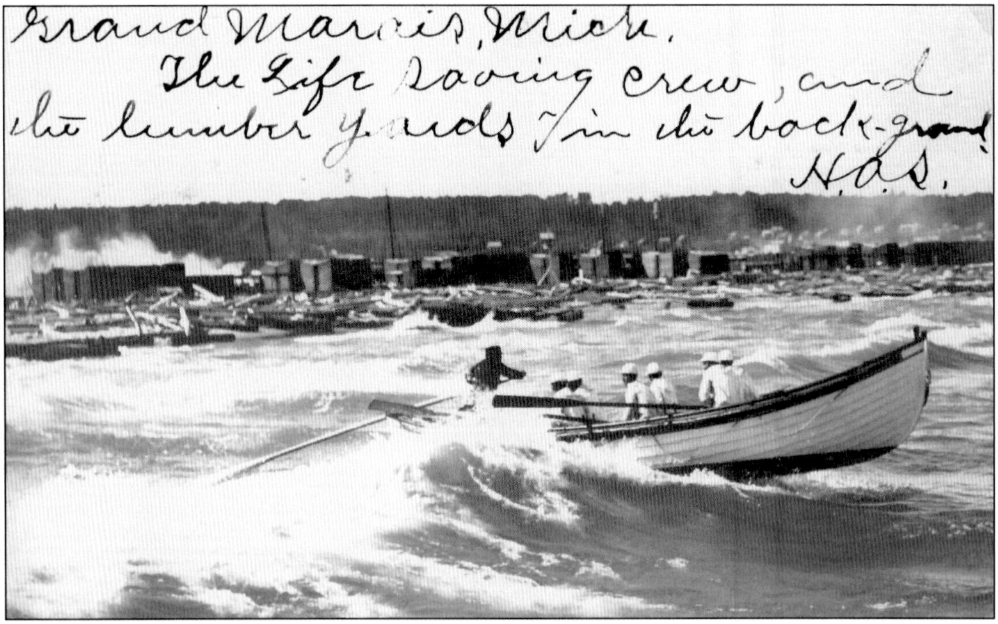

Another type of boat used by the lifesavers was this American-designed surfboat. Smaller and lighter than the lifeboat, it could be hauled across the sand on a cart and launched directly into shallow water, unlike the lifeboat, which had to be launched into the harbor and rowed out through the channel. Note the lumber docks in the background and the logs strewn on shore. (Doris Krempa.)

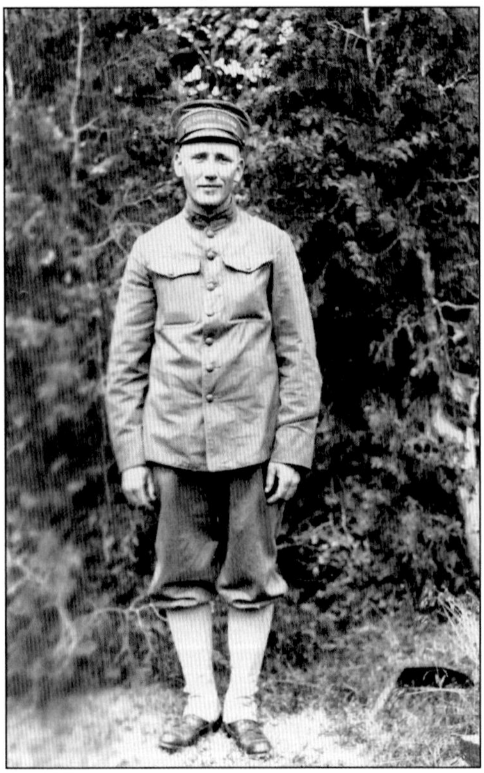

The surfmen were responsible for daily beach patrols. They would walk up to four miles on their shifts, checking the beach for wreckage and watching for ships in distress. At some stations, patrolmen met halfway and exchanged metal tokens. Many Grand Marais men such as John Soldenski, shown here in uniform, served with distinction in the U.S. Life-Saving Service; they were used to the harsh weather conditions. (Ted and Marge Soldenski.)

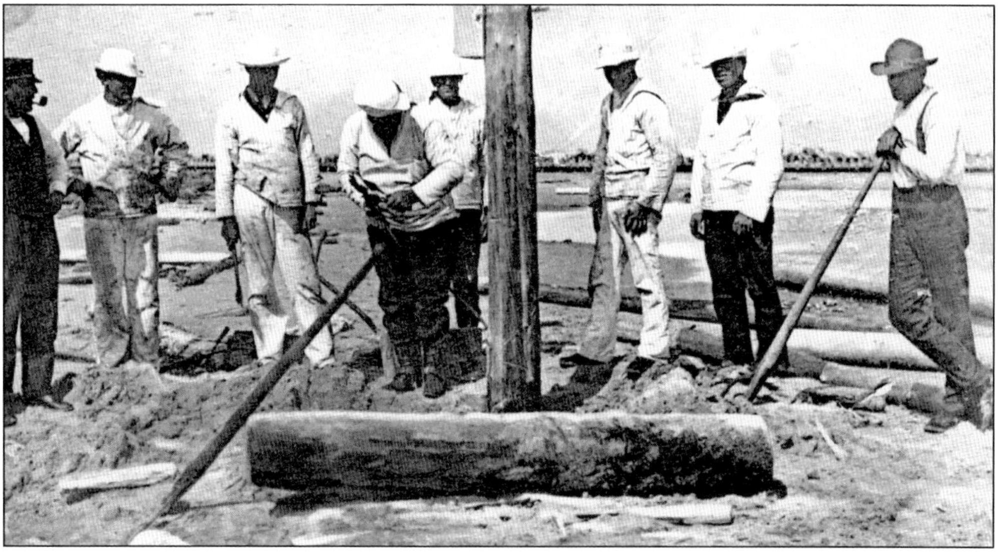

Lifesaving crews sometimes assisted with other government projects. This c. 1906 photograph shows the crew helping to bury a submarine telephone line. Capt. Benjamin Trudell, the station keeper, is at left with the pipe in his mouth. Station crews were expected to keep the grounds neat, do housekeeping, and maintain all the equipment. A crew member could be dismissed for failing to perform his duties. (GMHS.)

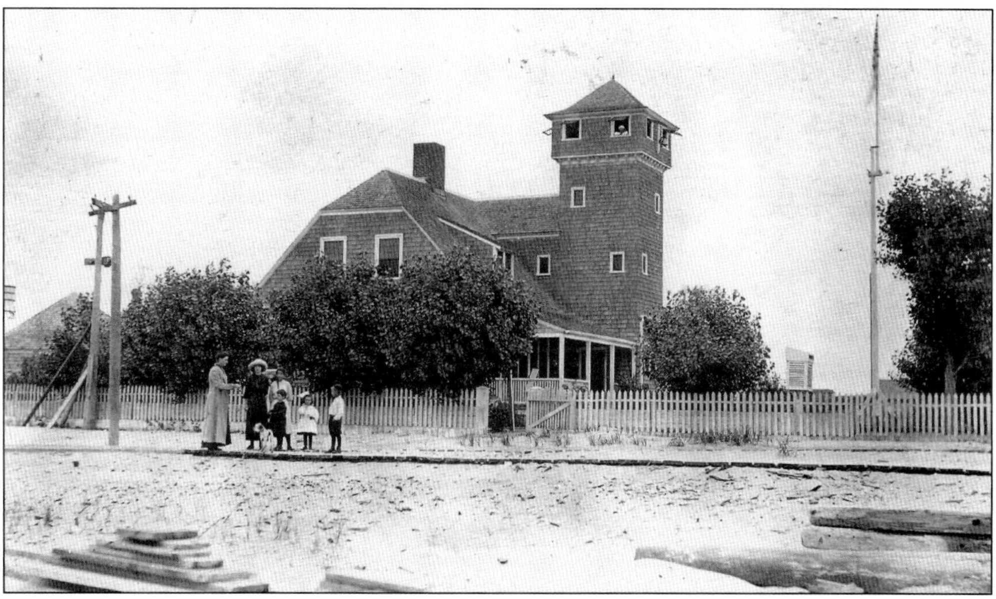

Married crew members often lived in town, although they were expected to spend their shifts at the station. This photograph shows the Grand Marais station about 1910. Note the water tower at the far left, the weather station next to the flagpole, and the crewman watching out of the lookout tower window. Boardwalks and a white picket fence give the station a more refined look. (Della Meldrum.)

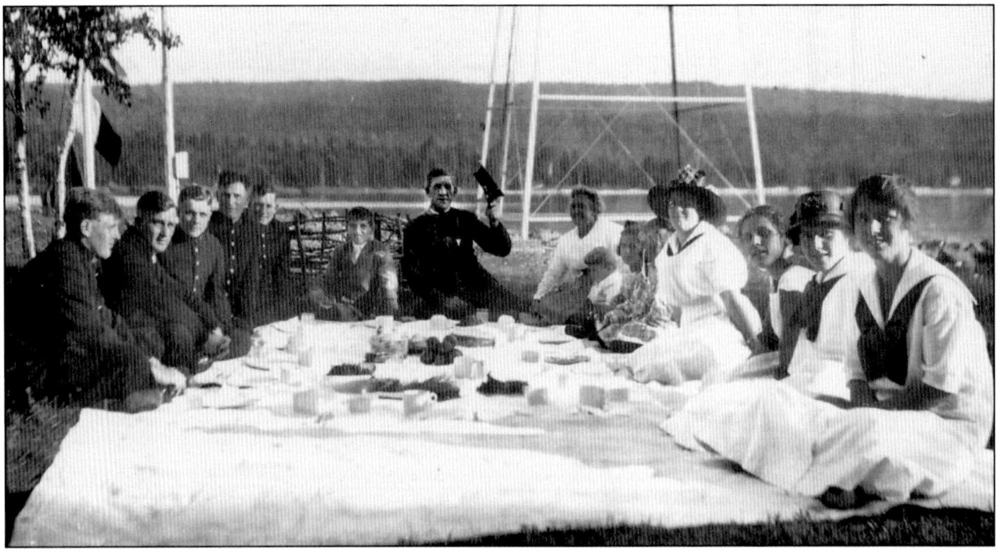

There was occasional time for fun, even if one was a surfman. Here the crew enjoys a picnic on the lawn for the Fourth of July 1917. Capt. Benjamin Trudell is shown at the rear. The woman and children around him are probably his family. Picnics like this were a way for young ladies in town to meet the surfmen under chaperoned conditions. Note their proper seating arrangement. (Della Meldrum.)

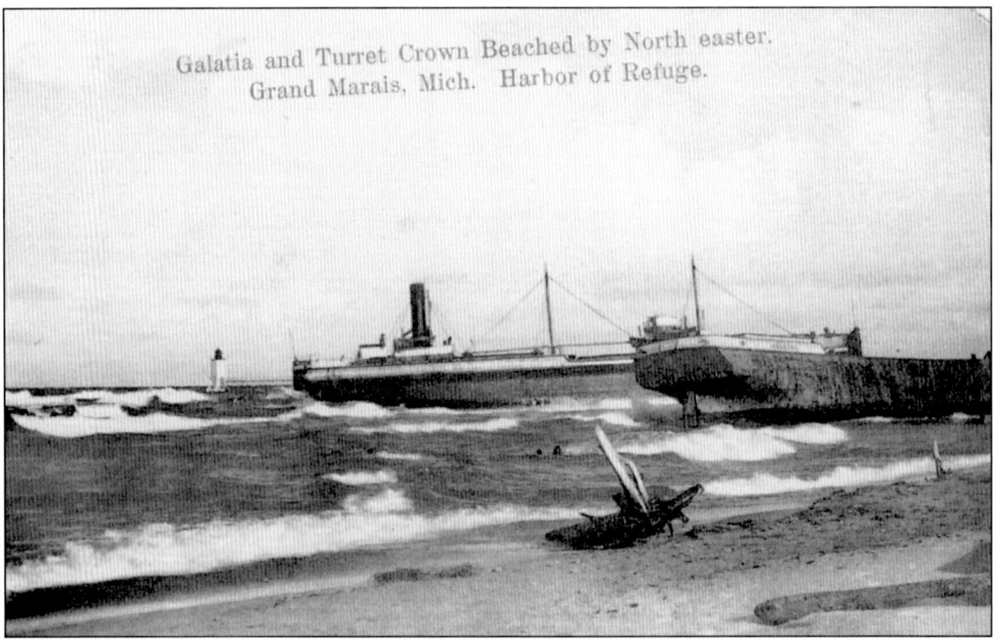

On October 2, 1905, the wooden schooner-barges *Nirvana* (incorrectly identified here as the *Turret Crown*) and *Galatea* (right) separated from the steamer *L. L. Barth* and collided with the piers during a gale. The *Galatea*'s crew simply clambered over the stern and walked ashore. The *Galatea* became a curiosity and townspeople visited the wreck throughout the winter. The *Nirvana* split from fore to aft and sank offshore. (GMHS.)

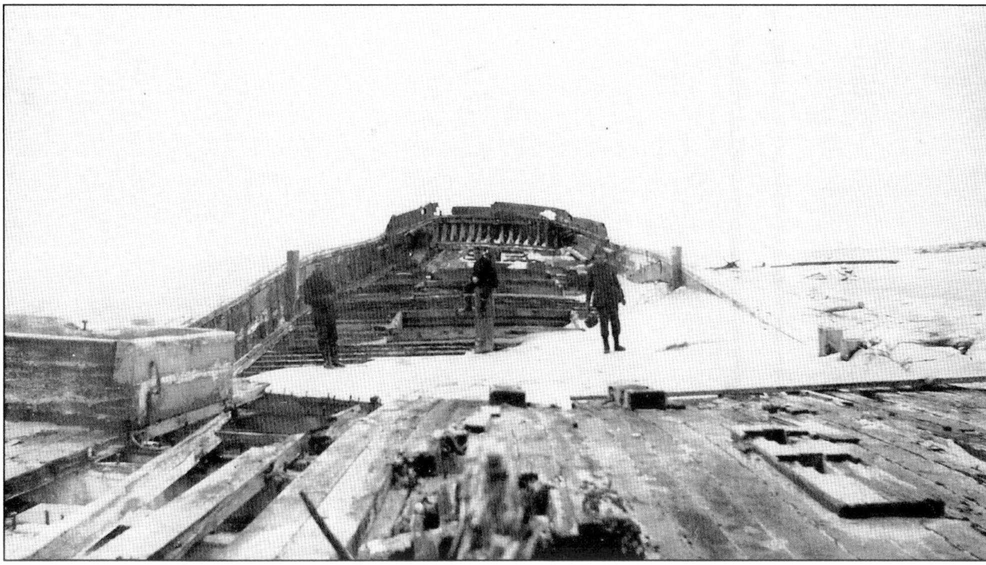

This barge is probably the *Galatea*, looking west along the beach toward the stern. Salvagers dug a 900-foot channel to the barge to try to float it off the beach but were unsuccessful. It broke up over the winter as it was pounded by waves and ice. People would often scavenge the timbers and use them for other purposes. (DVTC.)

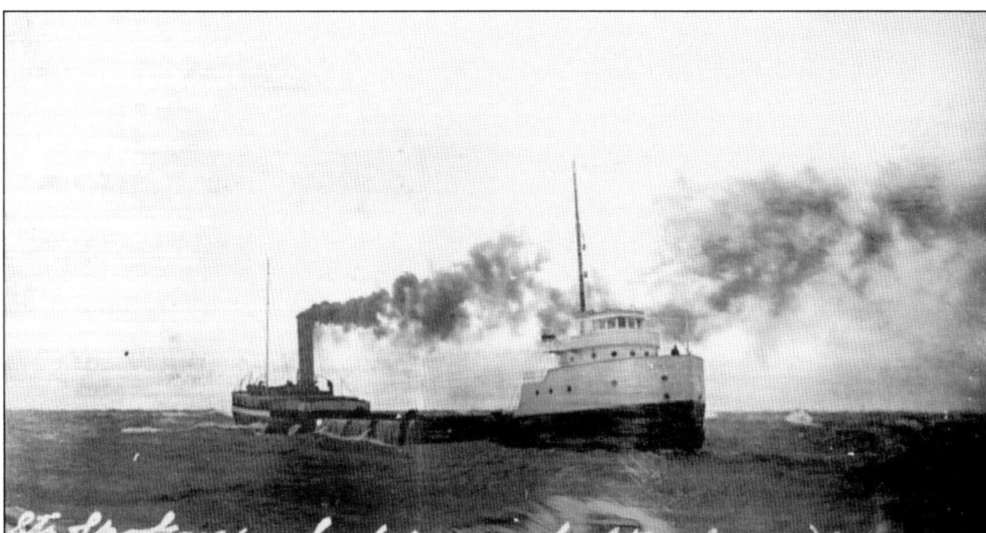

The steel steamer *Spokane*, reportedly the first steel ship to sail on Lake Superior, is shown here in the channel during a storm. Note the waves washing over the deck of the ship. The *Spokane* eventually did come to grief but not near Grand Marais. It was driven onto Gull Rock near Isle Royale in 1912 and broke in two. It was later recovered and rebuilt. (DVTC.)

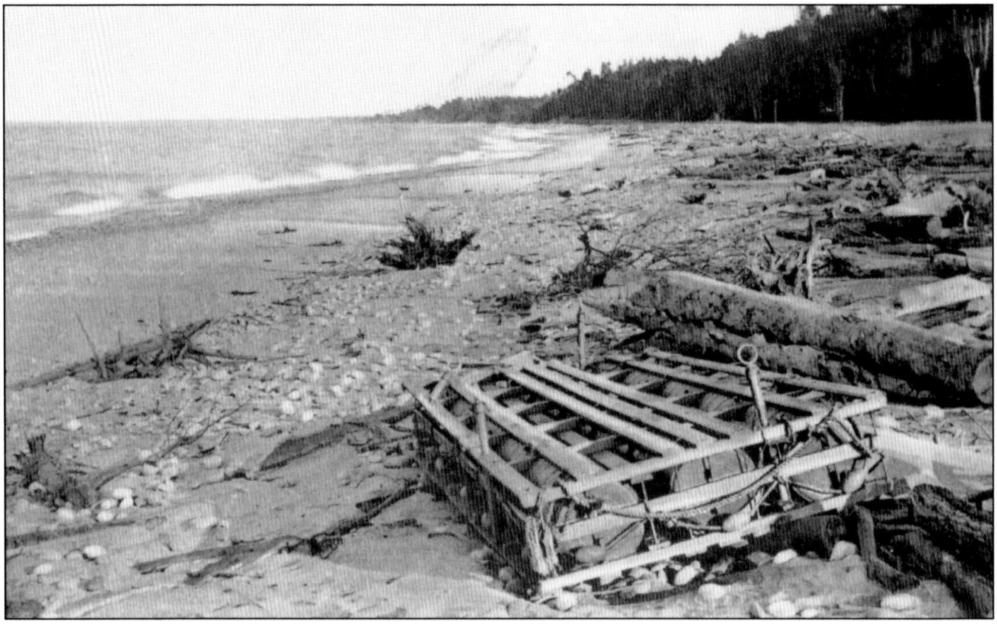

The lifesavers regularly combed the shore for wreckage and victims. This raft, washed up east of Grand Marais, was from the wreck of the *Cyprus* in 1907. Only 1 of the 22 men aboard made it to the beach, clinging to this raft. The steamer was just 21 days old and on its second voyage. The wreck was located exactly 100 years later, in 2007. (GMHS.)

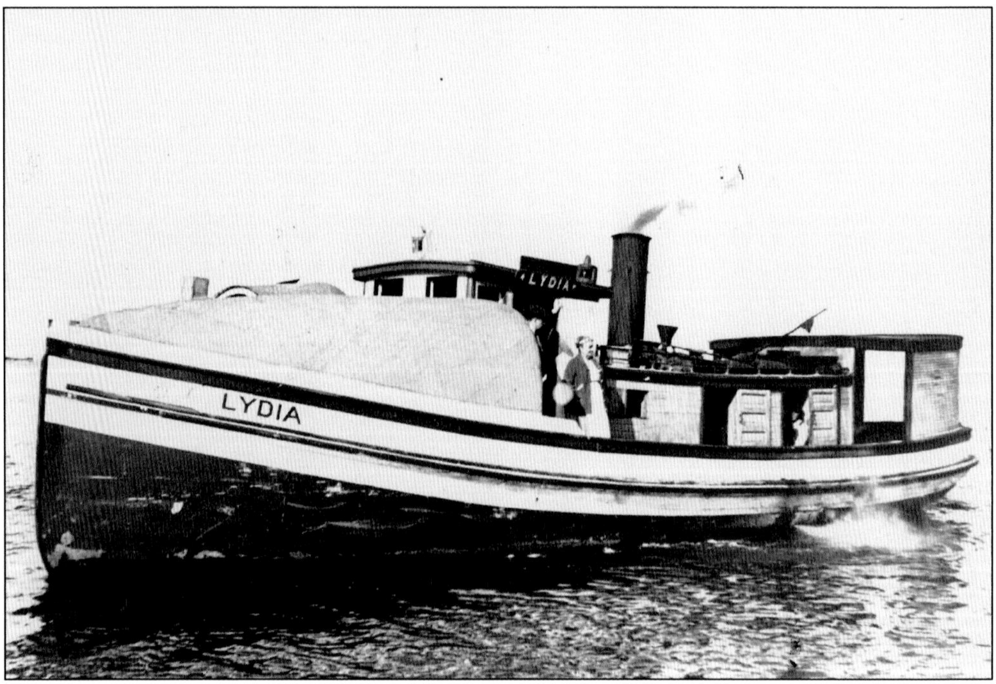

The *Lydia* was a fishing tug that tried to outrun a raging storm in November 1932. As the crew approached the Grand Marais break wall, heavy seas drove the boat to the bottom where it broke up on a sandbar. By the time the lifesavers from the Grand Marais station arrived on the scene, all five aboard were drowned. Many in Grand Marais lost a loved one that day. (PRNL.)

The outer and inner range lights for the Grand Marais Harbor channel were not built until 1895 and 1898, respectively. Captains lined up the two lights and then guided their ships through the channel into protected waters. It was the job of the lightkeeper to keep the lamps in good condition. This is the outer pier light tower in 1924. It was later replaced with a steel tower. (GMHS.)

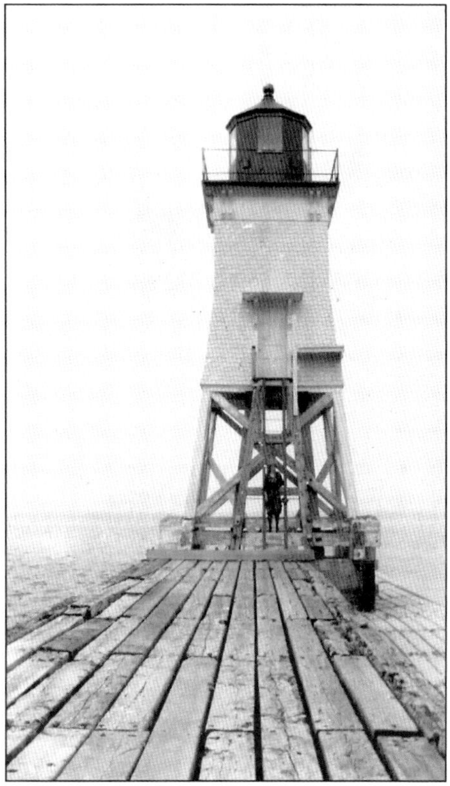

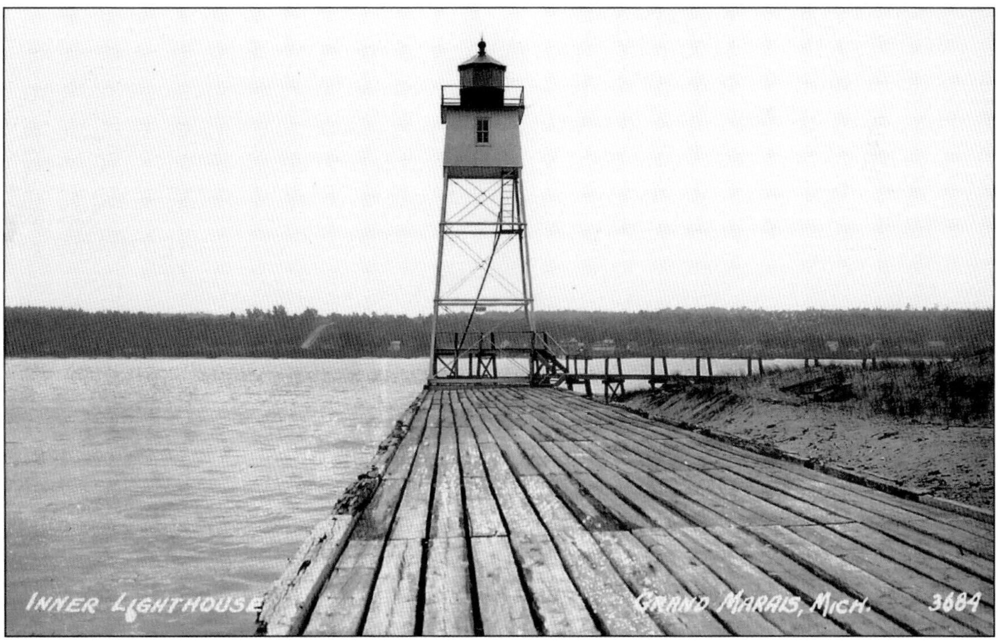

The inner range light sat at the harbor end of the shipping channel. A long wooden boardwalk connected the two lights. In 1905 both range lights were changed to red, making them easier to see. The lights were of a pyramidal skeleton tower design, and the lightkeeper had to climb the exposed ladders in all kinds of weather to carry out his duties. (DVTC.)

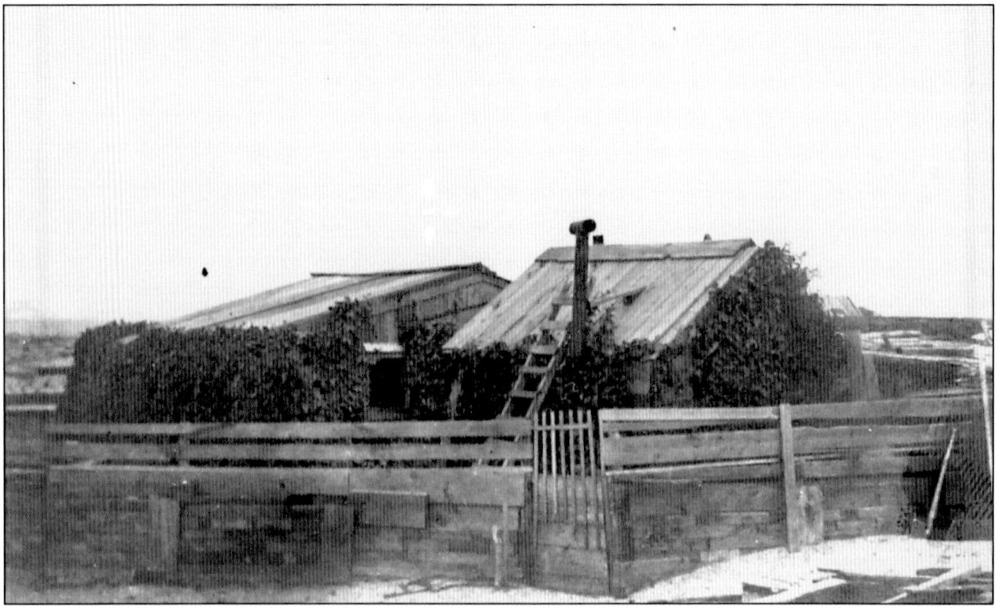

Samuel F. Rogers, the first lightkeeper, constructed this shack out of driftwood lumber and lived in it until 1904, when he resigned due to failing health. The district inspector began requesting a real house for the lightkeeper in 1901, referring to this structure as "a miserable shanty . . . neither decent nor healthful," "a disgraceful affair," and "the poorest kind of hut." (National Archives.)

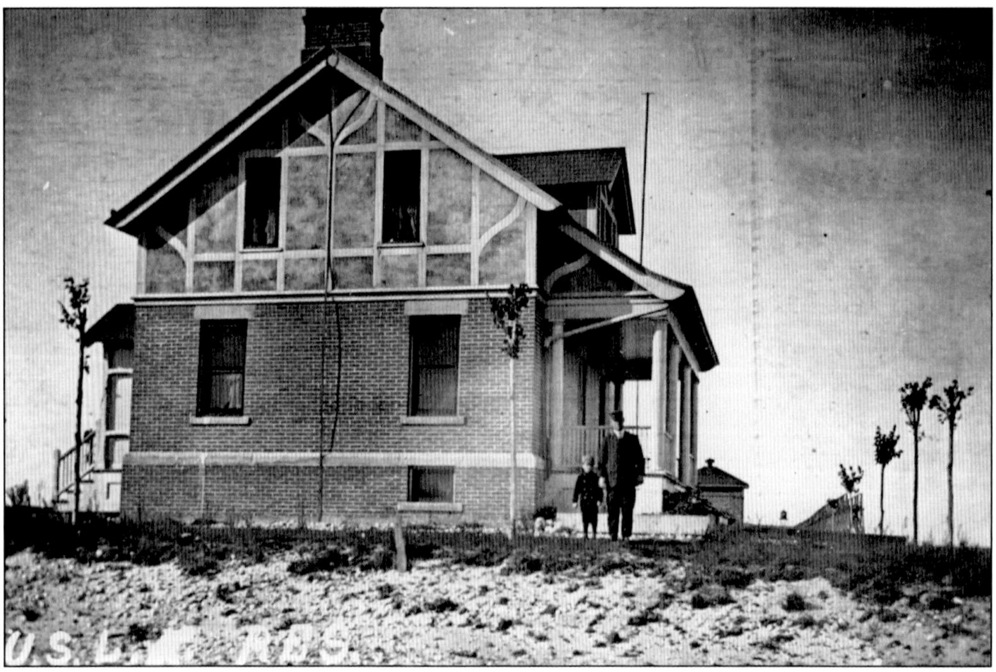

The lighthouse board finally built a house for the Grand Marais lightkeeper in 1908. In this photograph, lightkeeper George Barkley and his son, Russell, stand in front of the new keeper's dwelling. One of the first letters Barkley wrote to the lighthouse board was to request the building of a privy, which the board had overlooked. (GMHS.)

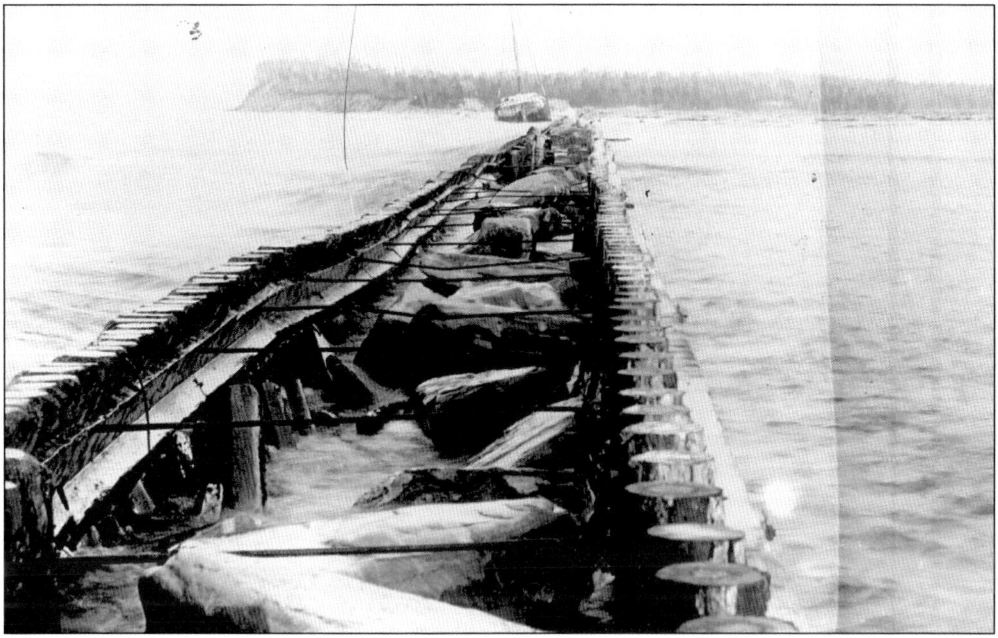

A mile-long pile dike was built in 1894 from the east pier to Lonesome Point. It fell into disrepair after World War II when the U.S. Army Corps of Engineers stopped maintaining it. The harbor has since filled with sand and could disappear completely. The ship in the distance is the schooner-barge *Saveland*, which broke its towline and wrecked against the pile dike in 1903. (PRNL.)

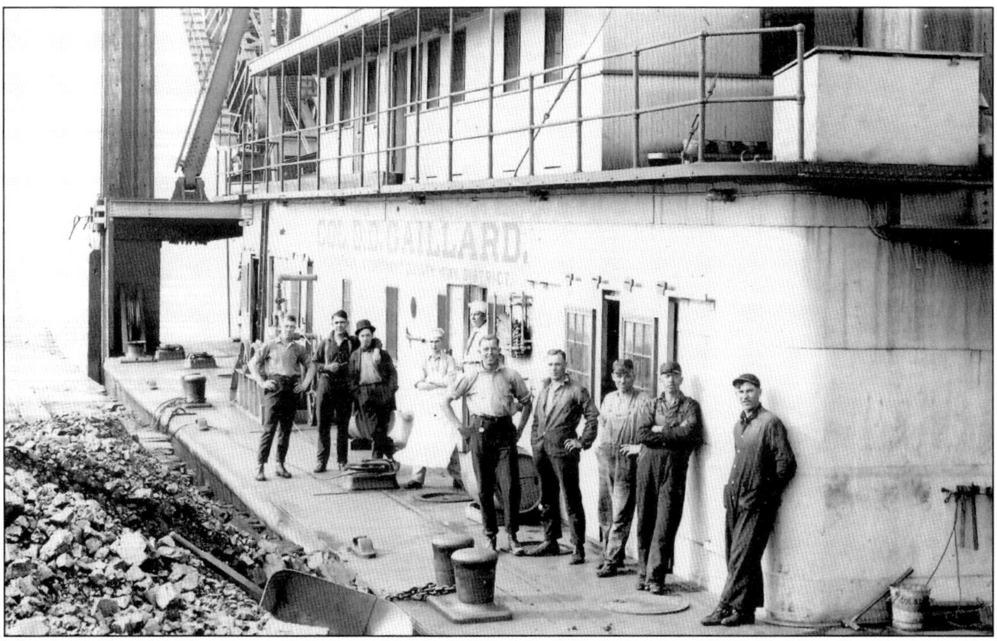

The steam dipper dredge *Col. D. D. Gaillard* was a frequent visitor to Grand Marais. It could remove sand, silt, and gravel at a rate of 2,000 cubic yards per eight-hour shift and could also dredge unusually heavy loads of rock. The *Col. D. D. Gaillard* was retired from the U.S. Army Corps of Engineers in 1982 and is now a floating museum in Superior, Wisconsin. (Della Meldrum.)

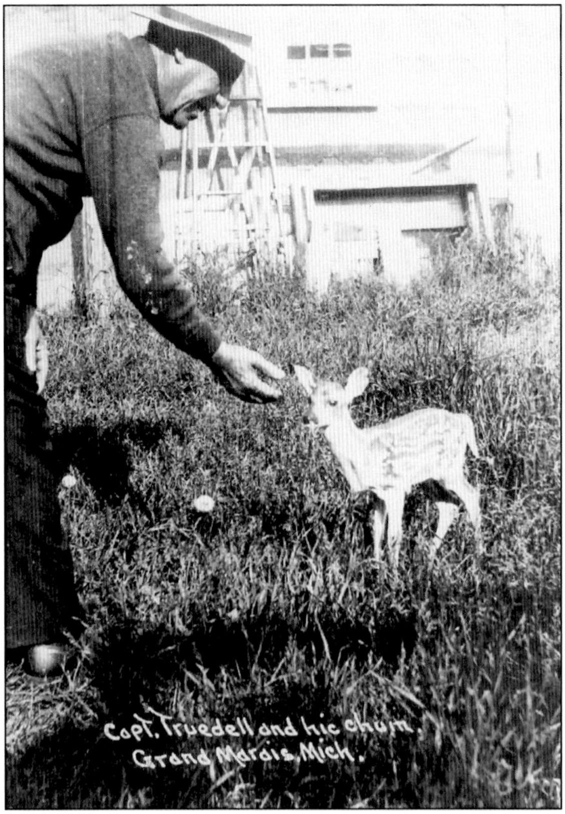

Capt. Benjamin Trudell was the head of the Grand Marais Life-Saving Station from 1900 to 1923. Upon his retirement, he purchased the Chisholm residence on the corner of Lake Avenue and Randolph Street and opened it as the Green Shingles Tavern. It was a hotel and restaurant until 1940. Trudell was much loved and respected in Grand Marais. Here he is shown with a small friend. (Doris Krempa.)

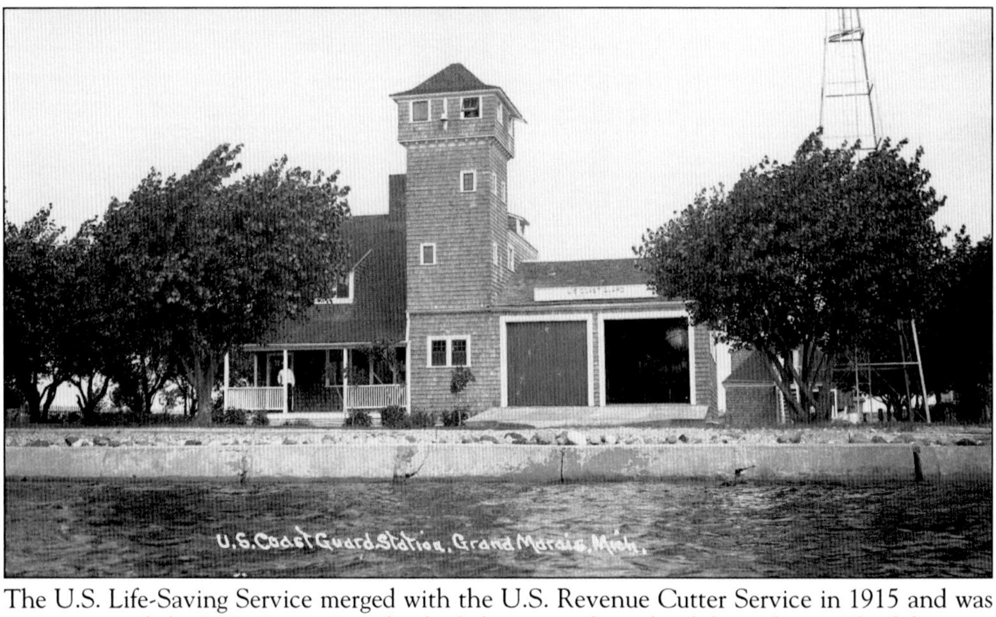

The U.S. Life-Saving Service merged with the U.S. Revenue Cutter Service in 1915 and was soon renamed the U.S. Coast Guard, which became a branch of the military. The lifesaving station, shown here in the 1920s, continued to operate until the late 1930s. By then wooden schooners had given way to steel steamers, which traveled too far out in the lake for a lifesaving crew to reach. (Great Lakes Pilot.)

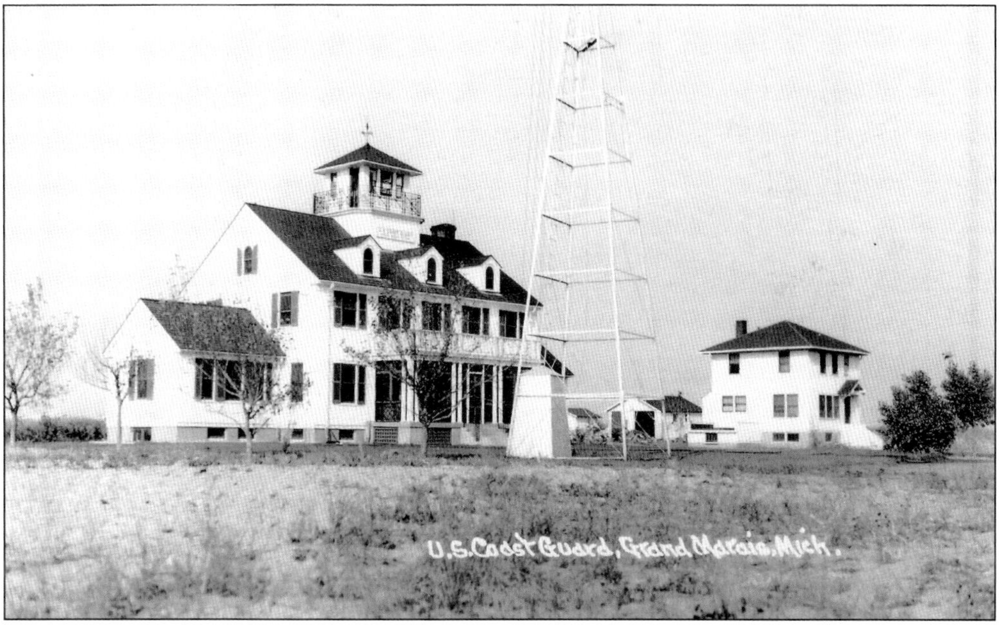

The Coast Guard erected two new buildings in Grand Marais in 1938. The building at left is the main quarters, and the building at right was used for housing. These structures offered modern amenities and more comfort for the crew. With the opening of these buildings, the old lifesaving station across the road soon became obsolete. (Doris Krempa.)

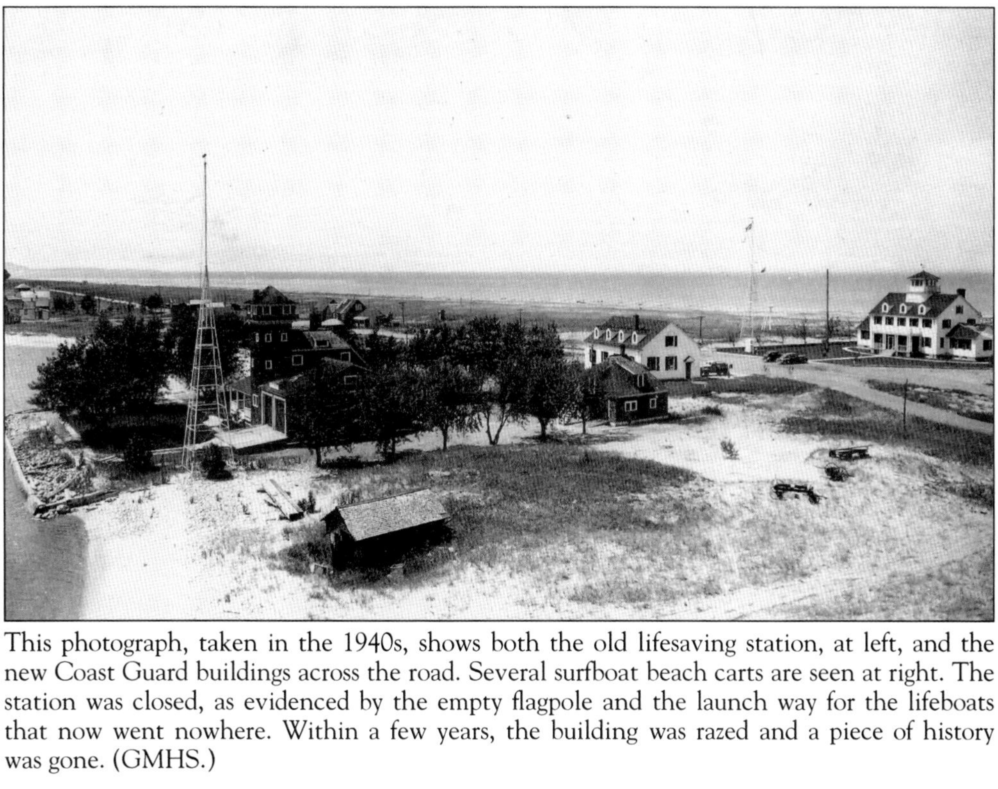

This photograph, taken in the 1940s, shows both the old lifesaving station, at left, and the new Coast Guard buildings across the road. Several surfboat beach carts are seen at right. The station was closed, as evidenced by the empty flagpole and the launch way for the lifeboats that now went nowhere. Within a few years, the building was razed and a piece of history was gone. (GMHS.)

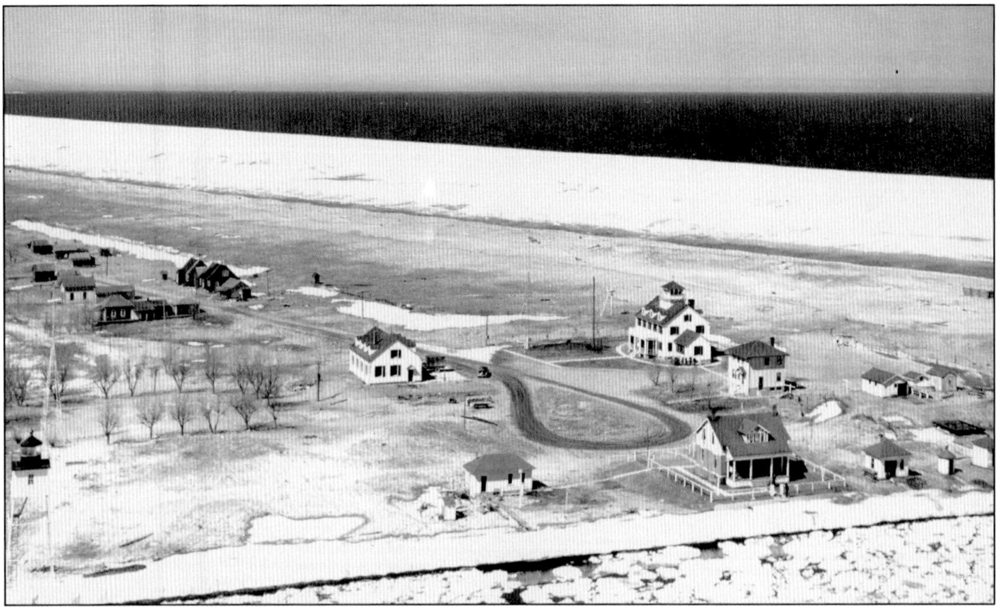

This aerial view of Coast Guard Point in winter was taken about 1950. The only reminder of the lifesaving station is the ring of trees surrounding the empty space where the buildings once stood. The Coast Guard Auxiliary group in Grand Marais uses the small two-story building in the center today and operates a rescue boat out of the harbor. (GMHS.)

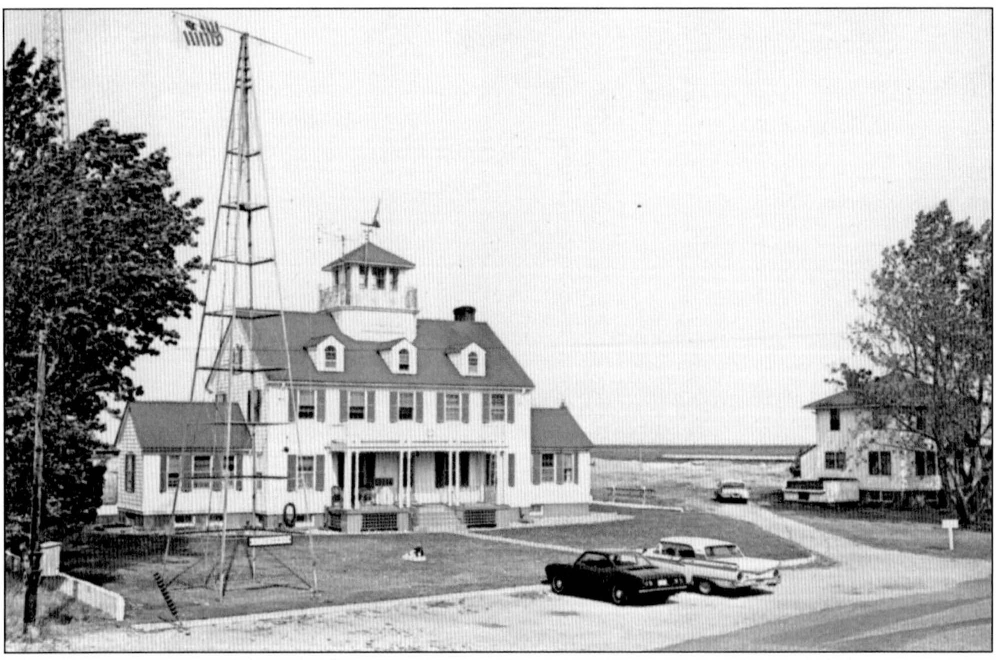

The Coast Guard used these buildings to house officers and crew from 1938 until the station was deactivated in 1981. The structures were given to the National Park Service in 1984, and today the Grand Marais ranger station for Pictured Rocks National Lakeshore operates out of here. This photograph was taken in the 1960s. (Doris Krempa.)

Six

The Fishing Industry

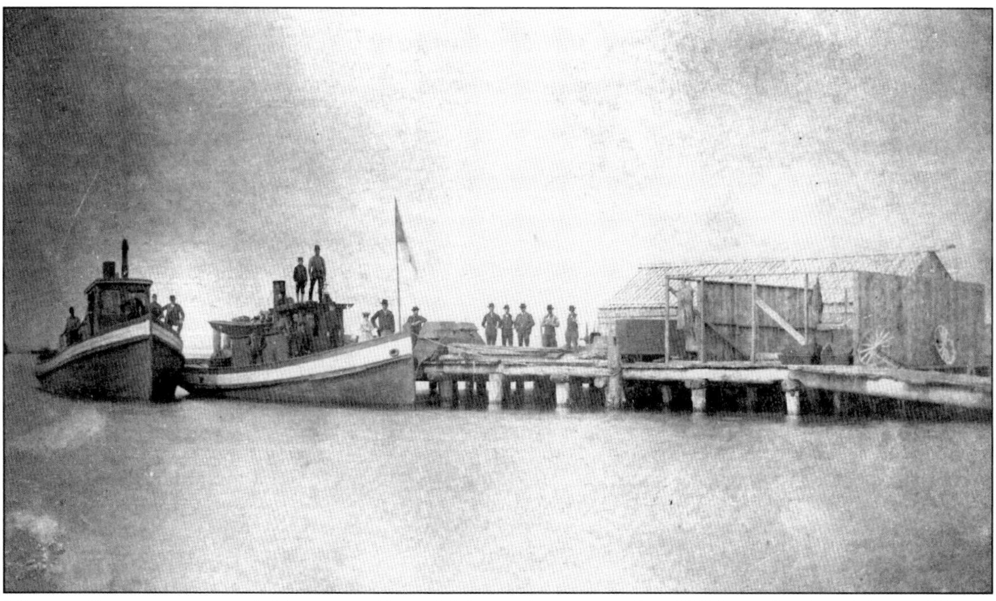

The earliest commercial fishing in Grand Marais began in the 1860s with Conable and Sons. In 1871, Emil Endress arrived from Sault Ste. Marie and set up fishing operations on the south shore of the bay. This photograph from the 1880s was taken at that location. The Endress family continued to fish commercially in Grand Marais for almost 100 years. (GMHS.)

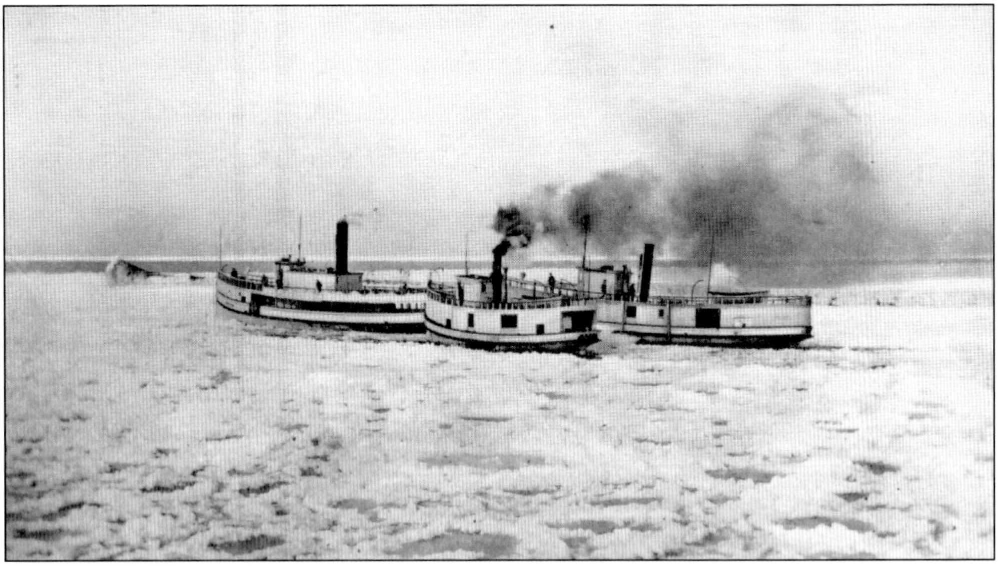

The first commercial fishing operation came to Grand Marais in the late 1860s, and by 1907, when this photograph was taken, a number of small fleets were based in the harbor. Each spring, fishing tugs from several fleets would break a channel through the ice for the rest of the boats. Here three tugs break through ice in the channel on their way to Lake Superior to start setting their nets. (GMHS.)

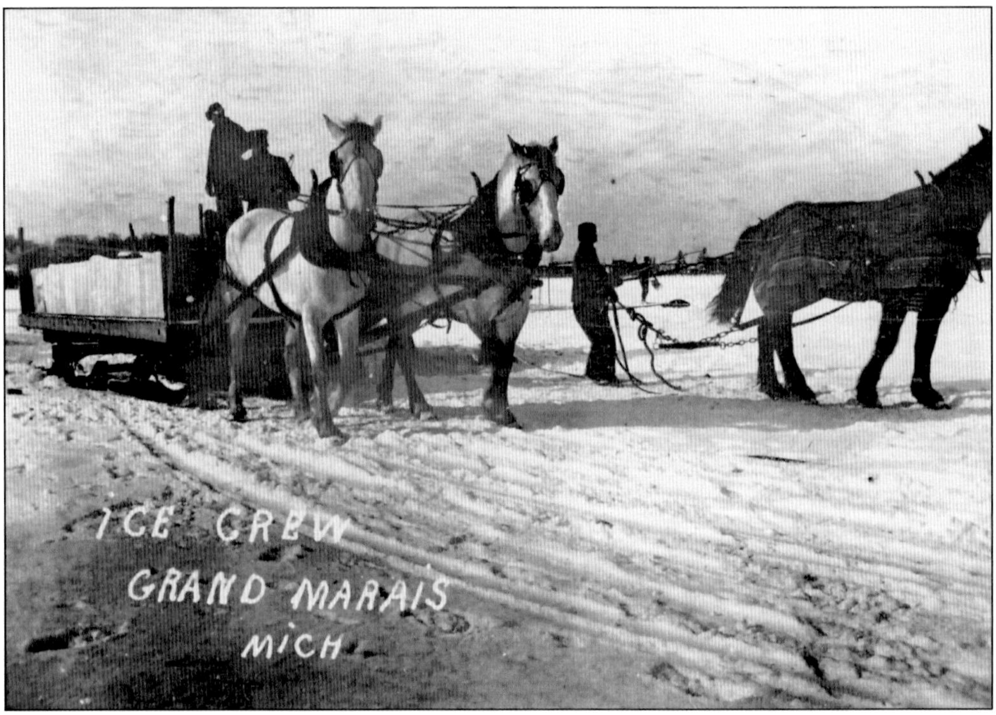

In winter, fishermen cut ice blocks from the bay and stored them in icehouses until the spring. Storing the ice in sawdust insulated it well and kept it from melting, even in summer. Fish were then packed in the ice for shipment to markets around the Great Lakes. In this 1910 photograph, horses pull an ice sledge loaded with cut blocks of ice. (ACHS.)

The first *South Shore*, shown here about 1910, was a passenger and cargo freighter that ran from Sault Ste. Marie to Marquette several times a week along what was known as the South Shore route. It would stop along the way and lift nets of fish. Emil Endress, son of pioneer commercial fisherman Charles Endress, operated the boat. This *South Shore* was wrecked in a storm in 1912. (DVTC.)

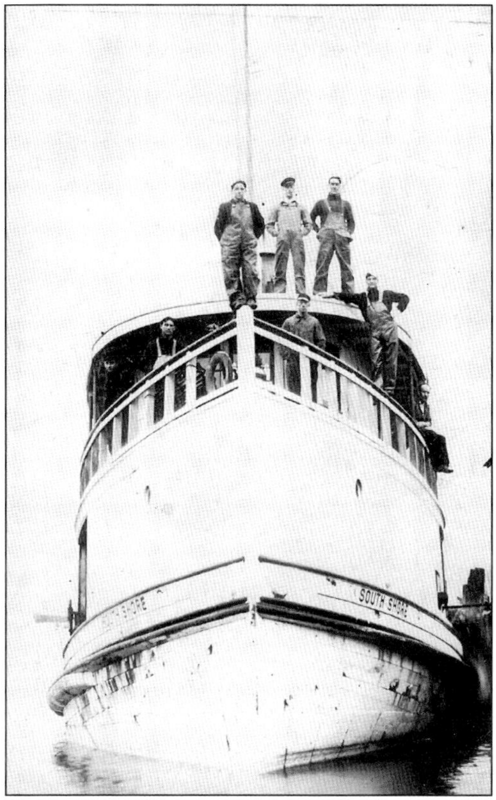

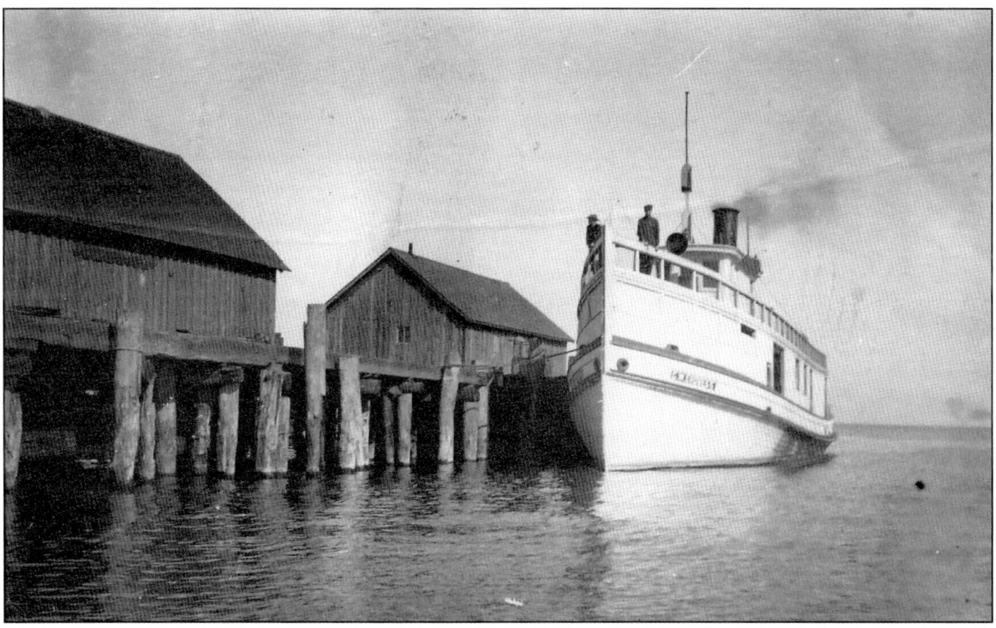

When the lumbering in the area ended in 1910, commercial fishing was one of the few businesses still active in Grand Marais. The years from 1910 to 1912 were lean, due to a decline in fish stocks on the lake, but the fish soon rebounded. The C. *W. Endress*, shown here at the Endress dock about 1914, was one of the larger tugs operating out of Grand Marais. (Della Meldrum.)

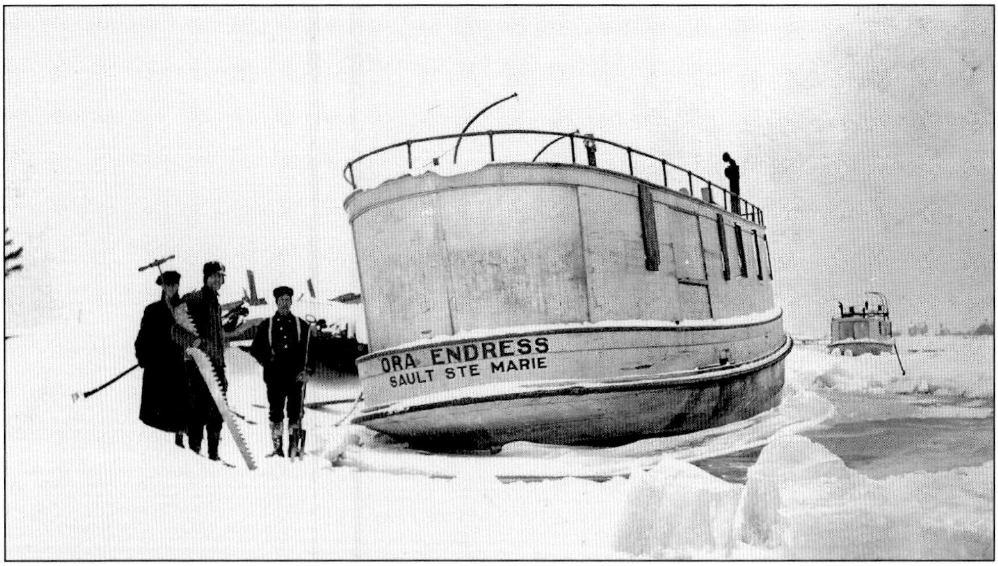

The fish tug *Ora Endress*, shown here in winter ice, capsized off Whitefish Point in 1914. The crew was rescued by the Whitefish Point lightkeeper. The boat was considered a total loss but was later recovered. It was rebuilt and enlarged and in 1928 was renamed the *South Shore*. It sank in Lake Michigan in 1932. (DVTC.)

The harsh northern winters took their toll on the fishing boats, and every spring they had to be inspected for damage from ice. Here the Endress packet freighter *South Shore* is frozen in the bay, waiting for the spring thaw. Some damage to the railing is already visible. The packet freighters were profitable because they combined fishing operations with delivery of passengers and freight. (ACHS.)

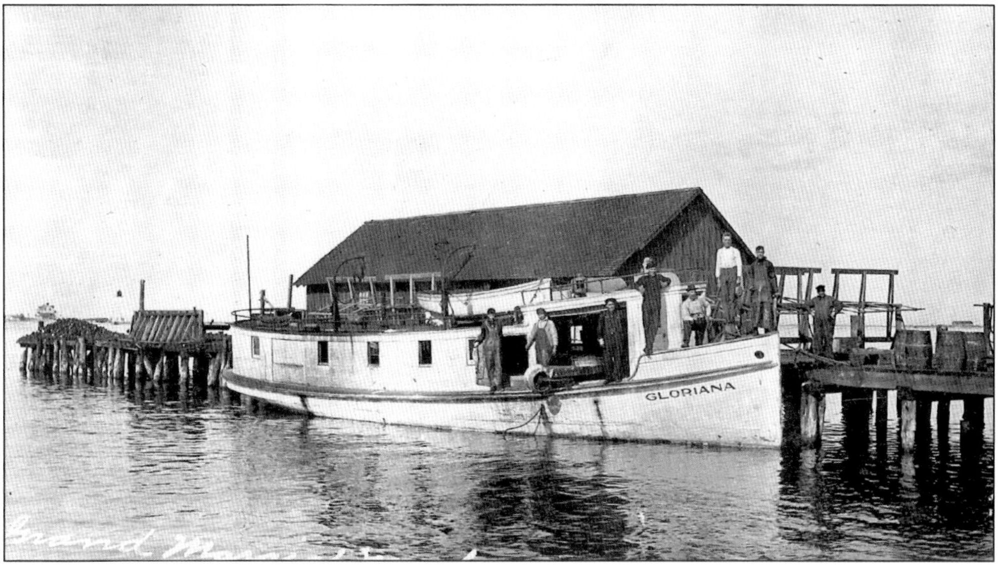

The fishing docks were busy places with plenty of work to be done. Here the *Gloriana* ties up at the Endress dock. Every fishery had large net reels for winding the nets to dry, along with buildings for packing the fish in ice to ship. Much of the fish was sent to Chicago. Each tug carried a crew of five to seven men, and there was room onboard for the crew to eat and sleep. (DVTC.)

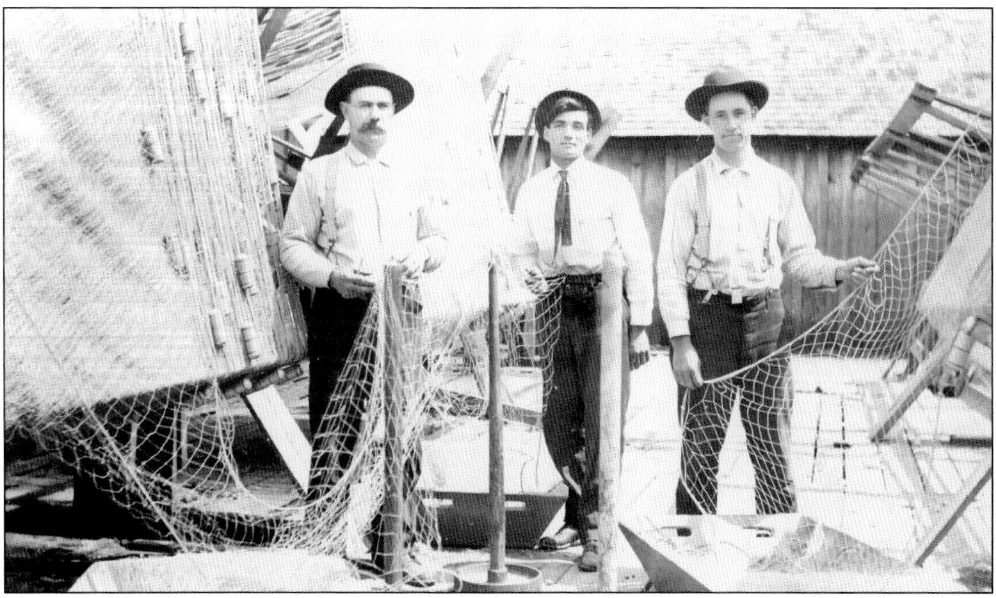

A fishing tug was only as good as its nets, and they were continually inspected for tears and mended as needed. From left to right are Dolph Meldrum, Jim McDonald, and Elzie Rouleau standing by the net reels. Note the fully wound reel at the left rear. These men are not wearing typical crew clothing; this must have been a posed photograph. (ACHS.)

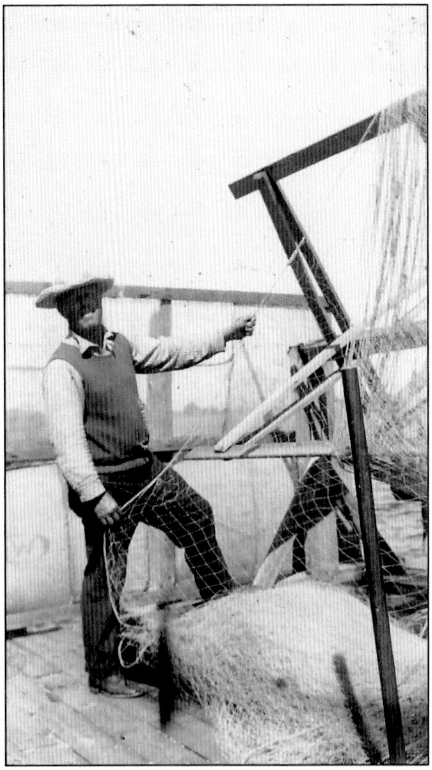

The fishing nets were made of cotton, and they had to be wound onto net reels and dried after every trip to prevent damage from rot. Here Dolph Meldrum winds a net out of a net box onto a large wooden reel. Every fishery had a number of reels for this purpose, and a few still survive today. (Petitpren family.)

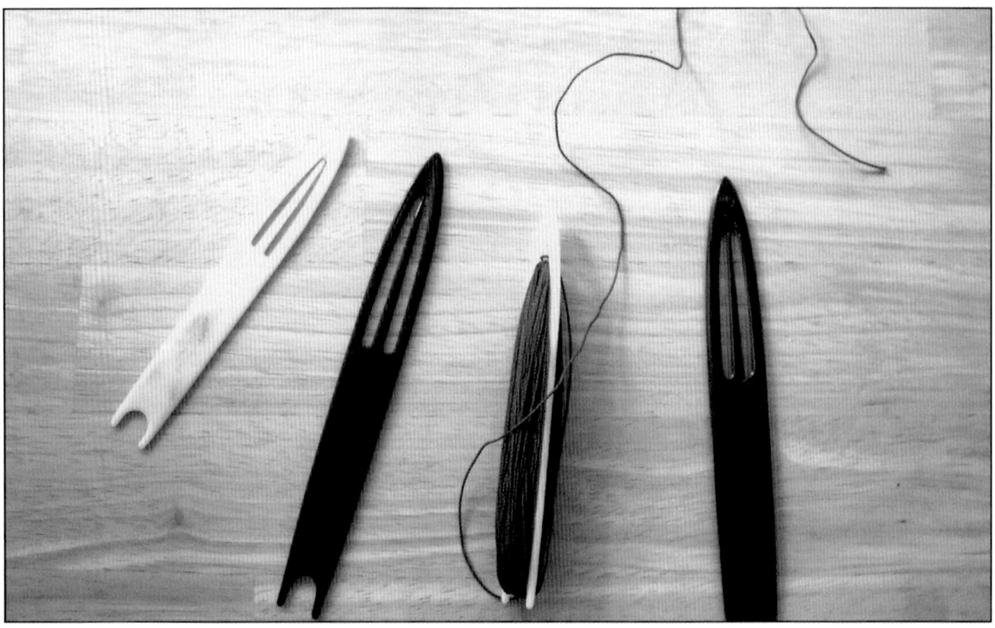

Grand Marais fishermen spent many hours mending nets using special net needles like these. The needles were loaded with the appropriate type of cord, and a seasoned fisherman could literally mend nets with his eyes closed. Net mending was a necessary skill, and nets were kept in top condition. Early needles were made of wood and often hand carved. These later needles are plastic. (Al Tornovish.)

Net reels were not only used for winding nets. Children soon discovered that the reels made excellent swings, and they loved to swing on them and spin them around. Even adults got into the act. This woman is enjoying a swing on one of the larger net reels, which is fully wound with nets. On a slow summer day, this was quite an enjoyable pastime. (GMHS.)

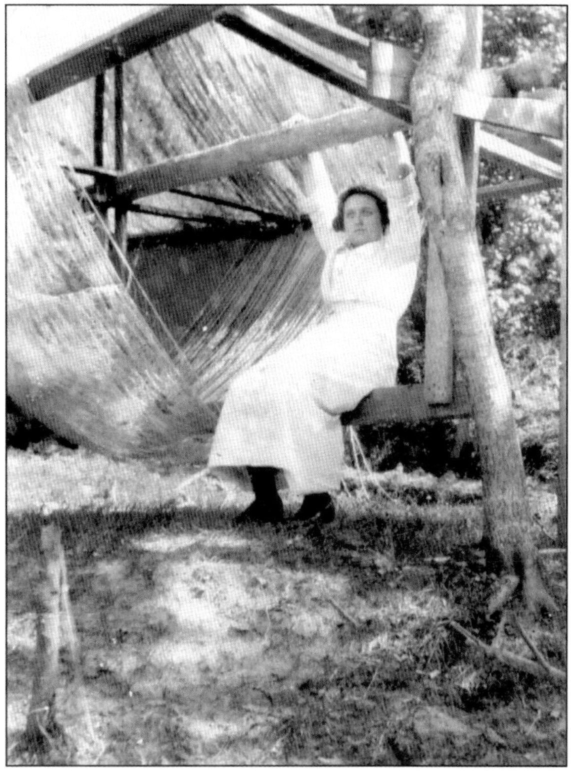

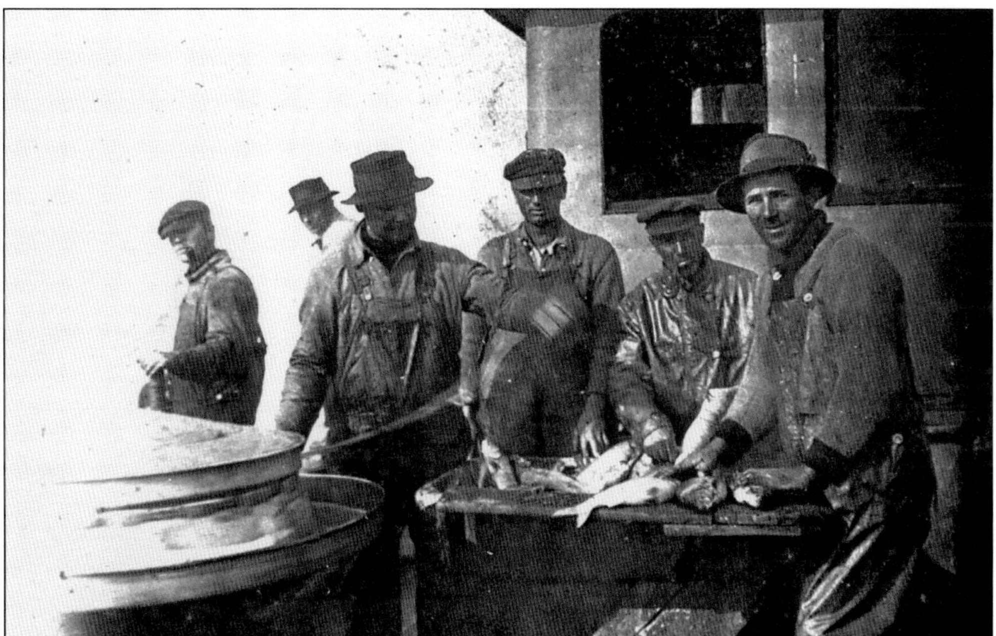

Once the day's catch was brought in, the fish had to be cleaned and packed in ice for shipment. These men are working aboard the Endress fish tug *Fashion* around 1910. Ora Endress, owner of the fishery, is second from left. The *Fashion* was a familiar sight around Grand Marais for many years. (GMHS.)

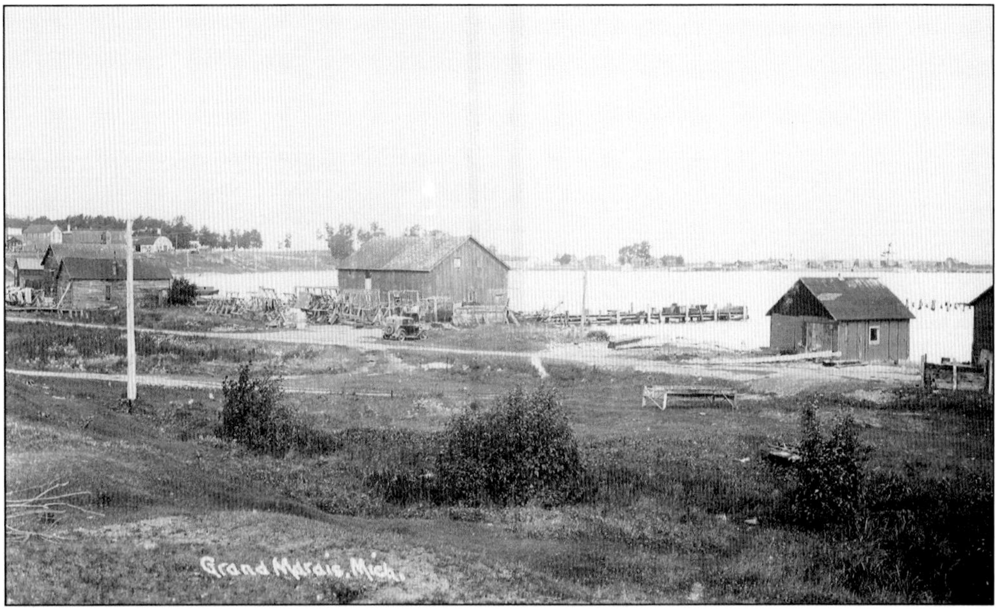

At its peak, Grand Marais boasted at least 11 commercial fishing operations. This photograph from the 1930s shows the Smith brothers dock, at center. Note the many net reels in front of the building. Fisheries owned by the Vaudreil and Petitpren families and the Chambers brothers lay along the same stretch of the harbor. The sawmills and railroad had given way to fishing docks and boats. (GMHS.)

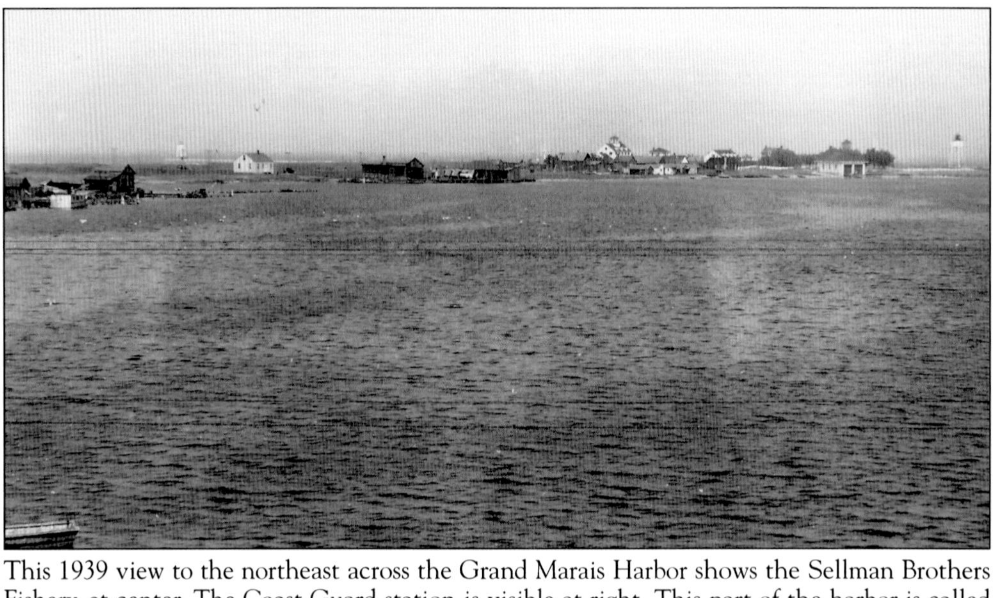

This 1939 view to the northeast across the Grand Marais Harbor shows the Sellman Brothers Fishery, at center. The Coast Guard station is visible at right. This part of the harbor is called Coast Guard Point. Very few houses existed on the point at this time, as the winters were particularly harsh on this exposed area and the point was isolated from town. (GMHS.)

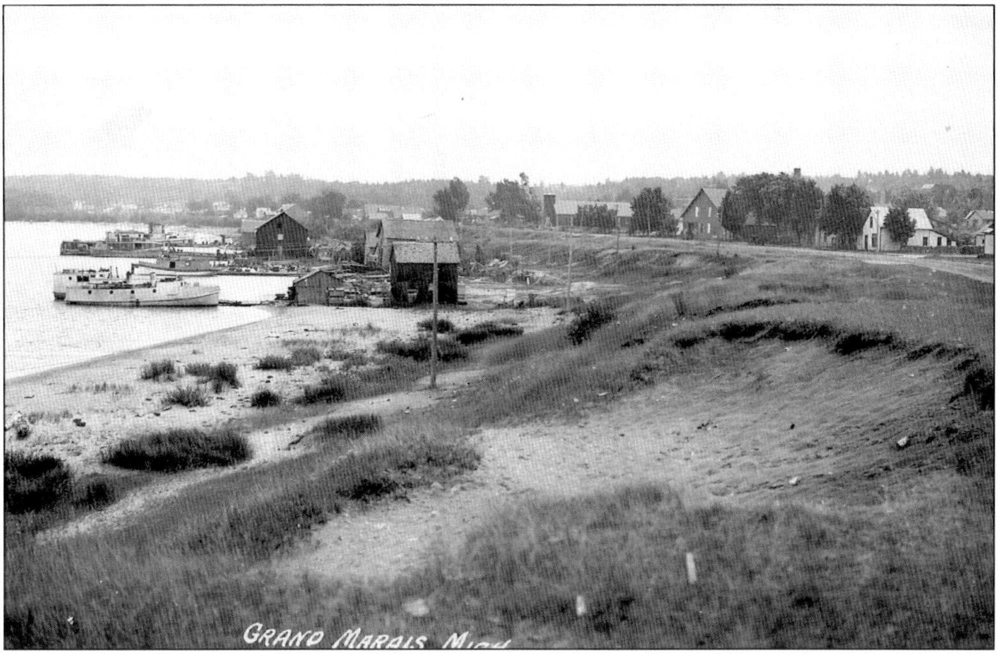

In this 1930s photograph, the *Flying Cloud* and the *Rambler* are docked along the shore of the bay. These small fisheries employed many of the townspeople and were a vital part of the area's economy. The large two-story building at center right is the opera house; beyond it is the Catholic church. This view looks southeast along Grand Marais Avenue. (DVTC.)

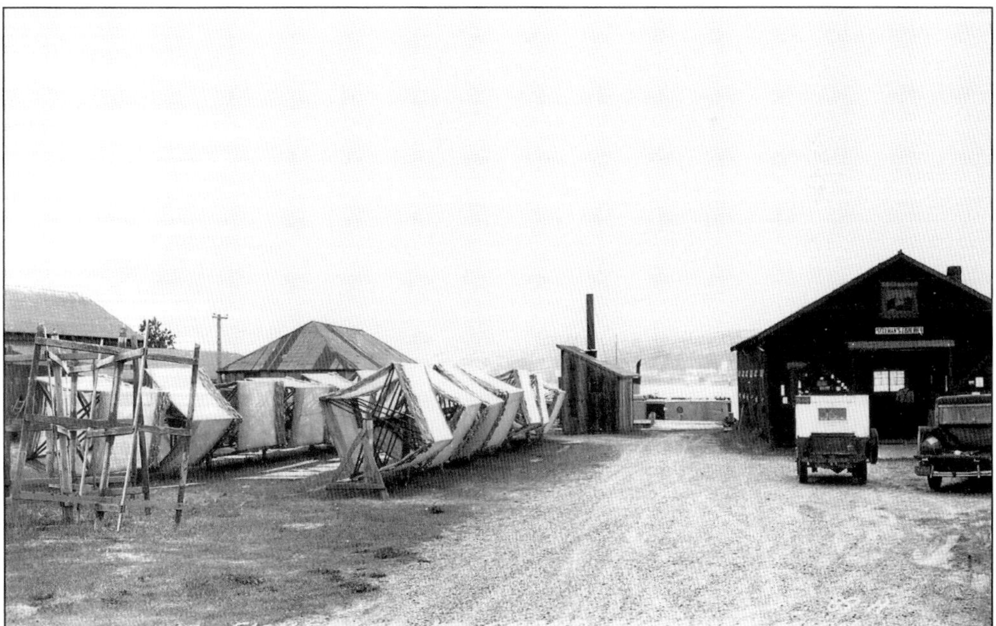

Sellman Brothers Fishery was one of the longest-lasting commercial fishing operations in Grand Marais. The fishery was located on the north side of the harbor on Coast Guard Point. From left to right are the net reels, one of the Sellmans' fish tugs at the dock, and the fishery building where the fish were unloaded and cleaned. (DVTC.)

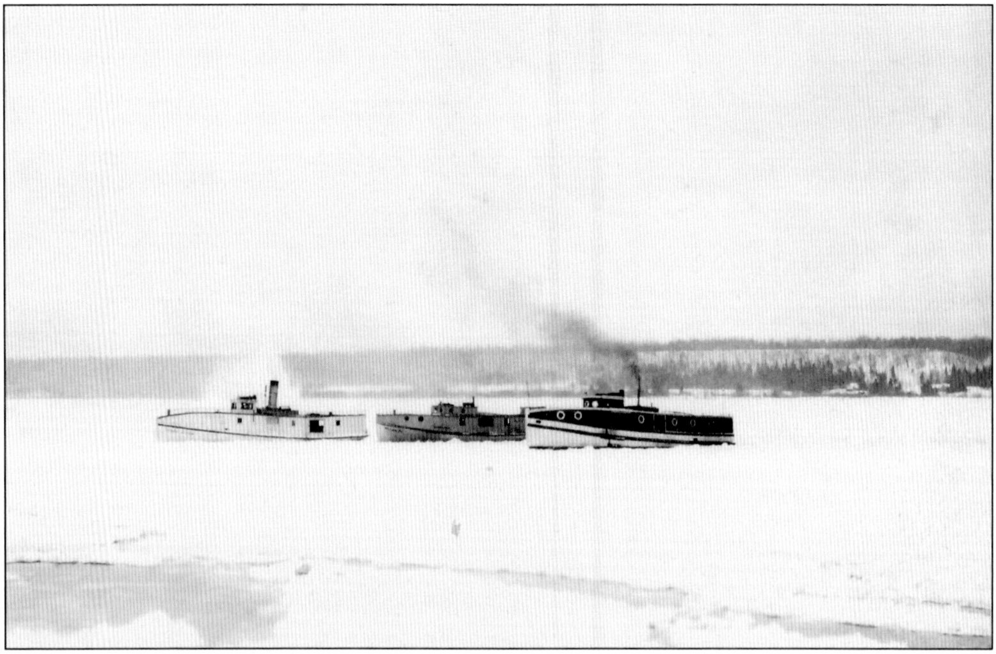

The fishing industry carried on in Grand Marais during World War II, although a number of young men went off to war. Tugs still needed to break the ice out of the harbor and channel each spring. Here, from left to right, the *Josephine Addison*, the *William Jr.*, and an unnamed tug from the Sellman Brothers Fishery break their way out of the bay in 1944. (Della Meldrum.)

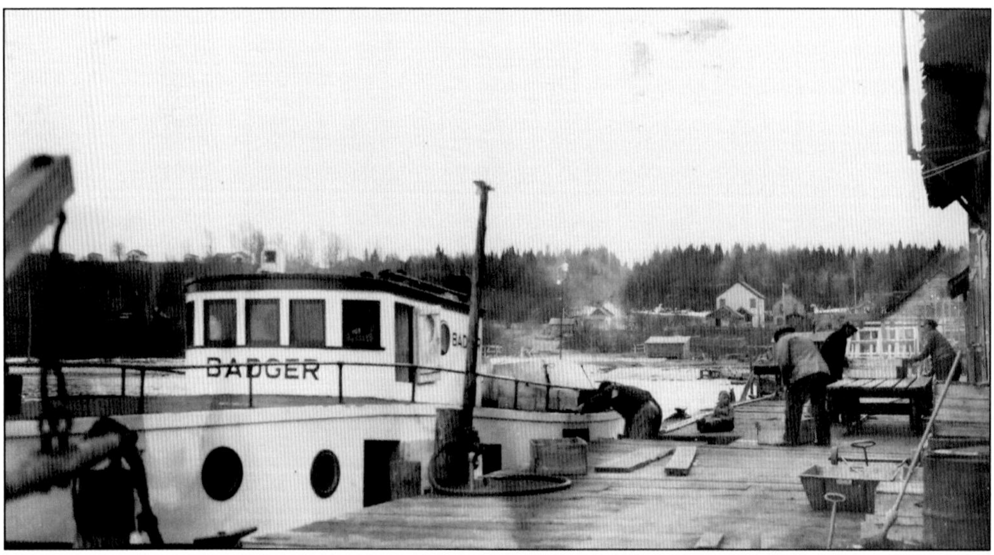

The commercial fishing operations employed many townspeople. This photograph shows the Endress and Masse fishing dock during the 1940s. The *Badger* had a crew of five, with more men working on the dock. The *Badger* burned in 1953, and the fishery carried on operations with the tug *Peter A.* By then the commercial fishing industry was in decline due to sea lamprey infestation, overfishing, and competition from sport fishermen. (GMHS.)

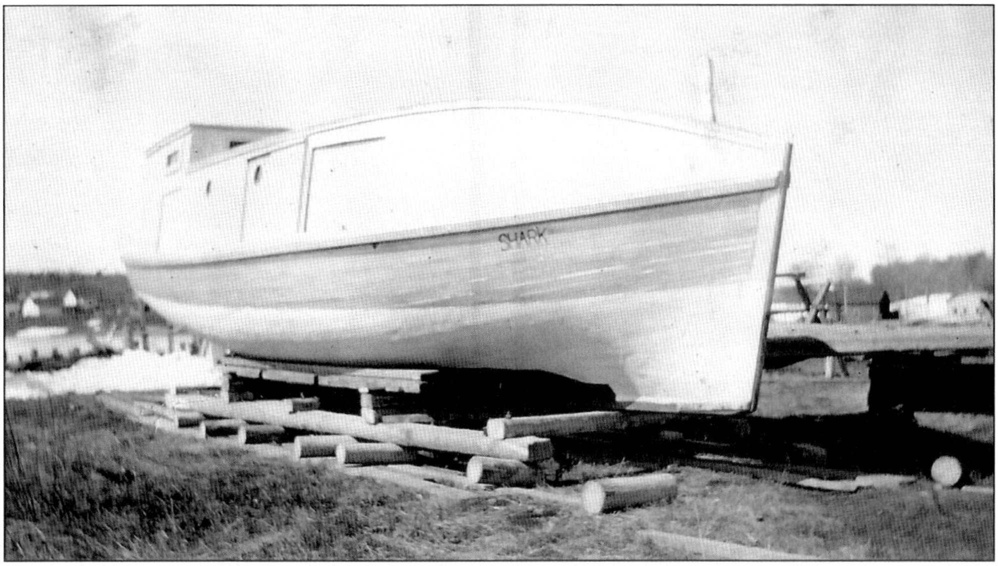

The *Shark* was a fishing tug specially designed by Otto Niemi for Lake Superior's rugged waters. Built in 1940, the Niemis used it until 1953, when commercial fishing had declined. It was sold several times and finally returned to Grand Marais in the late 1990s as a museum exhibit. The *Shark* is the last hand-built fish tug left in the Great Lakes region. (Petitpren family.)

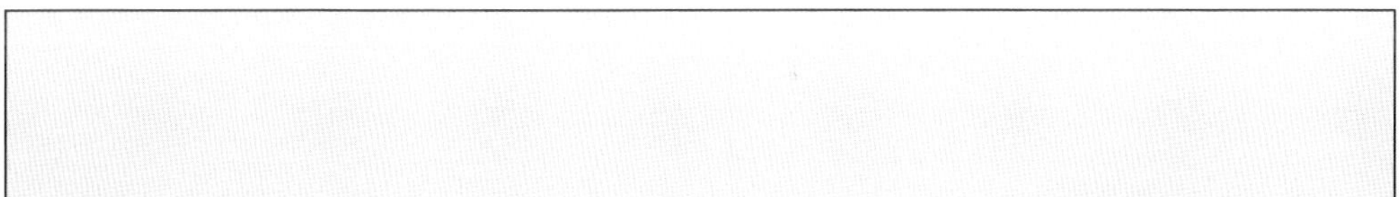

During the 1940s, the commercial fishing operations began to disappear. An influx of sport fishermen after World War II created tension between the two groups, and the invasion of the sea lamprey decimated the native trout population. As the fishing stocks declined, so did the fisheries. Gradually the docks were abandoned and the shoreline began to take on a completely different look. (Peoples State Bank.)

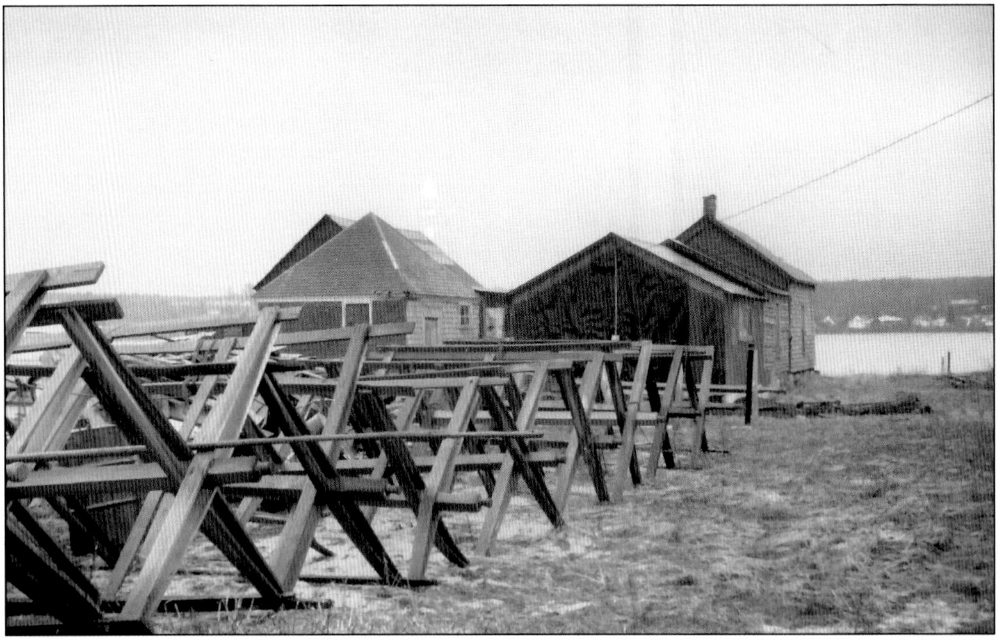

By the 1960s, commercial fishing in Grand Marais was nearly finished. Few of the fisheries remained open, and only a small fleet operated out of the harbor. The Sellman Brothers Fishery, shown here, was one of the last to close. By 1962, commercial trout fishing was prohibited in Lake Superior due to the sea lamprey predation, and herring was the major catch. (GMHS.)

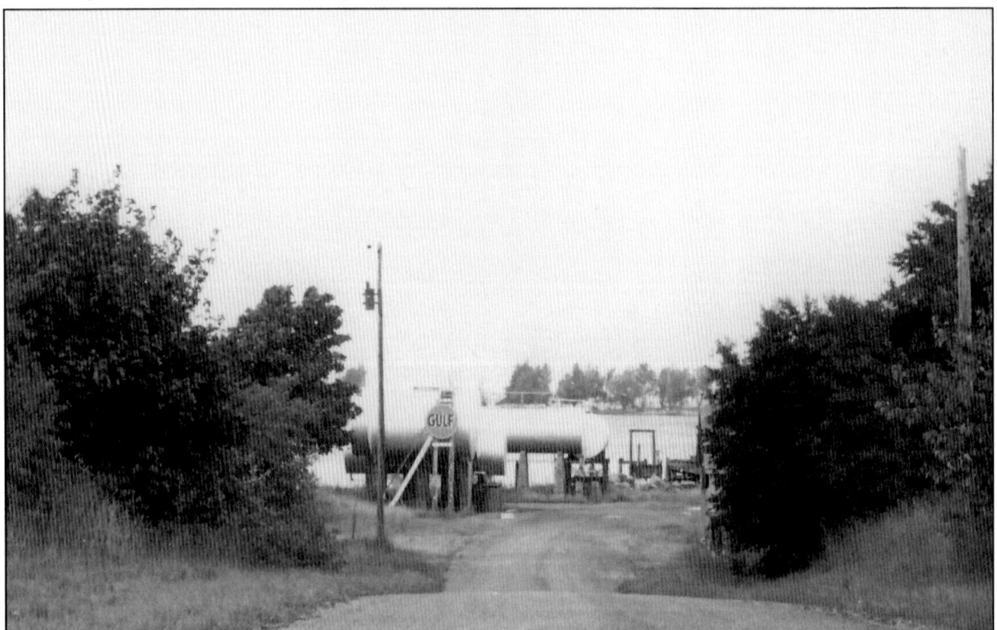

In 1961, the Endress fishery ceased its commercial fishing operations due to the poor fishing and turned to supplying oil to the townspeople. Endress Oil was located at the former fishing docks on Grand Marais Avenue. The business continued operations for over 20 years, and in 1971, the Endress family celebrated 100 years in business in Grand Marais. (GMHS.)

Seven

Life in Grand Marais

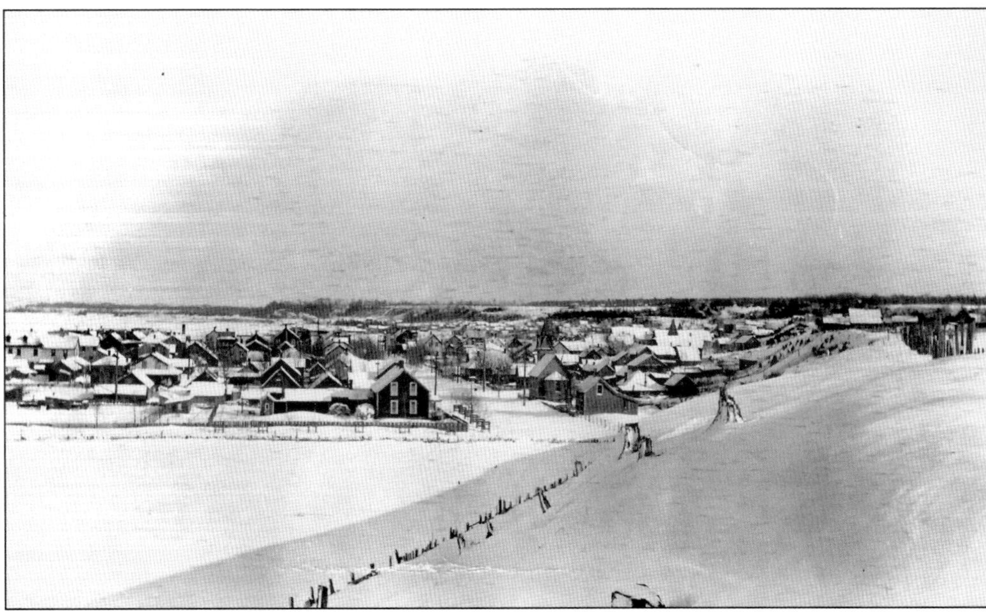

By the early 1900s, Grand Marais was a bustling town of over 2,000 people. Shipping ceased in winter and the railroad became the only major link to other towns. Blizzards were often fierce, and the citizens dealt with the harsh climate by depending on one another. When the railroad left in 1910, the need for some form of transportation drove the locals to new levels of inventiveness. (Della Meldrum.)

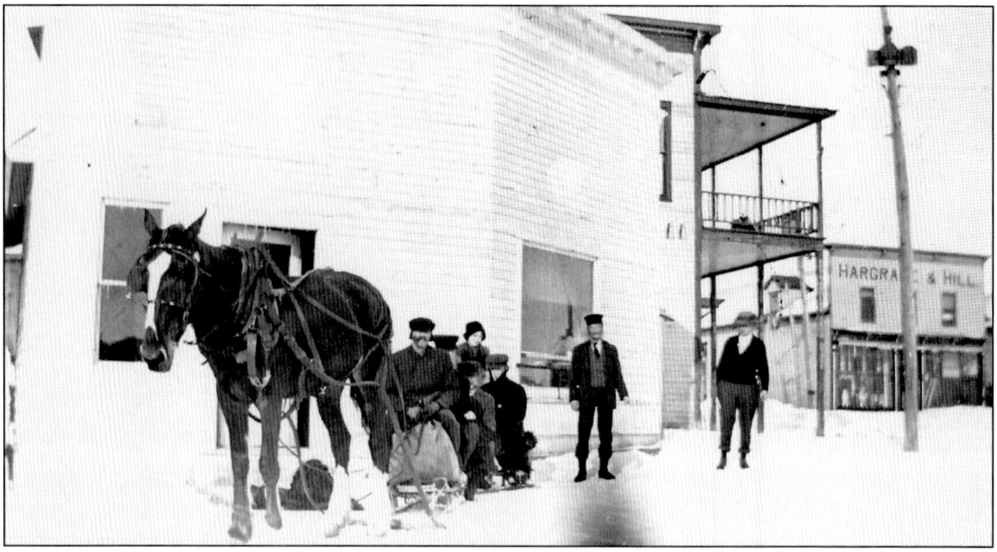

Before the road was put through from Seney in the mid-1920s, the mail and passengers were delivered to town by wagon in summer and by sleigh in the winter. The winter conveyances ranged from wagon boxes on runners to toboggans. One of the drivers was such a notorious flirt that many women in town did not like to ride with him. This one-horse sled is shown in front of the old post office. (ACHS.)

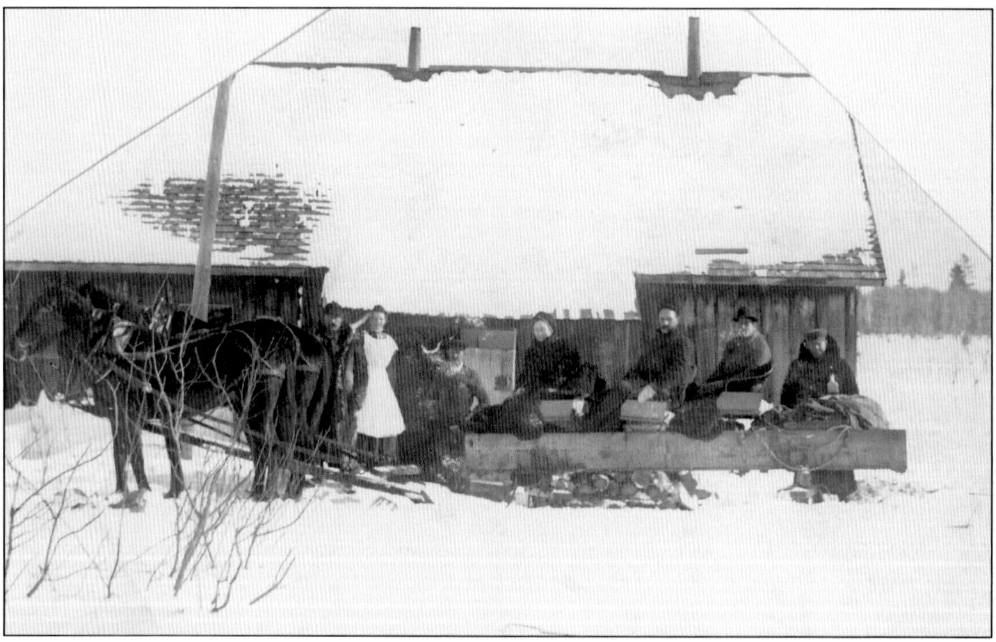

The winter stage is at the halfway point, about 12 miles from town. The driver and passengers stopped here to warm up, eat, and change horses. In 1928, the town was isolated for several weeks after a huge blizzard blocked the roads. Oxy Mattson snowshoed to the halfway point each day carrying the mail pouch and a flask of whiskey in his pocket, then returned the same way. (ACHS.)

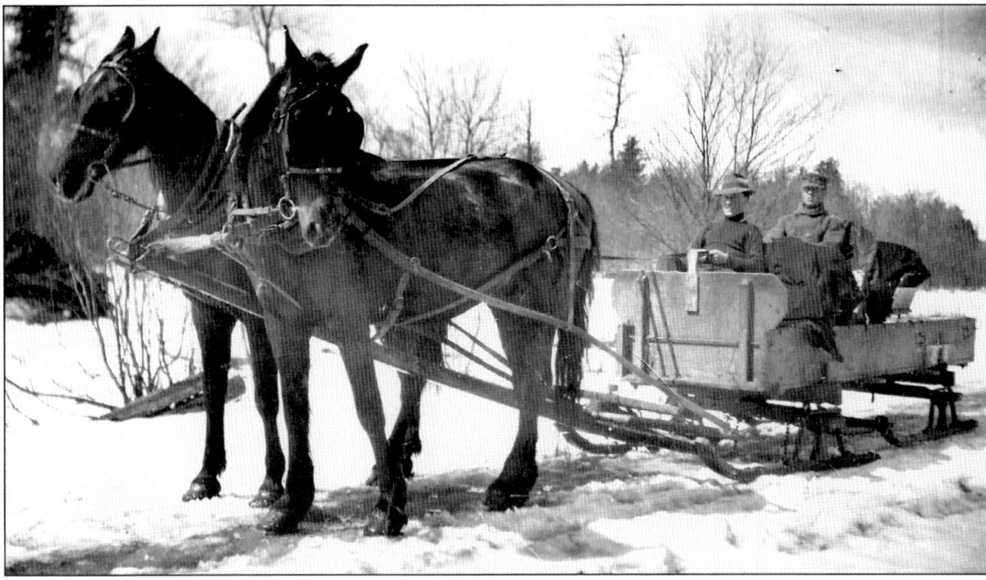

This late-winter photograph of a winter stage run shows a man in uniform making a trip as a passenger. The driver is coatless, but there are plenty of blankets on the seats. Since the road to Seney was not completed until 1925, this may have been taken around the time of World War I and may show a soldier coming home from the war. (Della Meldrum.)

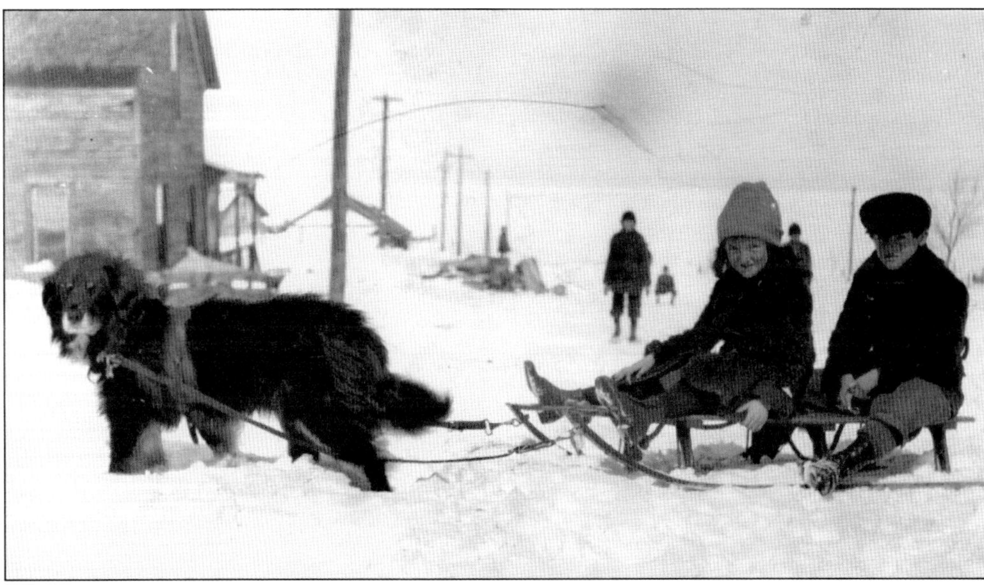

People were creative when it came to dealing with the harsh winters in Grand Marais, and not all winter sleds were horse drawn. Sometimes the family dog was pressed into service for transportation, for play, and for running errands. Maybelle and Earl Morrissey are enjoying a ride in this photograph from the early 1900s. It was taken in East Town, looking north toward Lake Superior. (Della Meldrum.)

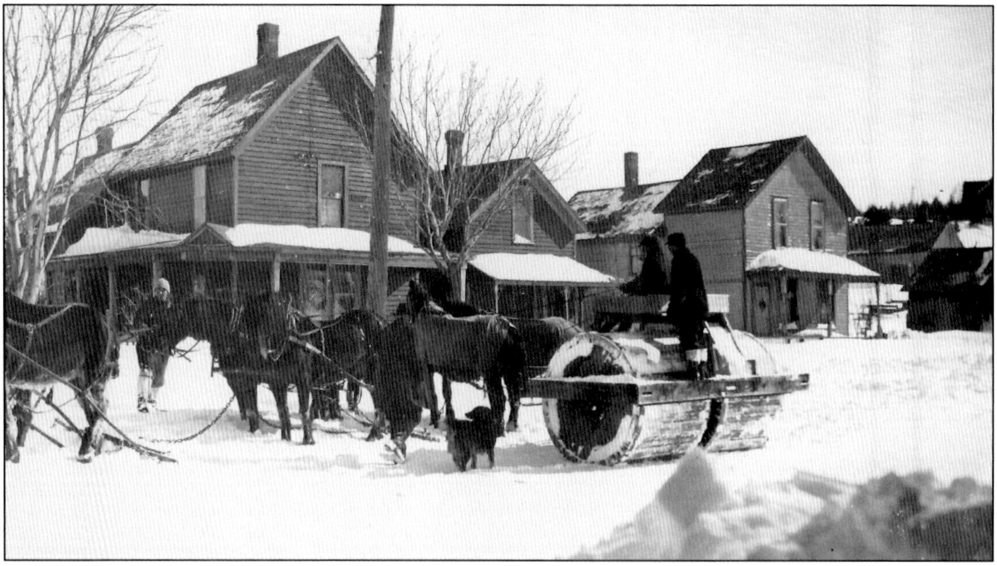

In the 1920s and 1930s, the streets and roads in and around Grand Marais were not plowed; instead, they were rolled. This large roller wagon, pulled by a six-horse team, packed the snow down so people, wagons, and horses could travel around town. The roller was packed with sand and was extremely heavy. (ACHS.)

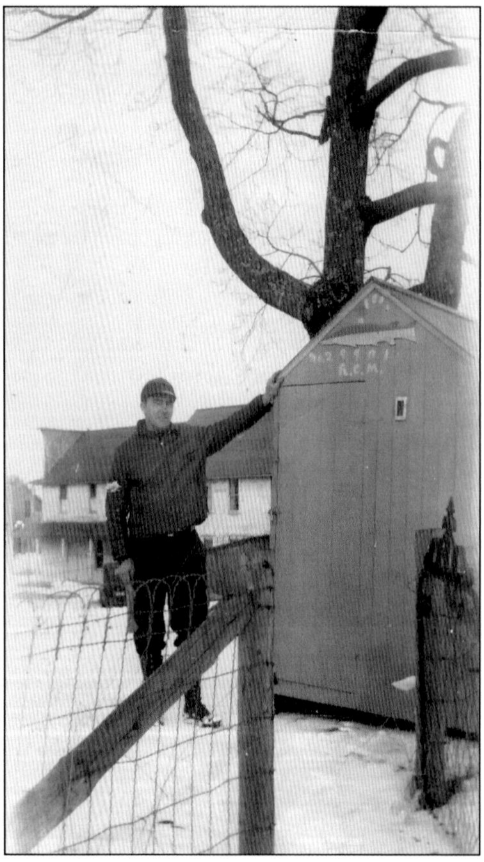

Winter ice fishing was not only a sport, it was also an important part of the winter food supply for many families. The protected ice of the bay was an ideal place to ice fish. Fishermen built their own fishing shacks, called shanties, and some of them were quite elaborate. This photograph shows Ray Meldrum with his ice-fishing shanty in the late 1920s. (Della Meldrum.)

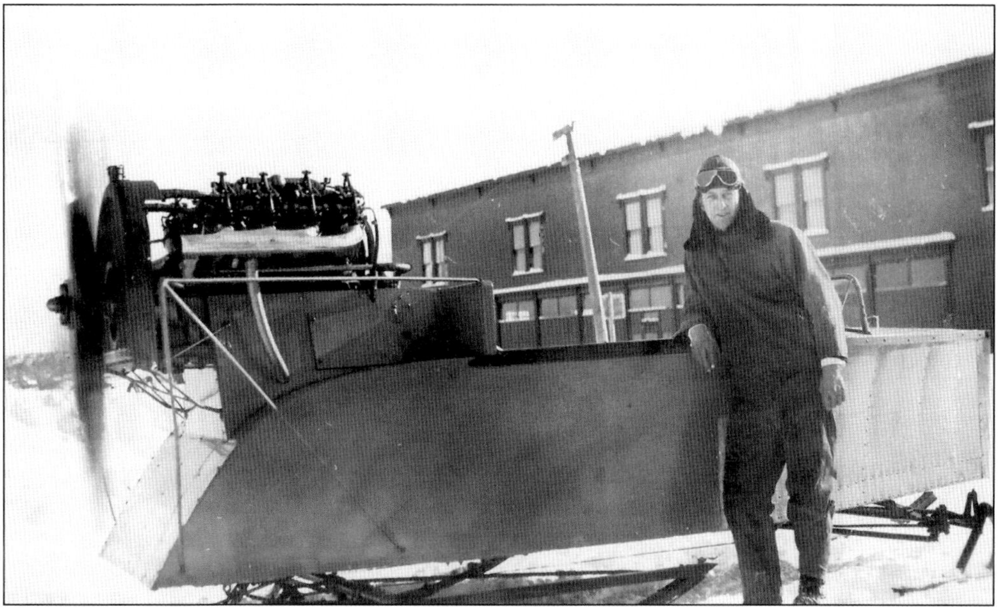

Ed Spencer, above, built this early snowmobile on a Model T undercarriage. The wooden body frame was covered with a canvas-type material and coated with airplane lacquer. The sled was powered by a Curtiss V-8 airplane engine with two propellers and could seat six people. Spencer used it to carry the mail in 1928 and wrecked it that winter when he hit a stump north of Seney. (GMHS.)

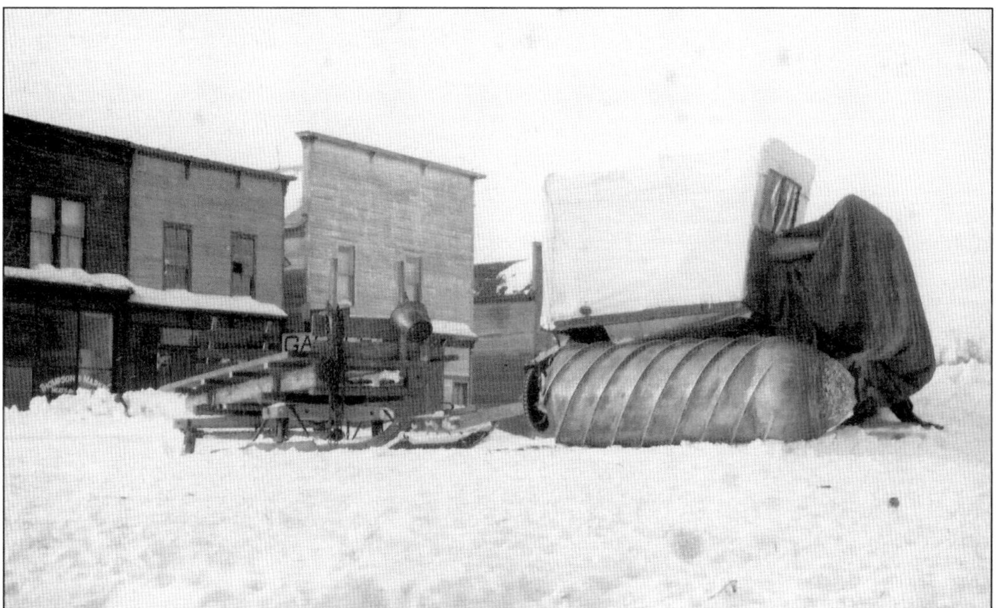

Snow has always been something to contend with in Grand Marais. This inventive early snow machine is a *c.* 1925 Fordson snowmobile, also known as an Armstead Snow-motor. This was a Fordson tractor with the tracks replaced by hollow screwlike cylinders that pushed through snow. It could haul up to five tons and could also traverse bare ground. It is shown here looking north on Lake Avenue. (GMHS.)

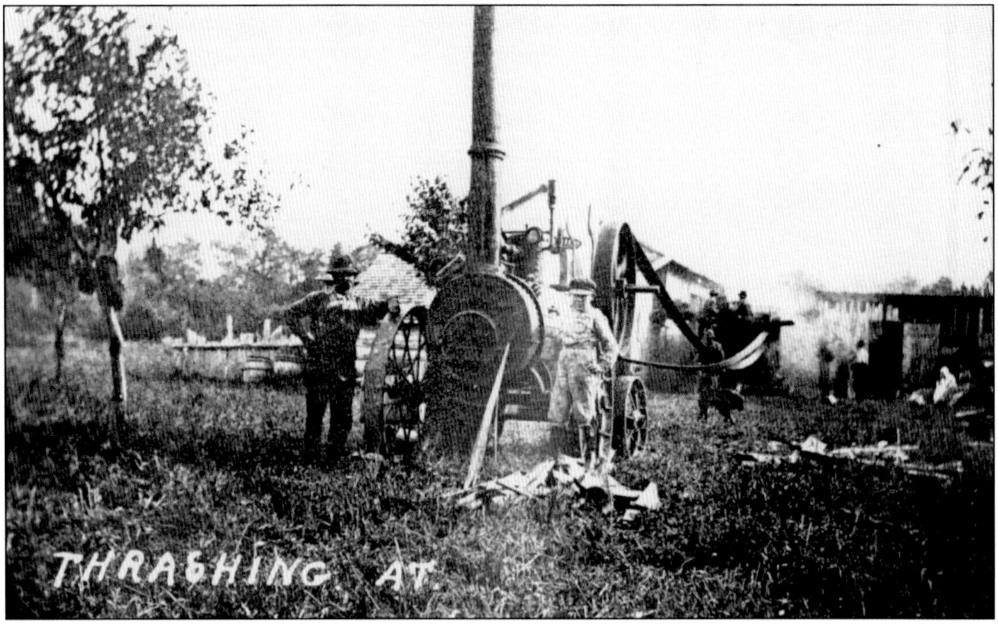

Numerous small farmers in the Grand Marais area grew potatoes and hay, two crops that would tolerate the short growing season and cool summers. Hay farmers were able to get two cuttings, three if the summer was warm. Other grains, such as oats and wheat, were also grown. A farm cooperative existed for a while, allowing farmers to share the cost of equipment like the thresher shown above. (ACHS.)

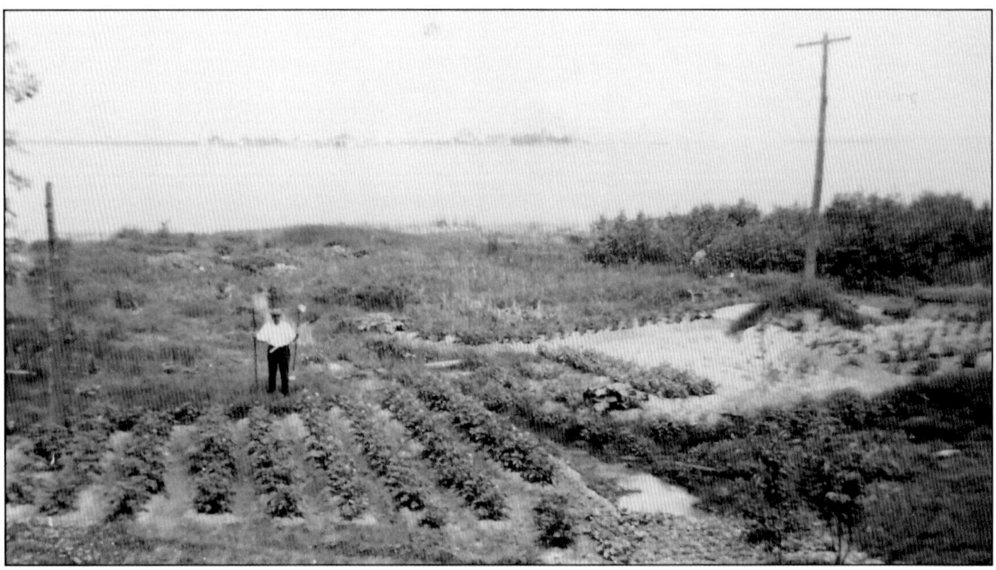

Many townspeople had large gardens, which provided fruits and vegetables for canning. Valentine Soldenski was the father of 16 children, and with that many mouths to feed, he cultivated a large garden plot behind his house. During the lean years after the lumber boom, families made do by growing substantial amounts of food to preserve for the winter. (Ted and Marge Soldenski.)

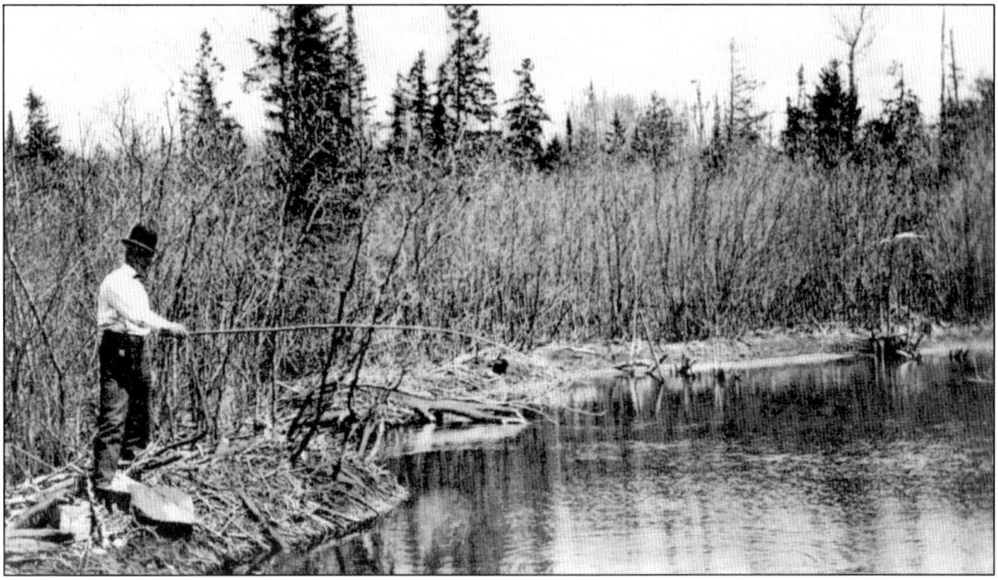

Fishing, whether commercially or for sport, has been a backbone of the Grand Marais economy since the earliest settlers arrived. The many streams and lakes in the area offered hours of pleasure, and a good catch would be canned or smoked for future use. Here a man fishes at a large beaver pond on Hurricane Creek. The dam was 500 feet long and 5 feet high. (GMHS.)

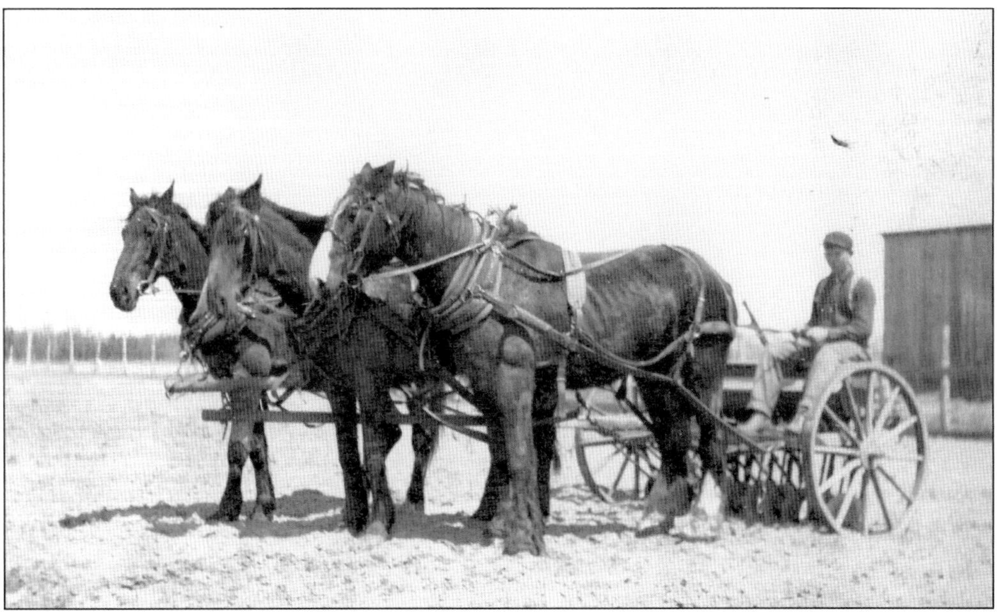

Local farms supplied the town with potatoes, corn, and other crops. This farmer is taking a break from his plowing to pose with his three-horse team. Farming in the Grand Marais area took skill, patience, and determination, as the growing season was short and fierce storms could blow in across Lake Superior at any time. (Ted and Marge Soldenski.)

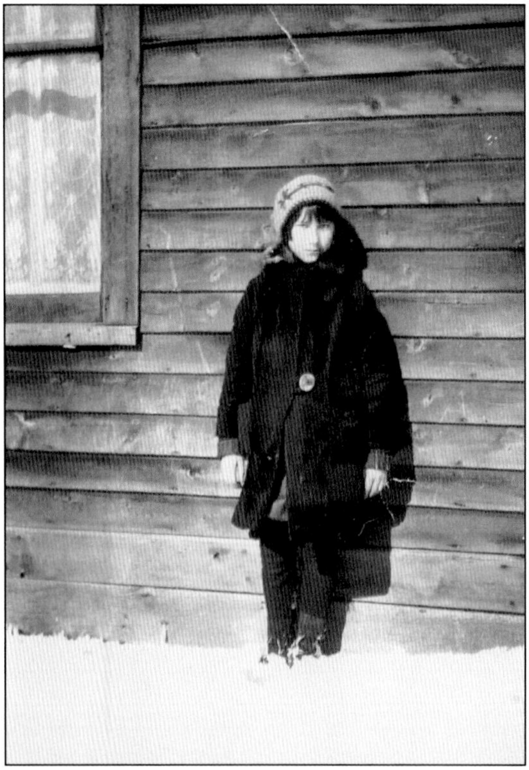

During hard times, mothers often refashioned used clothes to fit their children. Tudy Bugg (later Tornovish), shown here at age 11, called this her "coat of many colors." Her mother reworked a coat sent in a box of clothes from relatives in Detroit and lined it with a striped wool blanket. Bugg was especially proud of the big button on the front. The photograph was taken around 1926. (Tudy Tornovish.)

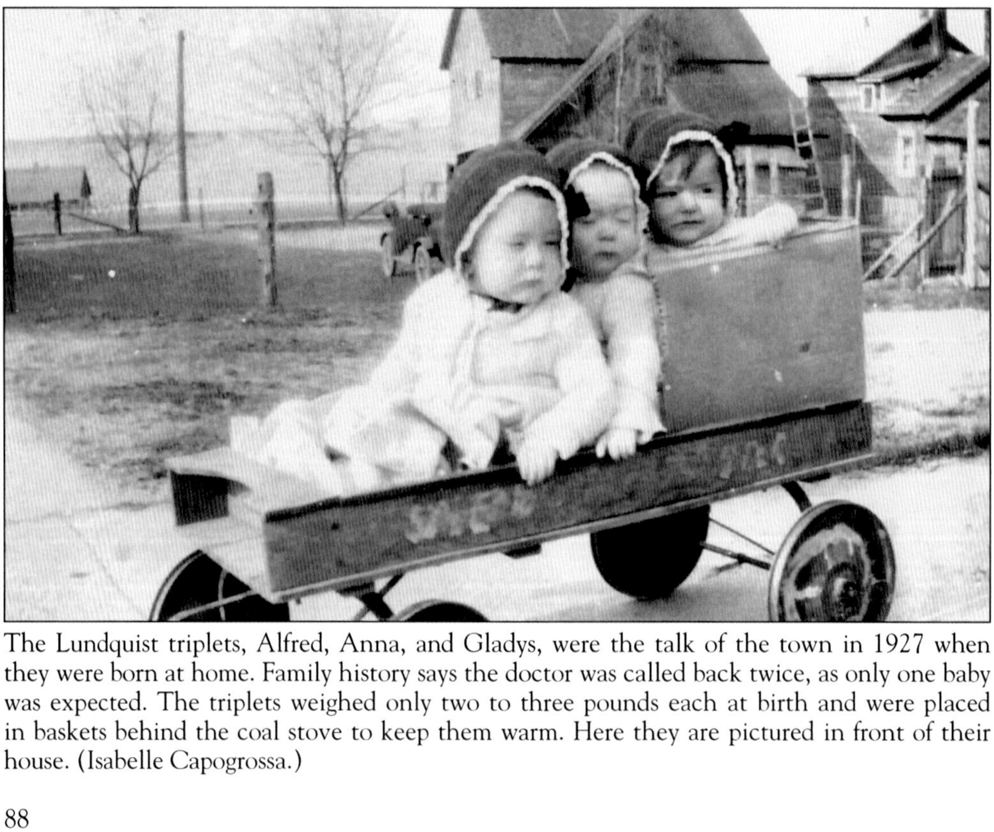

The Lundquist triplets, Alfred, Anna, and Gladys, were the talk of the town in 1927 when they were born at home. Family history says the doctor was called back twice, as only one baby was expected. The triplets weighed only two to three pounds each at birth and were placed in baskets behind the coal stove to keep them warm. Here they are pictured in front of their house. (Isabelle Capogrossa.)

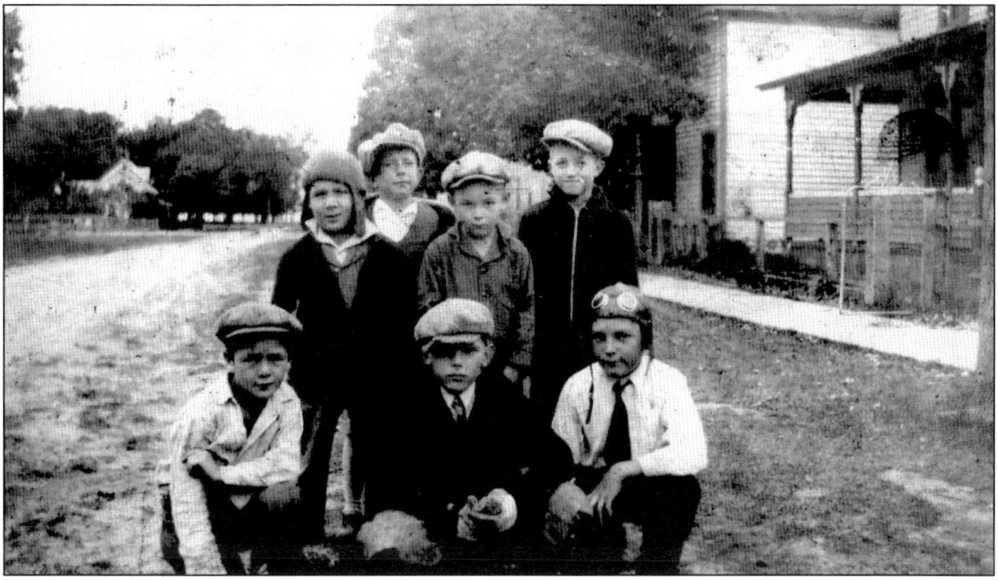

These seven well-groomed lads gather for a group photograph in the 1920s. Newsboy caps were the hats of choice, as was the stylish aviator cap with goggles worn by Harold "Pickle" Meldrum, front row at right. Boys were expected to wear a hat to school, and hats were also handy for carrying small items, such as marbles or frogs. (Della Meldrum.)

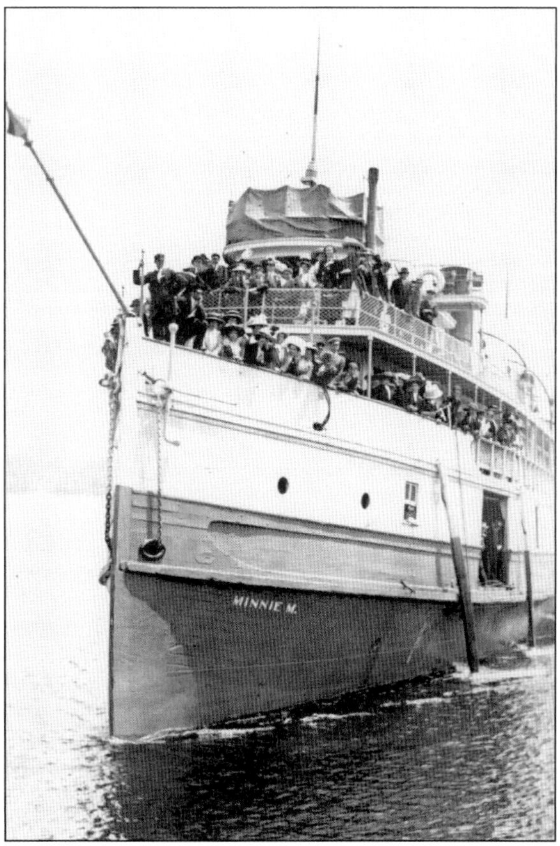

Grand Marais High School students take a trip on the excursion boat *Minnie M.* to Munising on June 10, 1911. Originally owned by the Algoma Steamship Company, the boat was eventually sold to the House of David religious sect of Beaver Island in 1913, which renamed it the *Rising Sun* and used it to haul lumber and produce. It broke up in a storm off Sleeping Bear Dunes in 1917. (GMHS.)

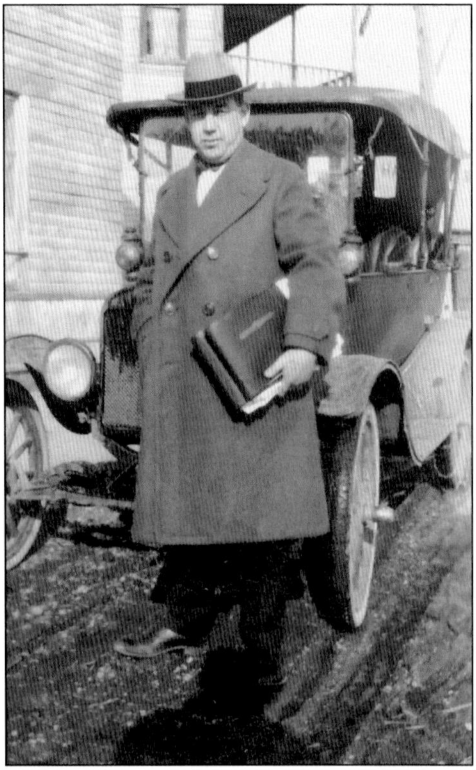

Grand Marais had an early movie theater, the Grand, on Lake Avenue. Later Alfred Lundquist opened the Palace Theater on the corner of Lake Avenue and Carlson Street. Movies were popular entertainment. Universal Pictures salesman Bob Winnig has come to town to book the latest releases. This photograph was taken in 1917, when silent films were still all the rage. (Isabelle Capogrossa.)

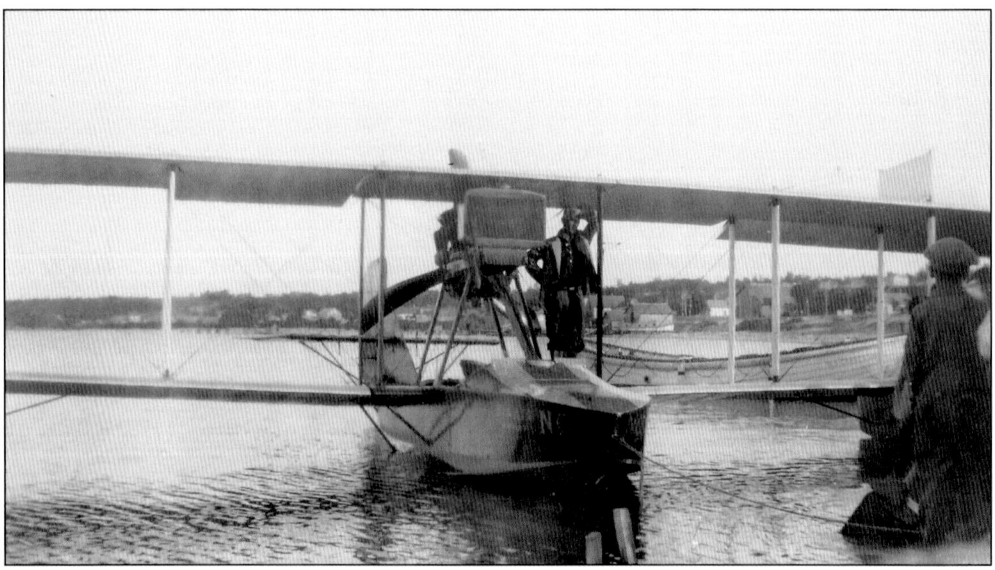

This undated photograph is likely from the late 1920s. A biwing flying boat has landed at the harbor, drawing interested kids. The plane is marked "Via Air No. 2 Detroit" on the fuselage. Note the Coast Guard boat behind the plane at right. Today seaplanes still land on the bay during the annual Grand Marais Splash-In, held in June each year. (Della Meldrum.)

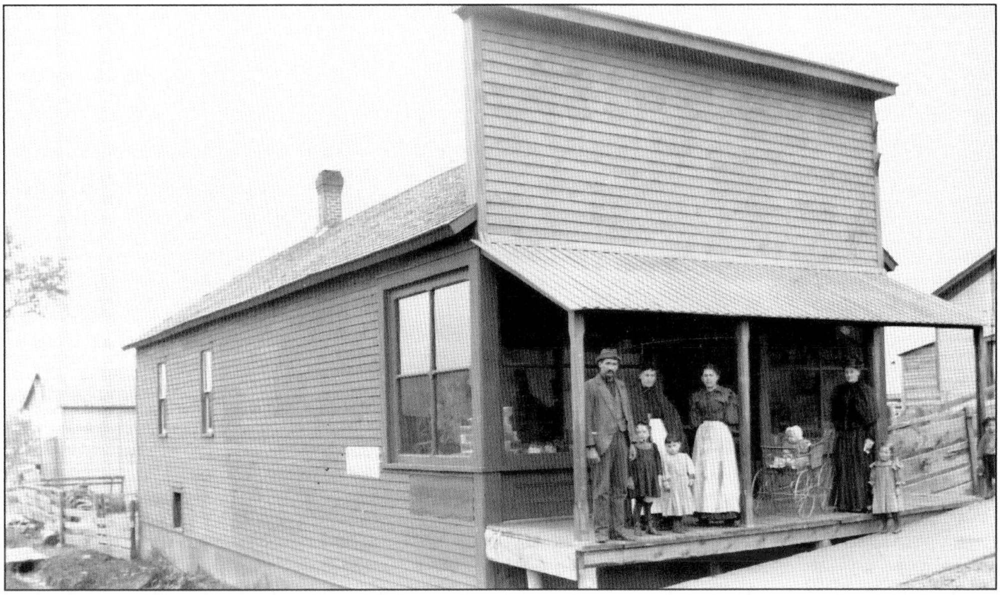

Charles Trembley, a Frenchman, ran a grocery store in East Town beginning in the 1890s. He is shown here on the porch of his store with his family. The store was located on Everett Avenue about a half mile east of downtown. Later Trembley used this building as an office for his ice delivery, People's Ice Service. The store was torn down in 1971. (Della Meldrum.)

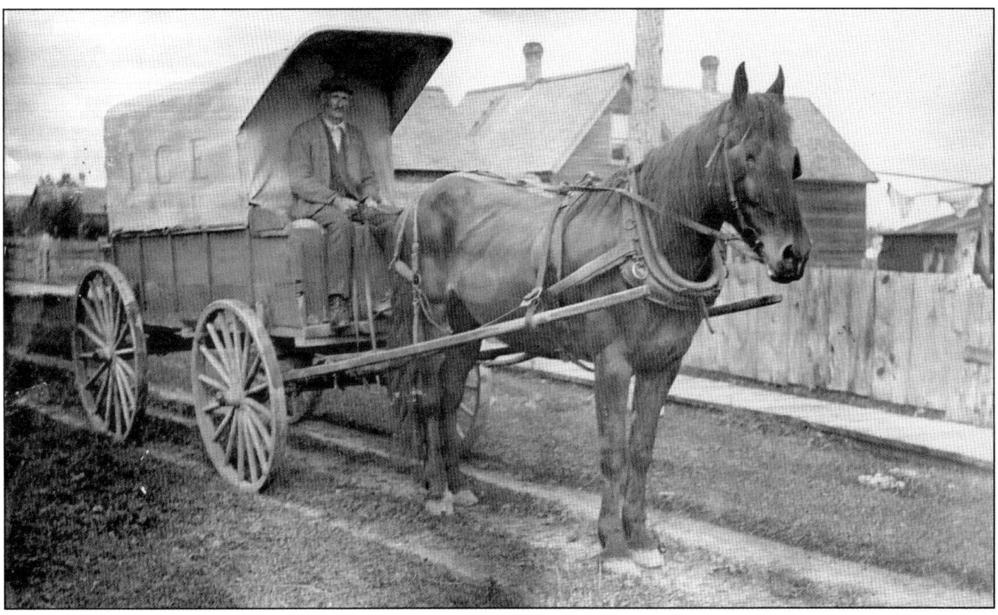

Charles Trembley delivered ice around Grand Marais via horse-drawn wagon until the 1940s. Ice was cut from the bay in winter and stored until summer. Children would run behind the wagon and beg for ice chips, and one frugal housewife even ordered her children to collect fallen ice chips for use in the family icebox. (Della Meldrum.)

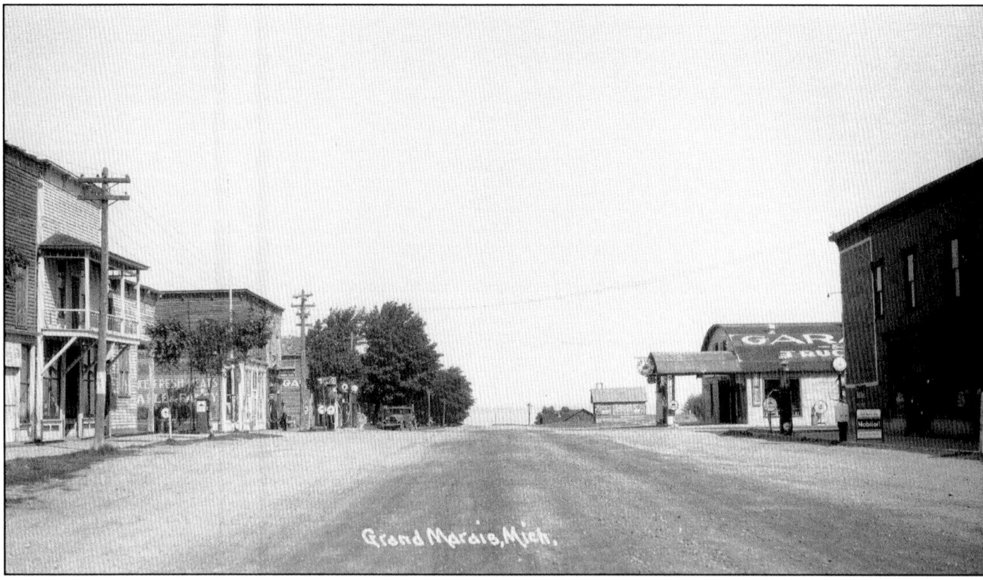

By the 1930s, Lake Avenue was undergoing a transformation. The mill was gone, and the old Schneider warehouse had burned down. Herman Wood and Milton Touzel opened a garage on the site in 1927. They began a daily freight service to Seney that lasted for over 30 years. With the opening of State Highway 77 in 1925, gas pumps sprang up in front of many businesses. (Great Lakes Pilot.)

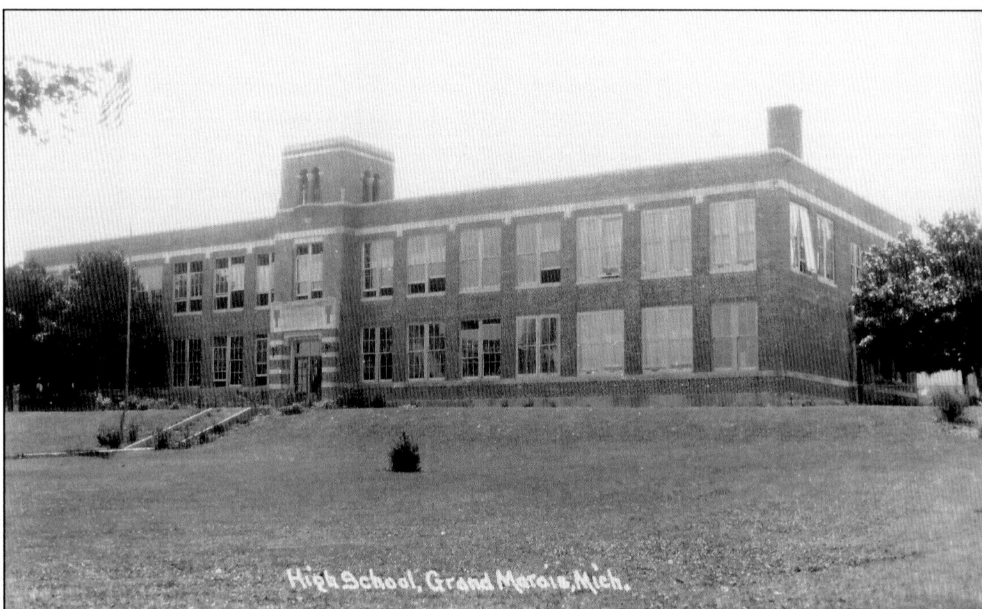

By the mid-1920s, the old school was deemed unsafe to use. The old building was torn down and replaced with a new two-story brick building. It was completed in 1926 at a cost of $125,000 and immediately opened as a school serving kindergarten through high school. The school is still in use today and is one of the last schools in the state of Michigan to serve kindergarten through 12th grade. (Doris Krempa.)

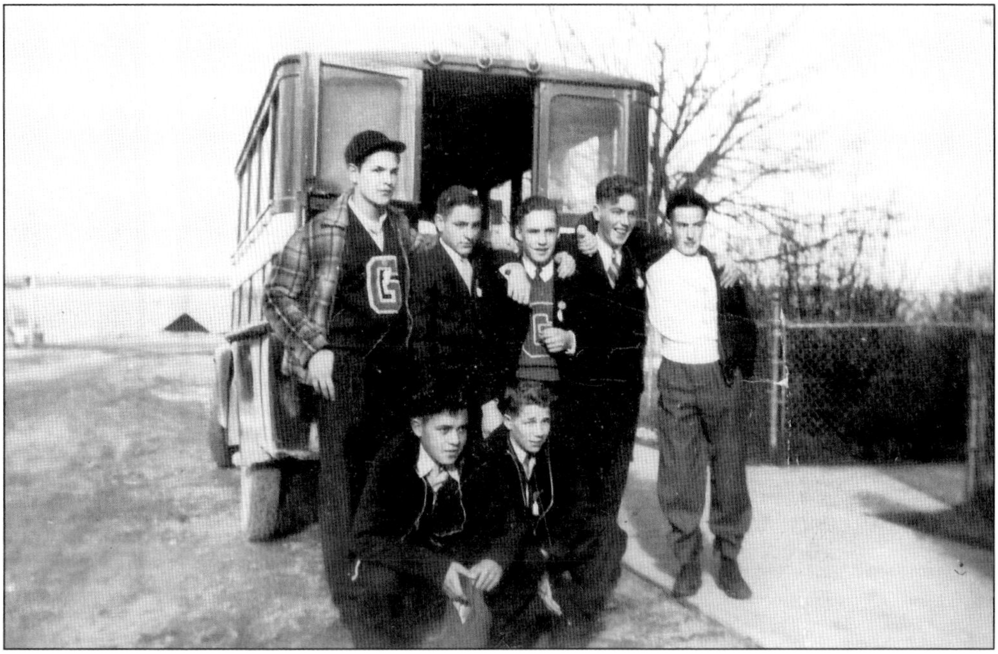

This 1930s basketball team poses in front of the school bus, ready to travel to an away game. The school enrollment had declined, but Grand Marais managed to field a team every year. From left to right are (first row) Jim "Mano" Cherrette and Art LeFebvre; (second row) James Martin, Francis Bleckiner, Ernie Erickson, Armas Kallio, and Richard Mulligan. (Della Meldrum.)

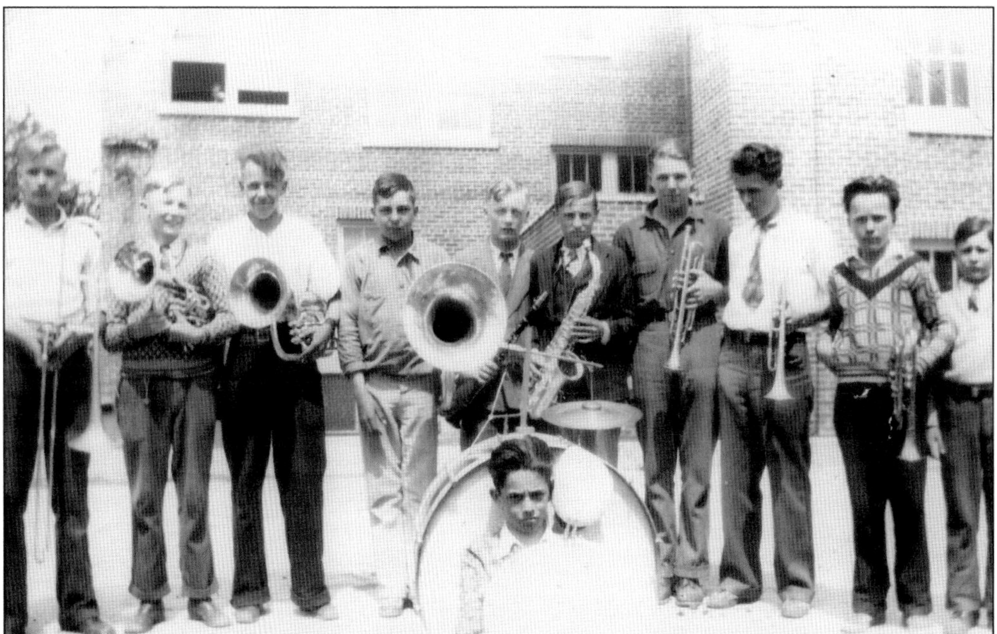

Students who were interested in music had a number of opportunities to learn to play an instrument. This high school band of the 1930s played at school functions and also marched each year in the annual Fourth of July parade. These boys are shown in back of the school building. (Della Meldrum.)

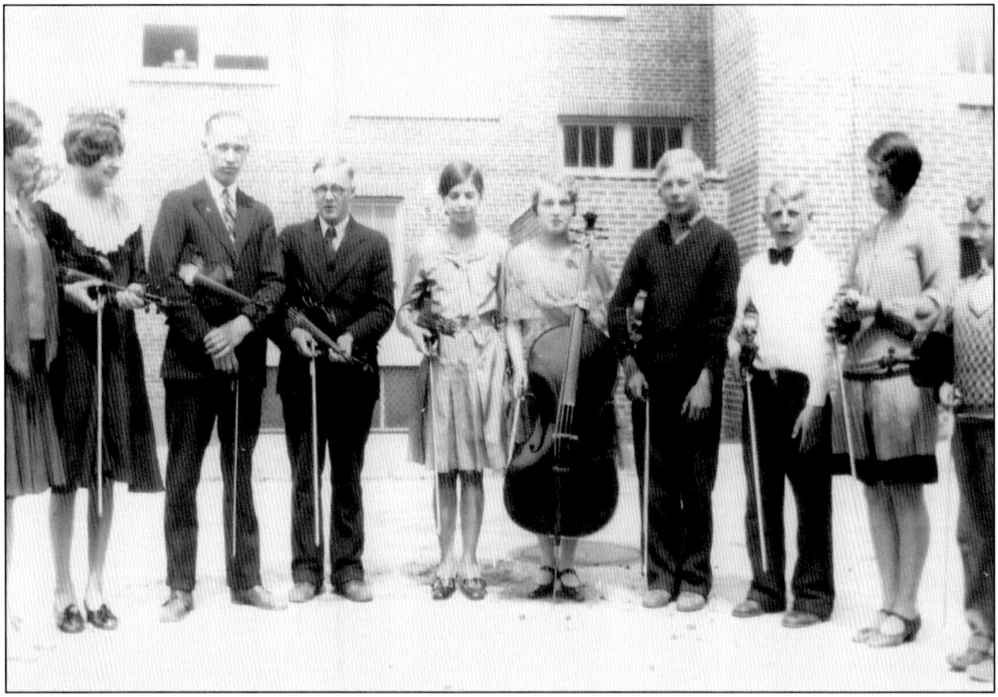

The high school offered an orchestra for interested students. Shown here in the 1930s are, from left to right, Rosalie Tomkiel, Margaret Tornovish, Carl Kallio, Ed Senecal, Frances Tomkiel, Aino Niemi, Vernon Newberg, Charles Senecal, Vivian Niles, and Axel Niemi. The band and orchestra played at school functions and parties. (Della Meldrum.)

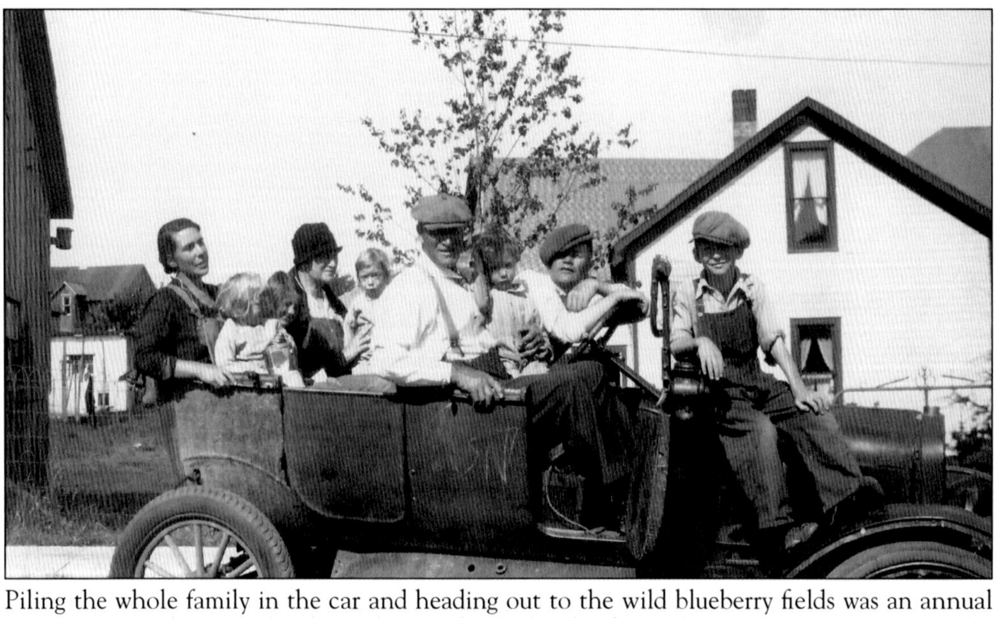

Piling the whole family in the car and heading out to the wild blueberry fields was an annual event for Grand Marais families. The Lundquist family, shown here in the late 1920s, had a favorite picking spot near Sullivan's Landing west of town. The triplets are seated on the adults' laps; one of the girls in the back holds a small picking pail. (Isabelle Capogrossa.)

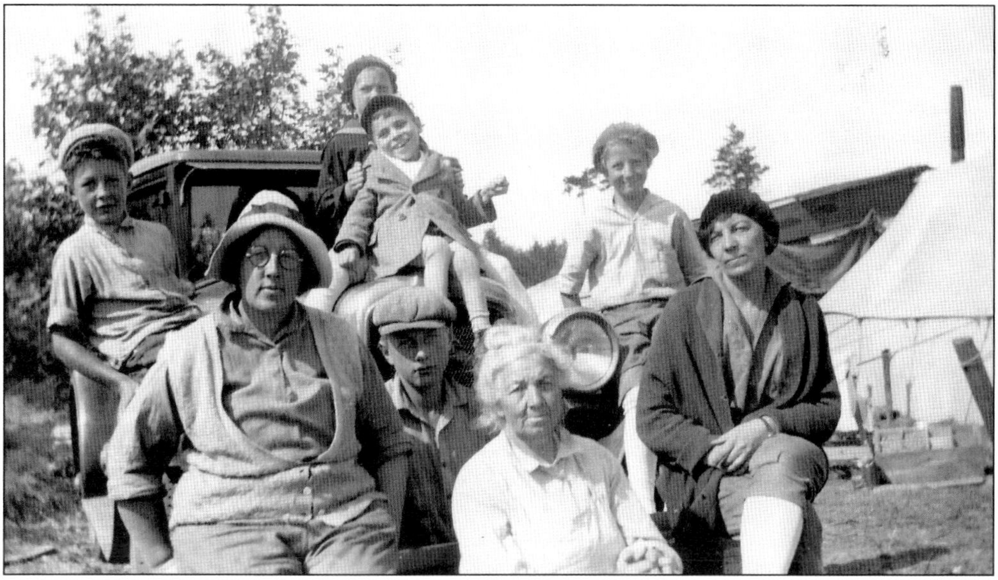

Picking ferns for florists and blueberries for sale to faraway markets helped families make ends meet. During the summer blueberry season, families would set up blueberry camps with tents and live out in the blueberry patches for several weeks. Some camps were quite elaborate. One Grand Marais resident remembers having real mattresses on the beds. This was true comfort! (Della Meldrum.)

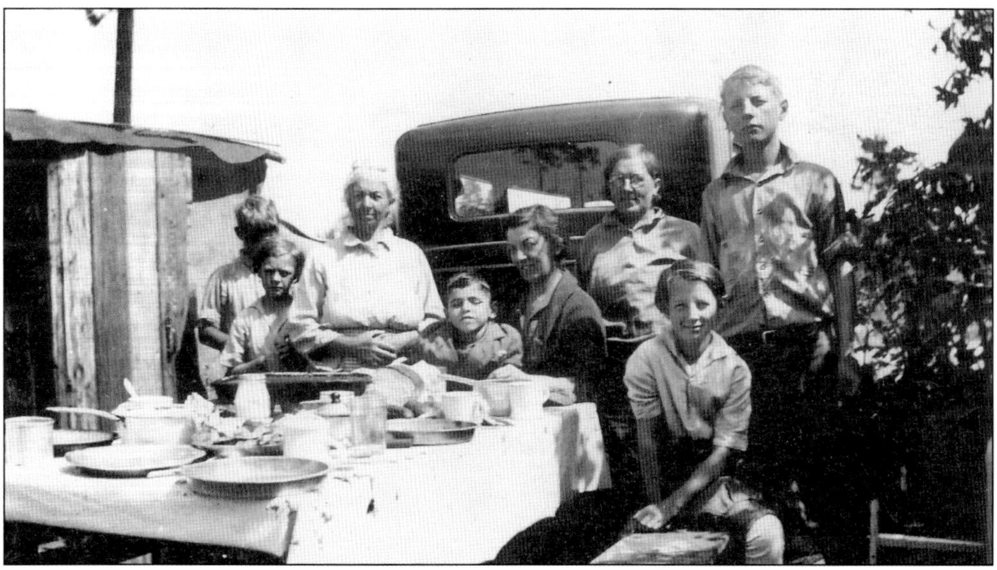

Blueberry picking was an activity for all generations, and everyone from grandparents to young children participated. The wild blueberries were packed in crates and taken by truck to Seney, then shipped by rail to markets in large cities. For the kids in the family, blueberry camp was a real adventure, although mothers faced some challenges in meal preparation. This family even has a small cook shack. (Della Meldrum.)

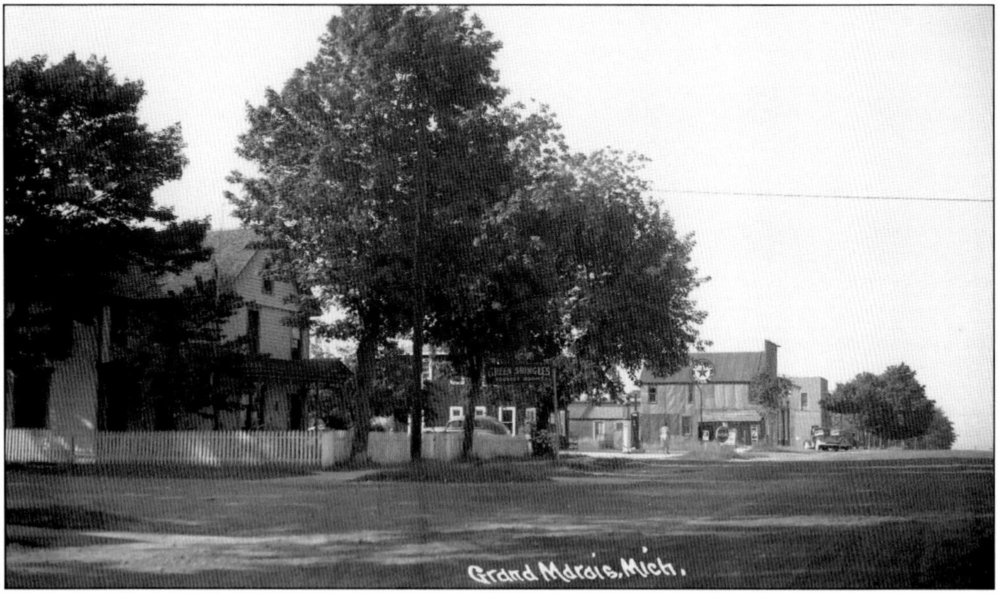

After the devastating fire that destroyed much of the western side of Lake Avenue in 1915, the lots stood empty for years. This photograph from the early 1940s shows the Texaco station, which was built on one of the empty lots. The building at left is the Green Shingles Tavern, which in this photograph is advertising "tourist rooms." It later became a rest home for adults. (Great Lakes Pilot.)

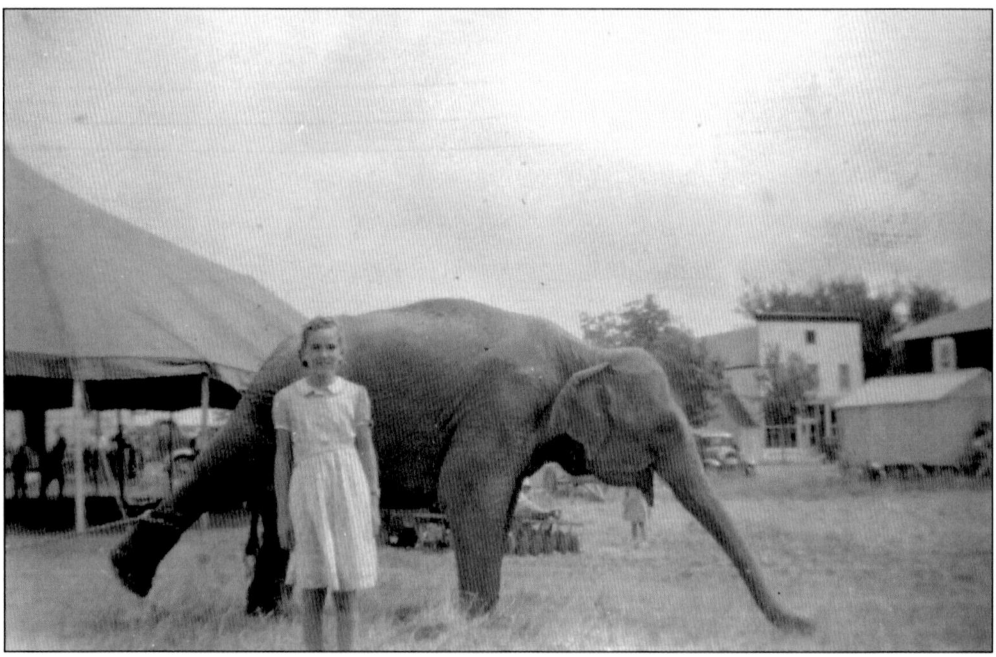

Occasionally entertainment would come to Grand Marais. In this undated photograph, a circus has come to town and has set up on the vacant land left from the 1915 fire. This girl poses next to a young elephant, which is straining at its tether ropes. The view looks southeast across Lake Avenue. The white building in the background is the old Saulson and Company Dry Goods store, now a restaurant. (GMHS.)

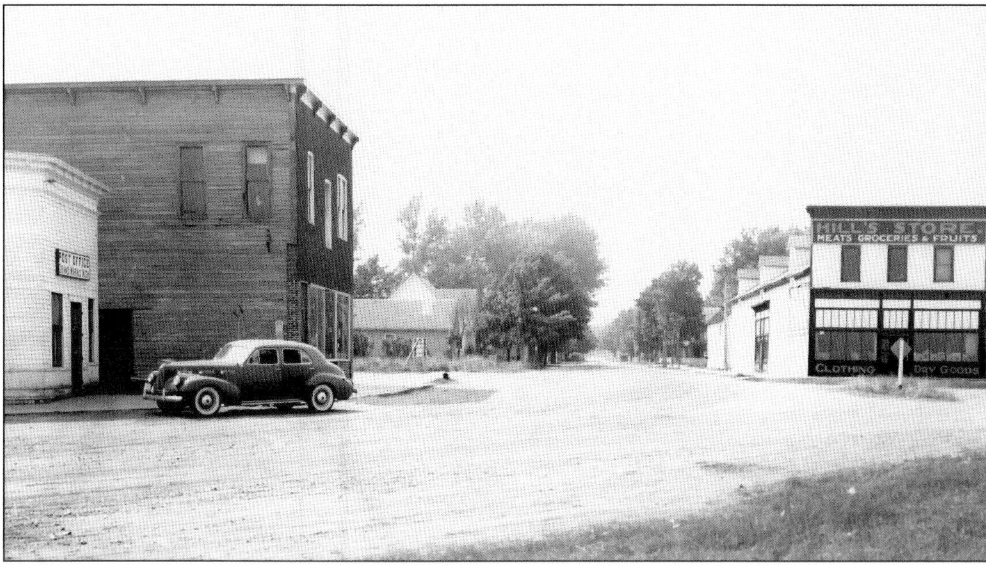

By the 1940s, Grand Marais was a quiet resort town. Hill's Store, at right, continued to serve the needs of the townspeople and provided a variety of goods, including meats and fruits. Some residents made a daily trip to the store to pick up groceries. World War II would soon call many young men away from Grand Marais. Some quit school to enlist in the military. (GMHS.)

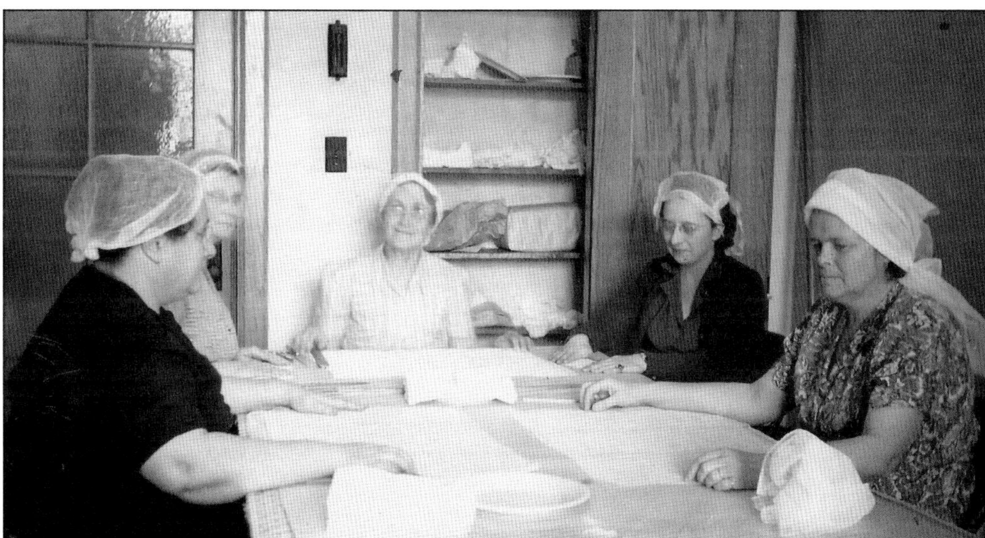

During World War II, women help the war effort by rolling bandages for the Red Cross. A number of Grand Marais men went off to join the armed forces, and people who stayed in Grand Marais helped by growing victory gardens and buying war bonds. Pictured are, clockwise from the lower left, Celina Bleckiner, Fern Erickson, Hilda Peterson, Bernice Bennett, and Mrs. Mattson. (Argie Thorrington.)

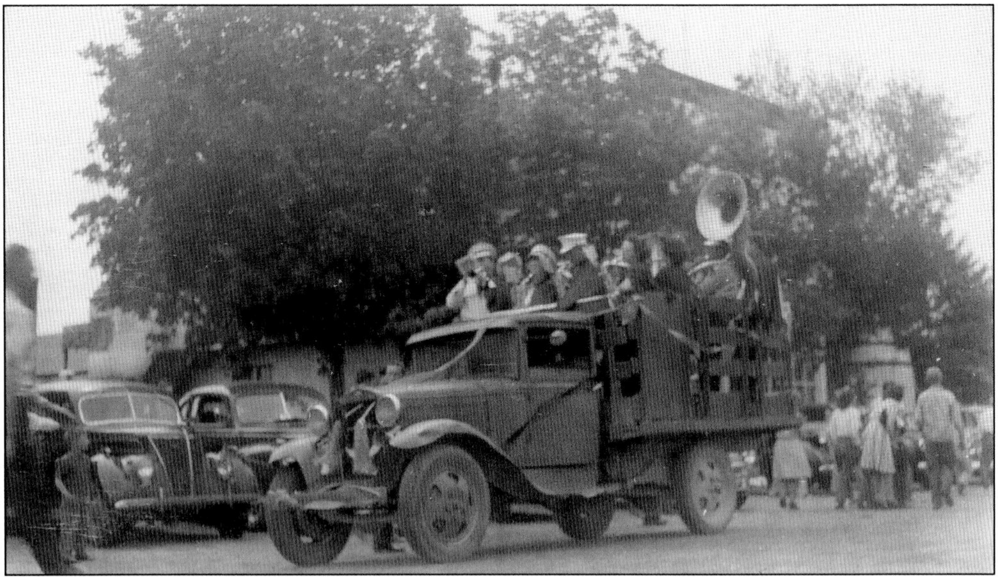

The annual Fourth of July parade draws hundreds of people from the surrounding areas into Grand Marais each year. This high school band piled into an open pickup truck and played as the parade wound around the streets of the town, starting with Lake Avenue, shown here looking southeast. At right is the famous Pickle Barrel House. This photograph dates to the 1940s. (Della Meldrum.)

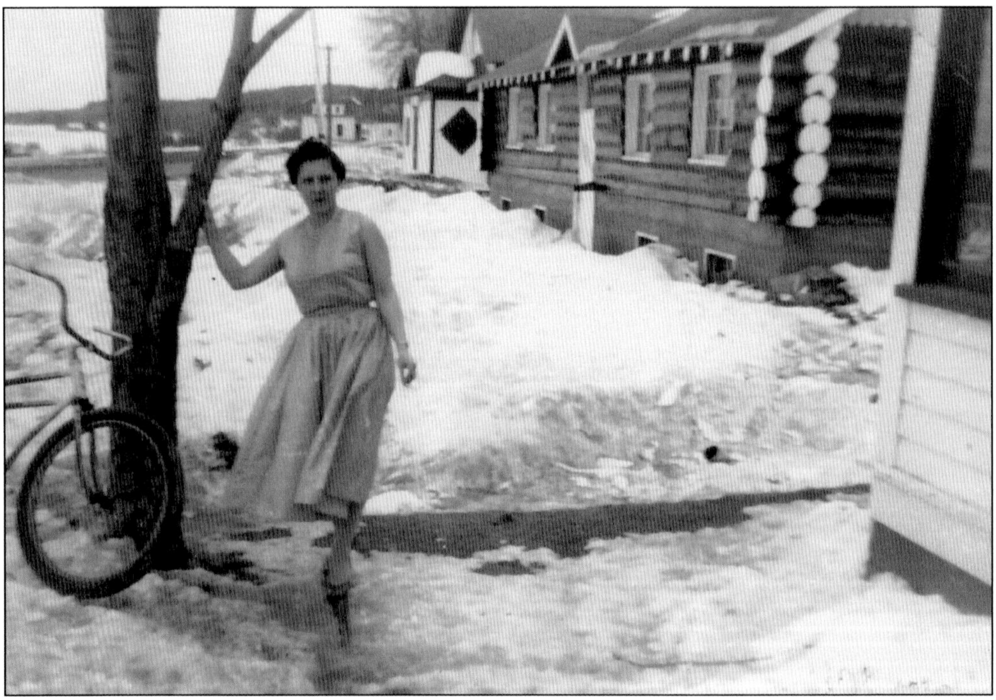

The log building at the right is the VFW hall, where dances were held on Saturday nights up until the 1960s. A bar was set up in the basement. Pictured here is Argie Thorrington, who played piano in the band that performed at the dances. Today the building houses the Burt Township offices. The building has a new exterior, but the original logs are underneath. (Argie Thorrington.)

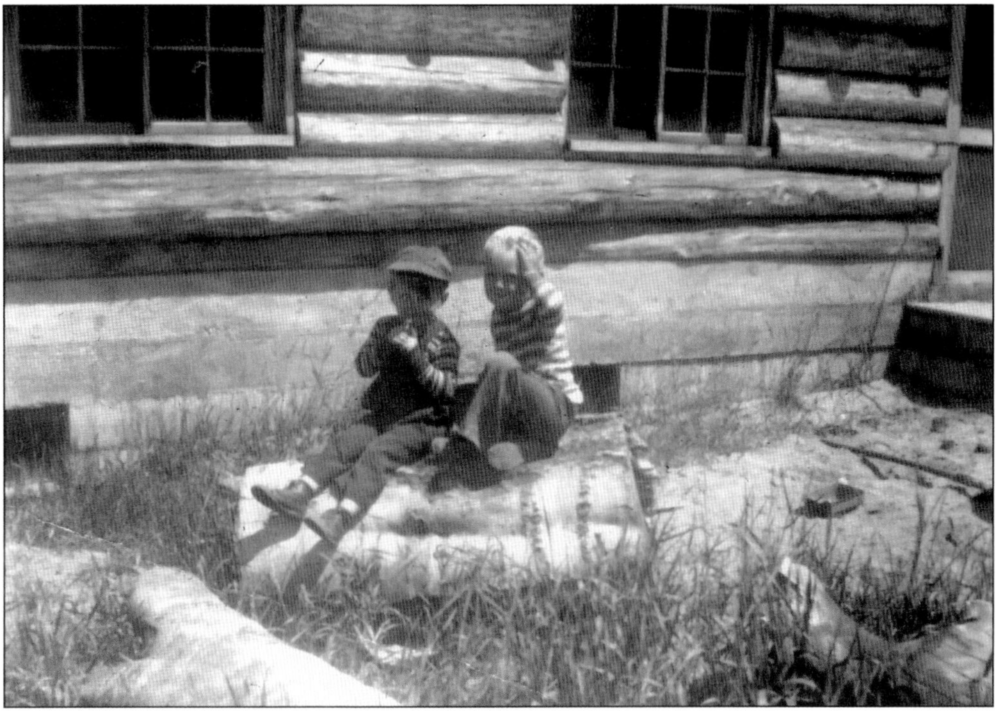

Scott Thorrington (left) and Greg Lundquist play in the sand behind the VFW hall in the early 1950s. The back of the hall was a perfect place for small boys to dig for treasure, climb on the leftover logs, and play in a somewhat protected area. This area was left untouched for many years. Note the cap and high-top shoes worn by Thorrington. (Argie Thorrington.)

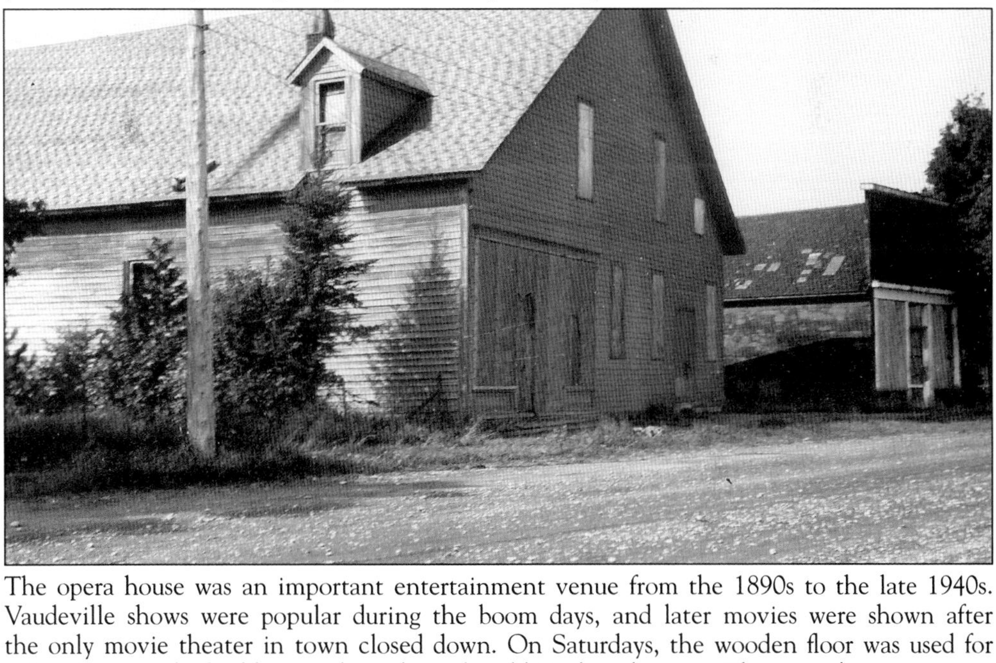

The opera house was an important entertainment venue from the 1890s to the late 1940s. Vaudeville shows were popular during the boom days, and later movies were shown after the only movie theater in town closed down. On Saturdays, the wooden floor was used for roller-skating. The building to the right is the old Norkowski store. The opera house was torn down about 1950. (GMHS.)

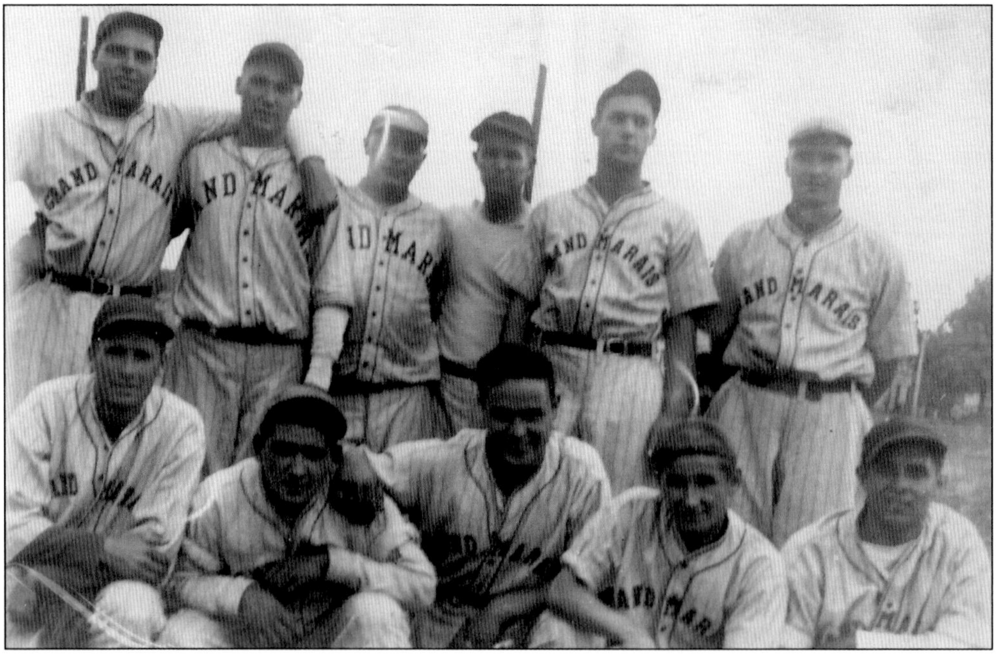

Baseball has always been a popular sport with great family appeal, and Grand Marais had its share of teams for both adults and kids. This Grand Marais men's team is ready to take the field against a local rival team in the 1930s. Today the town ball diamond is located behind the recreation center on Brazel Street. (Argie Thorrington.)

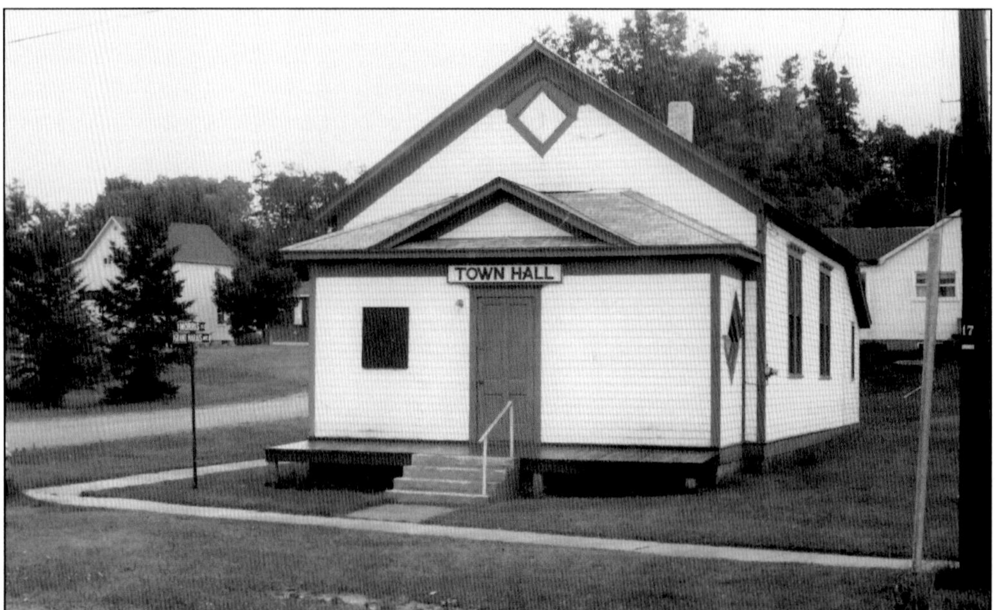

The town hall in the 1940s was a multipurpose building used mainly for meetings, although there was a small jail in the rear of the building. Today it is the township medical building, providing space in which visiting doctors and nurses can practice. The old VFW hall next door to this was re-sided and converted into the current township offices in the 1970s. (Peoples State Bank.)

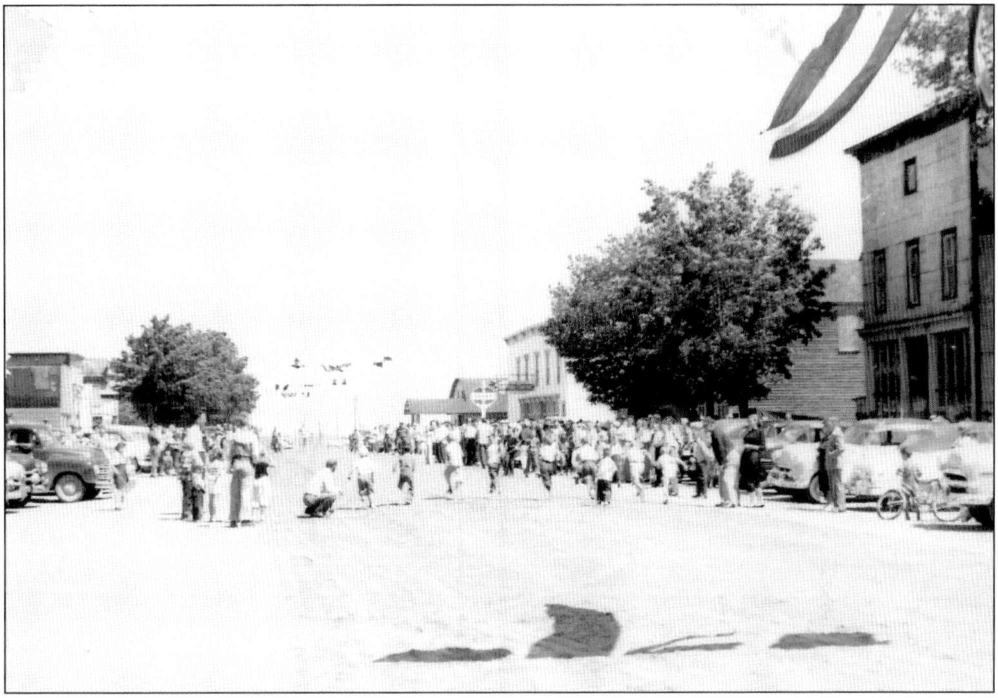

Fourth of July in Grand Marais has always been a day of celebration and fun. This photograph from the 1950s shows children running races down Lake Avenue after the annual parade. Games and contests are still held every year after the parade is over. The building at right dates to the 1890s; today it is a restaurant. (Argie Thorrington.)

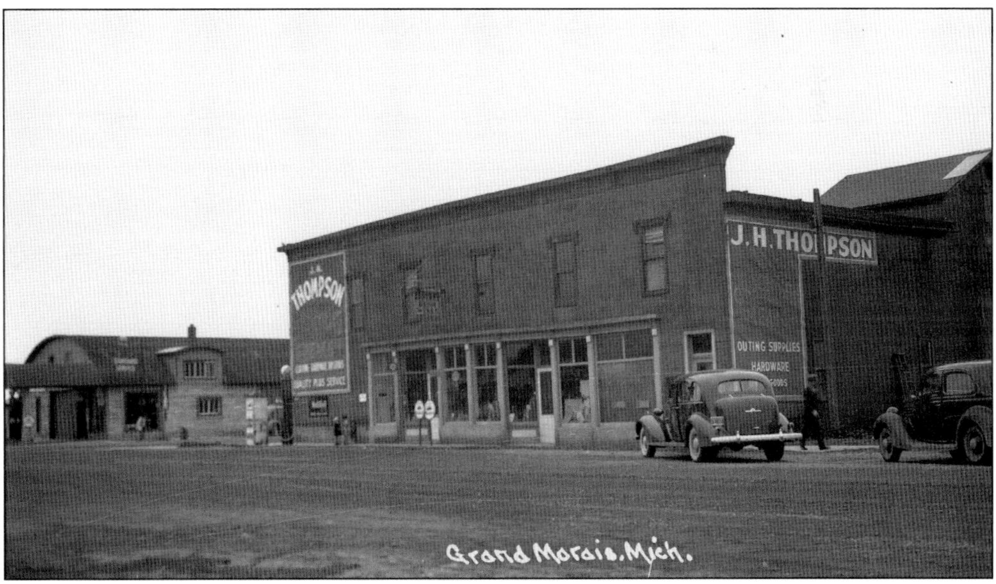

The Morse and Schneider store was a fixture in Grand Marais dating to the 1890s. It became the Schneider store in 1903, burned down in 1904, and was rebuilt shortly after. The business was sold to J. H. Thompson in the 1930s, and he continued to operate it as the department store shown here. For over 60 years, this was the largest building in Grand Marais. (Great Lakes Pilot.)

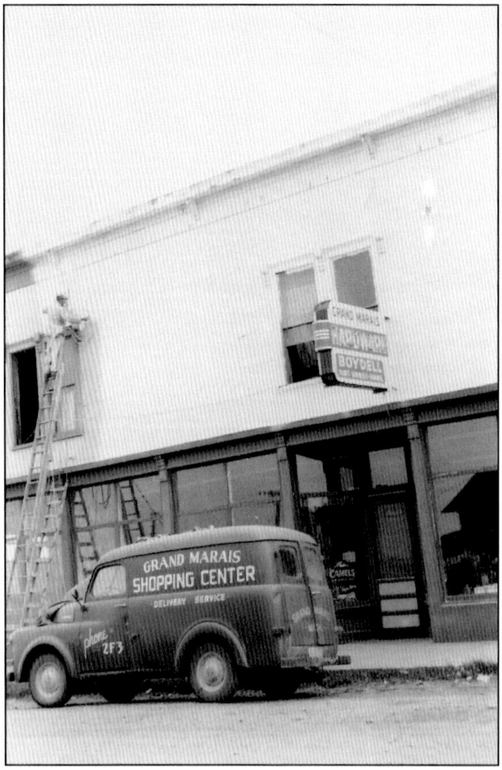

The J. H. Thompson department store was sold to Edmund Warren and Robert Jacobites in the late 1940s. They operated the store for a few years before closing it for good in 1953. The advertisement in the window is for Camel cigarettes and features singer Vaughan Monroe, which dates the photograph to about 1950. In 1962, the store burned to the ground, taking with it the garage to the north. (Della Meldrum.)

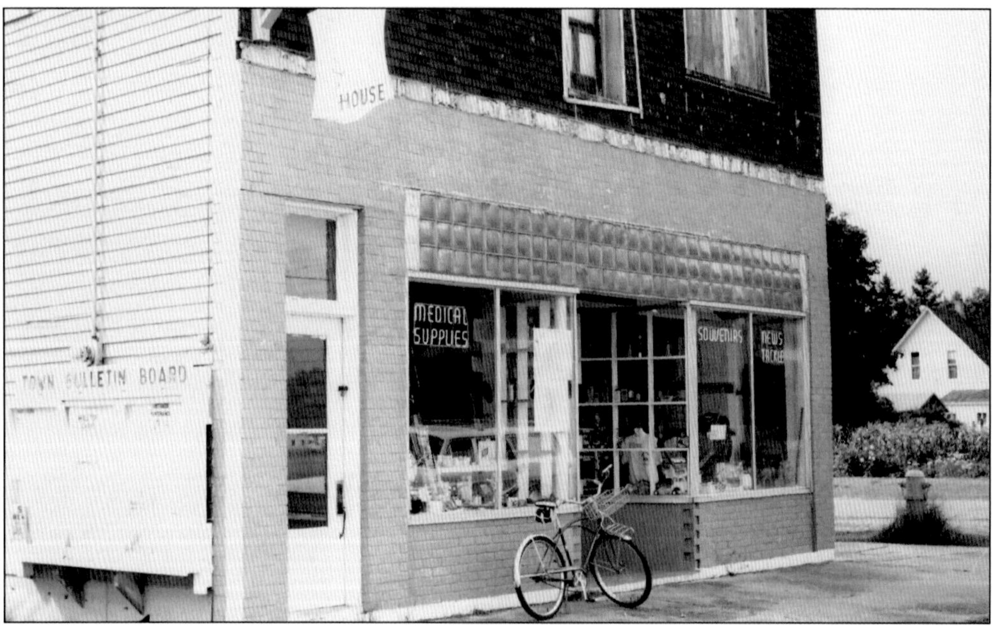

By the 1960s, the former Ostrander's Drug Store has become a general store. At right is the Mennonite Youth Mission Garden, run by Mary Handrich for the Mennonite Church. In its first year, the church raised $90 to purchase Bibles to send to Japan by selling potatoes from the garden. The building underwent a major renovation in 2007 and is now a private residence. (Peoples State Bank.)

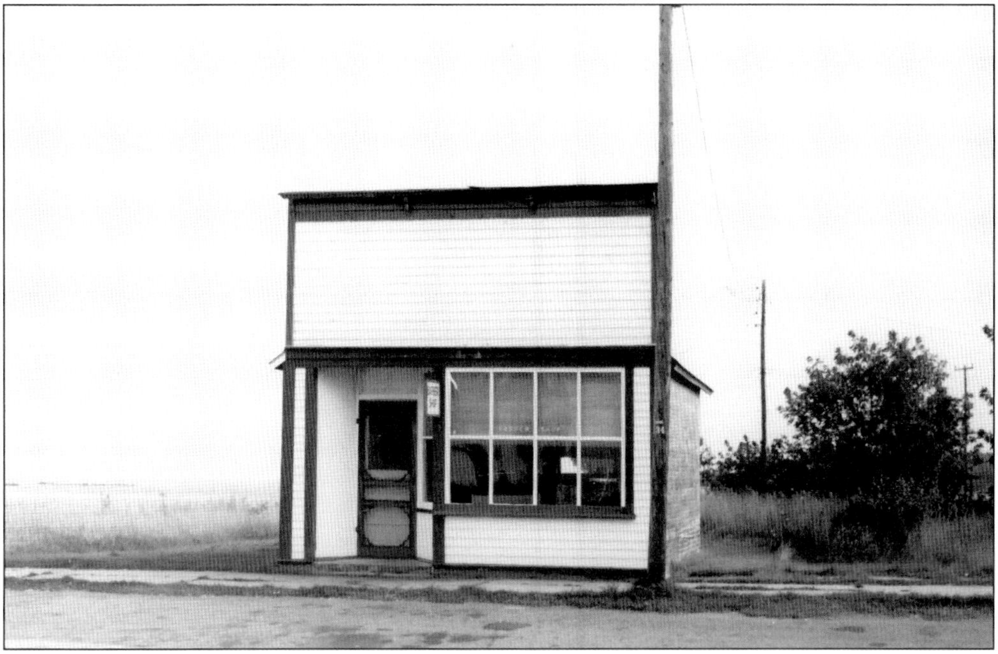

This building originally housed Teeter's Variety Store and was built in 1895. Dave Thomas, who owned a saloon next door, later used it to display a Ford Model A car. Ed Bennett ran a barbershop in this building for many years. It escaped the big fire of 1962 because the wind blew away from the building. Today this building houses an artists' cooperative. (Peoples State Bank.)

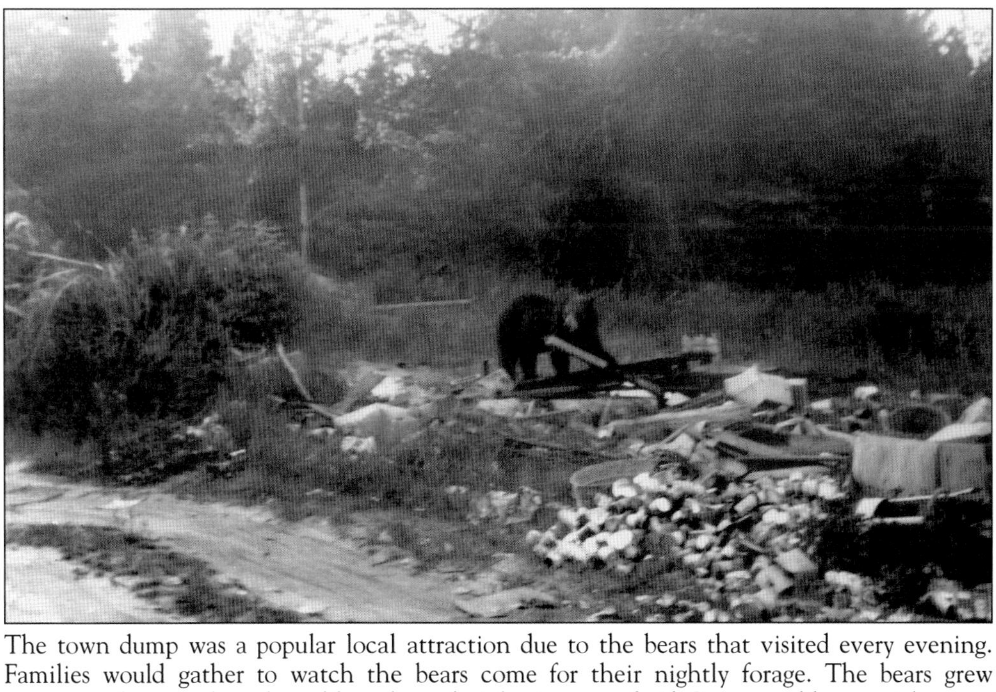

The town dump was a popular local attraction due to the bears that visited every evening. Families would gather to watch the bears come for their nightly forage. The bears grew accustomed to people and would go about their business unafraid. Some would come right up to the car windows. The dump closed in 1990, and the bears soon wandered off to look elsewhere for their evening meals. (Argie Thorrington.)

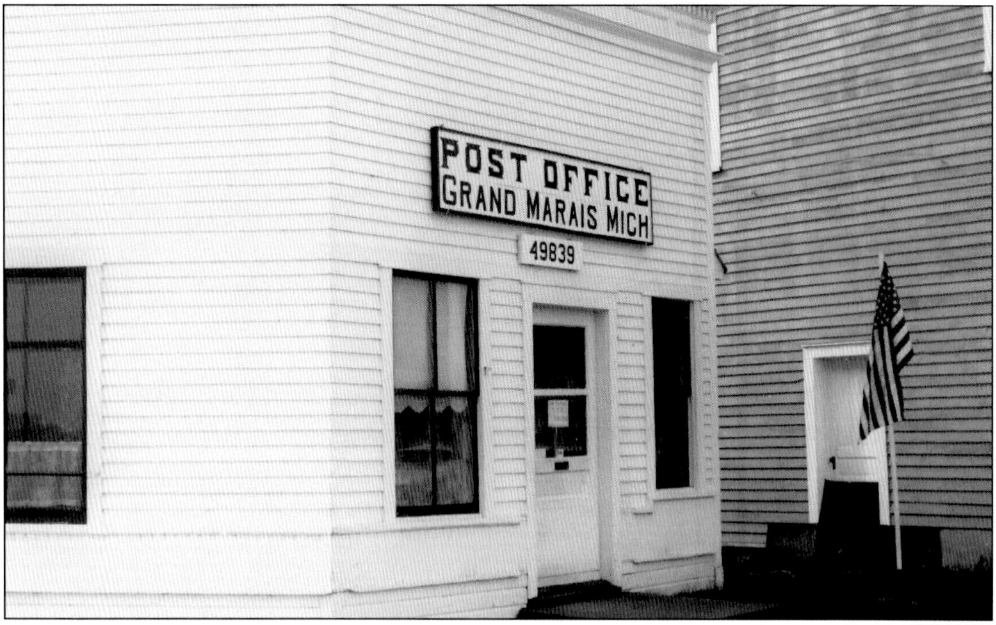

The post office moved into this unique, five-sided building in 1907 and stayed until 1978, when the postal service was relocated into a former self-service laundry down the street. This building became a gift shop and beauty salon. In 2007, the owners donated the historic structure to the Grand Marais Historical Society, which moved the building onto Lake Avenue to become a museum of Grand Marais history. (Peoples State Bank.)

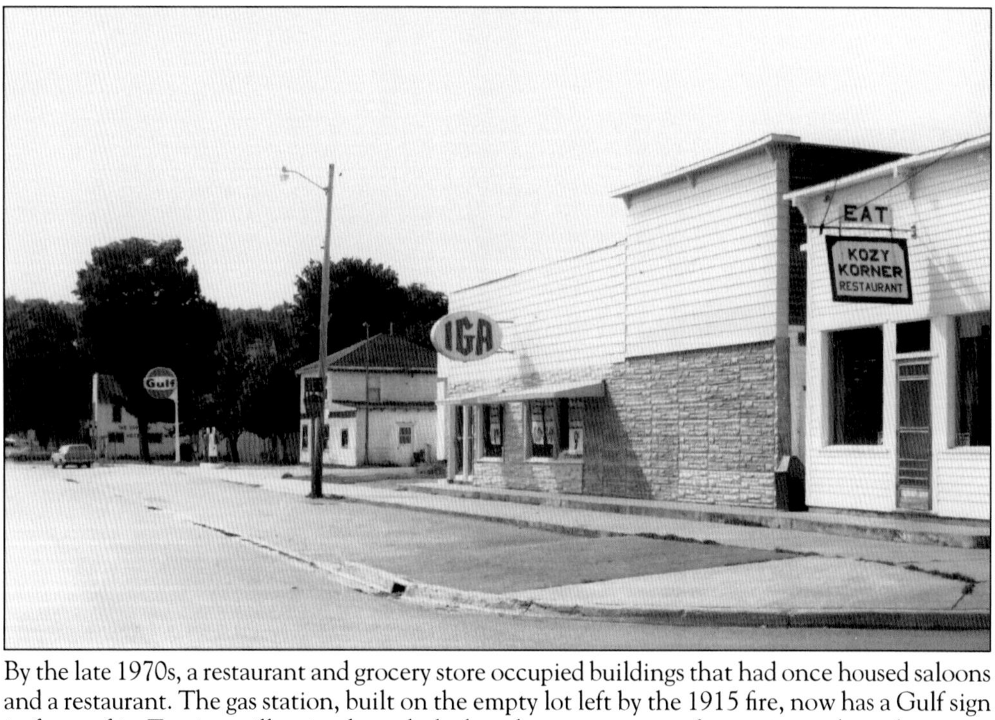

By the late 1970s, a restaurant and grocery store occupied buildings that had once housed saloons and a restaurant. The gas station, built on the empty lot left by the 1915 fire, now has a Gulf sign in front of it. Tourists still arrived regularly, but the streets were often quiet and nearly empty. This photograph looks south along the west side of Lake Avenue. (Peoples State Bank.)

Eight

Tourism Grows

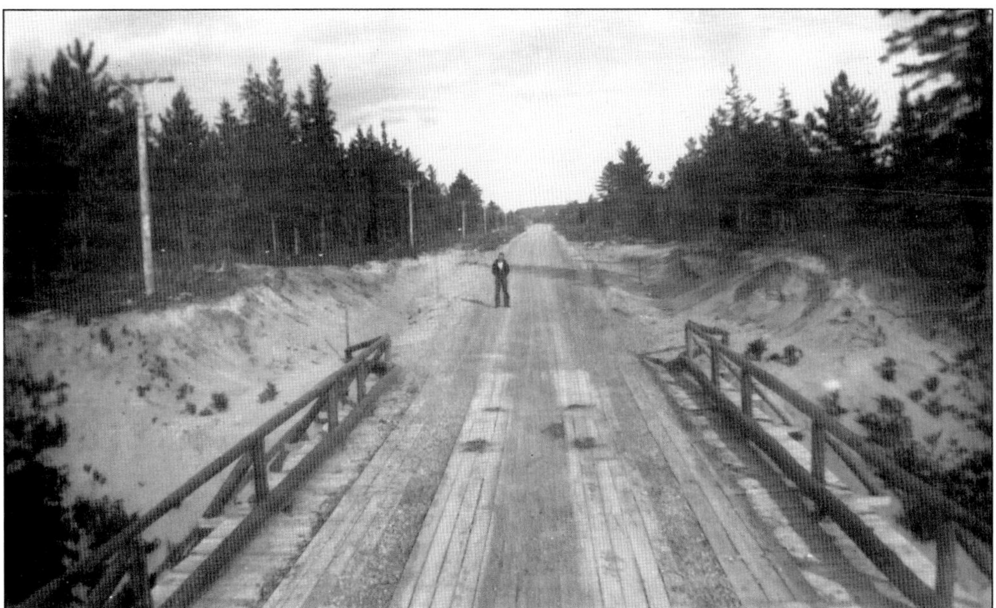

The year 1925 brought change to Grand Marais when the state road was completed all the way to Seney. Labeled State Highway 77, it enabled motor traffic to reach the town in all four seasons. Tourists would soon follow, and as they discovered the natural beauty of the area, the town was poised for an economic revival. (GMHS.)

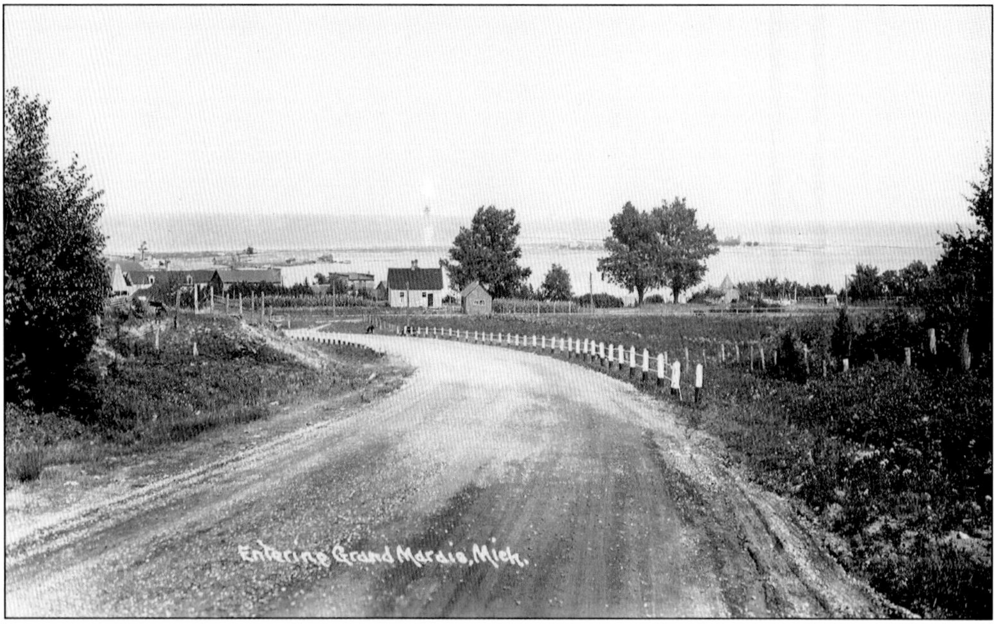

Because Grand Marais is nestled at the base of a high ridge, the first glimpse visitors received was of the harbor and range light as they came down the curving hill into town. This early view, taken not long after the state road was completed, has changed little over the years. The vast expanse of Lake Superior still astonishes first-time visitors. (GMHS.)

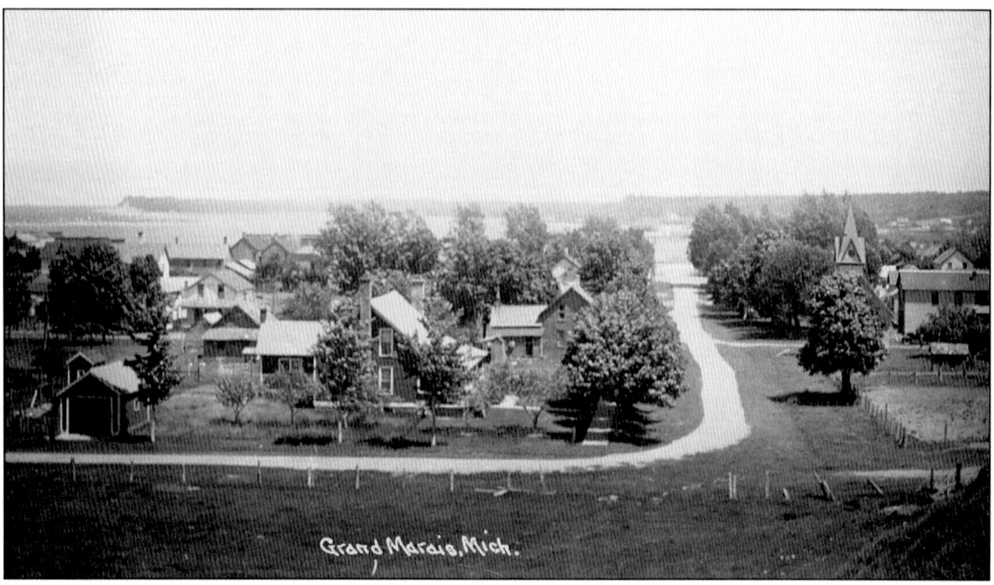

By 1927, Grand Marais was a quiet northern village with a population of only a few hundred, and little in the way of an economy except for commercial fishing. This view looks east down Randolph Street. Note the steeple of the Swedish Lutheran church at right and the fenced garden plot. Changes were coming as an influx of tourists brought a need for more services. (GMHS.)

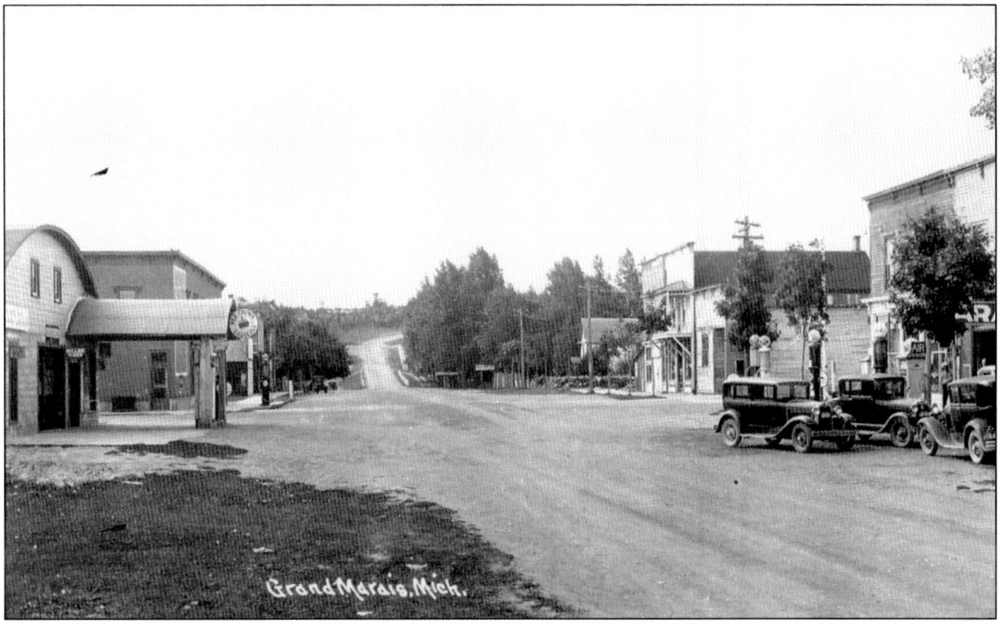

It did not take long for motorists to make their way into Grand Marais. This view looks south on Lake Avenue in the late 1920s. The Wood and Touzel Garage is at left. Shortly after the road was completed, Wood and Touzel started a delivery service to Seney, sometimes making several trips per day in its van. Note the many gas pumps in town. (GMHS.)

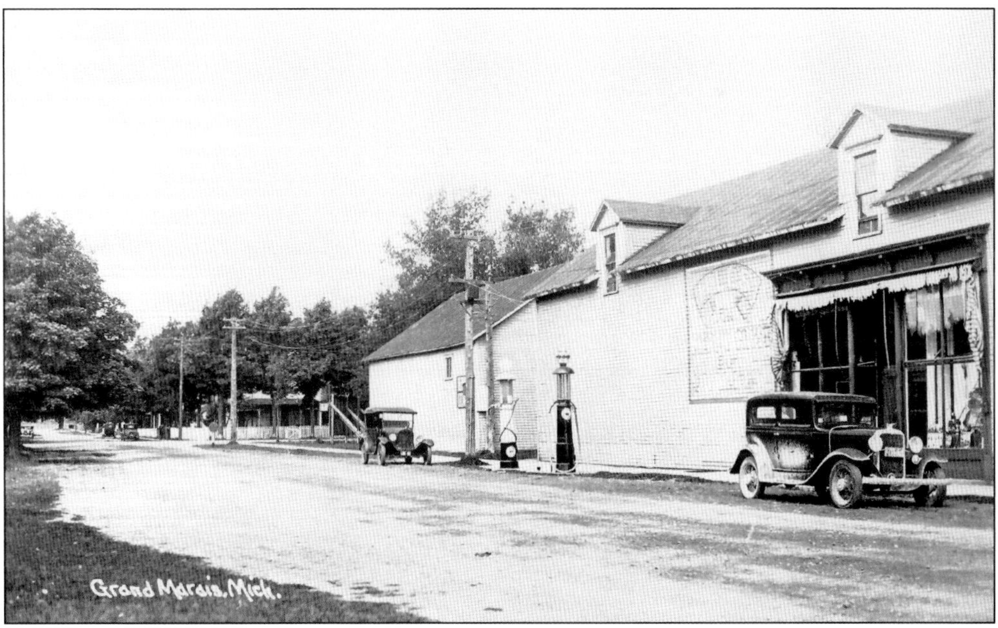

One of the larger stores in town was Hill's Store, shown here in the late 1920s. With the increase in motor traffic, every proprietor in town tried to install a gas pump or two. Standard Oil had Red Crown, White Crown, and Blue Crown gas; Shell and Mobil also had pumps in town. Hill's Store also provided tourists with groceries, clothing, and other items they might need. (GMHS.)

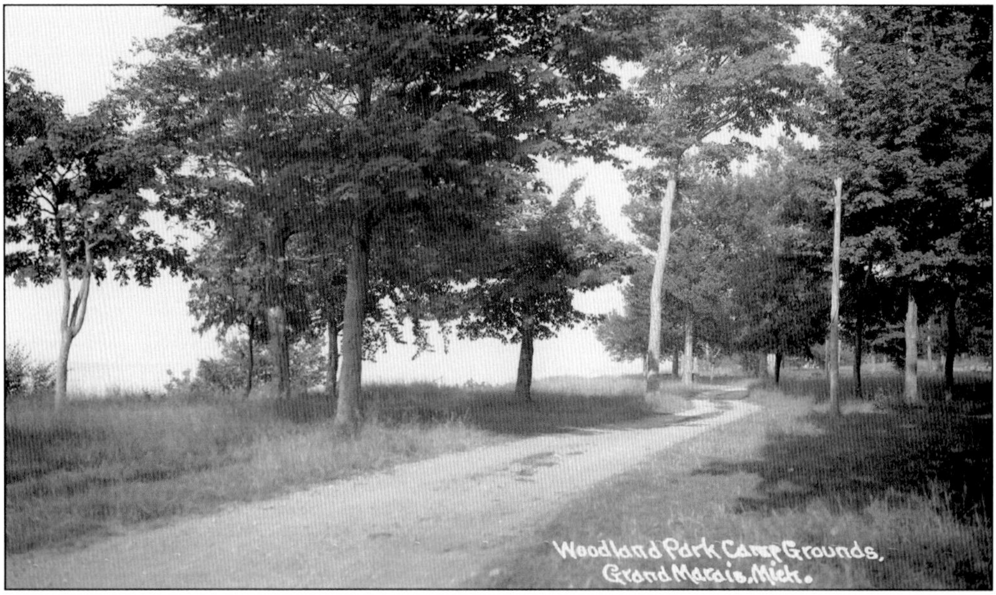

Woodland Park, the township campground, was established in 1902 on land donated to the township by several prominent lumbermen. It stretches for a half mile along Lake Superior and was an instant draw for campers. Swimming, walking, and agate hunting on the beach have always been the biggest draw to this historic location. Tourists soon discovered its pristine beauty and convenient proximity to downtown. (Great Lakes Pilot.)

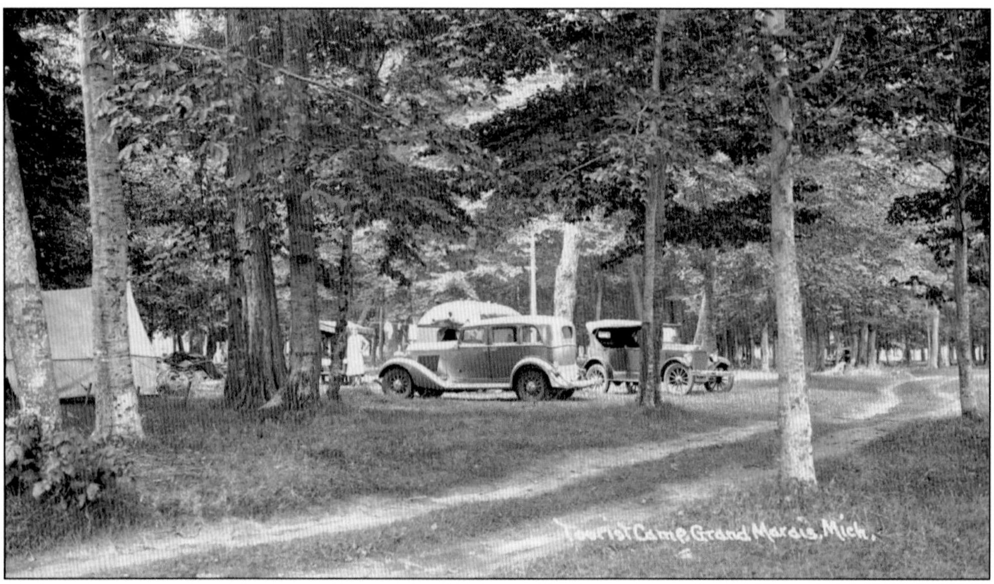

By the early 1930s, campers arrived in Grand Marais for extended stays at the campground. Most brought tents; a few had early types of travel trailers. The campground provided few amenities beyond water and outhouses, but the campers did not seem to mind. Groceries and supplies were available in town, and the local businesses found they had a new customer base. (Great Lakes Pilot.)

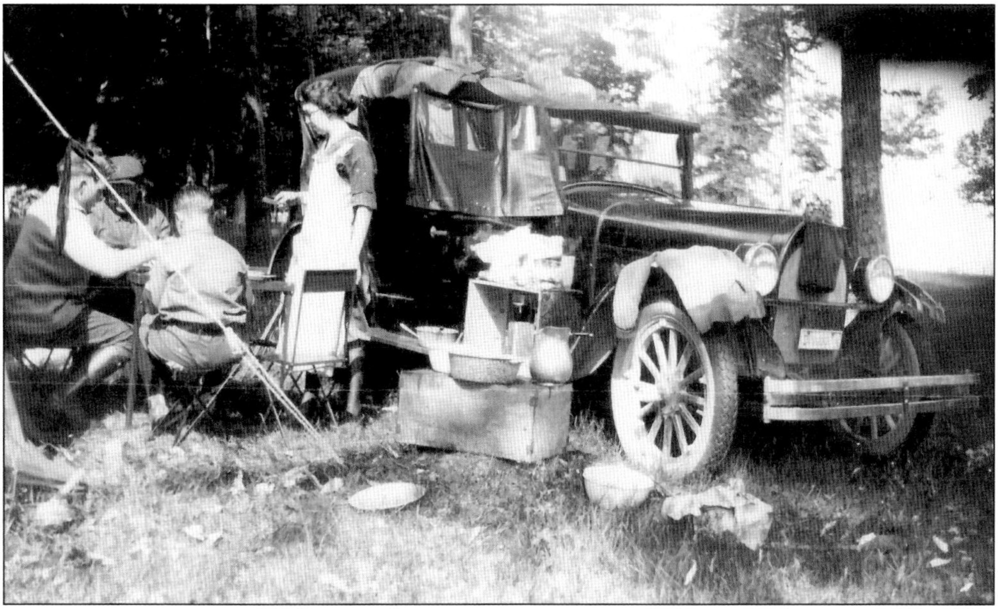

Camping in the 1930s was a bit of a challenge, as everything had to be packed in boxes or crates and brought along. Even folding tables and chairs were needed for the trip. Cooking was done over an open fire, and the family car might even double as a clothesline. If the fishing was good, fresh trout or whitefish would appear on the dinner menu. (GMHS.)

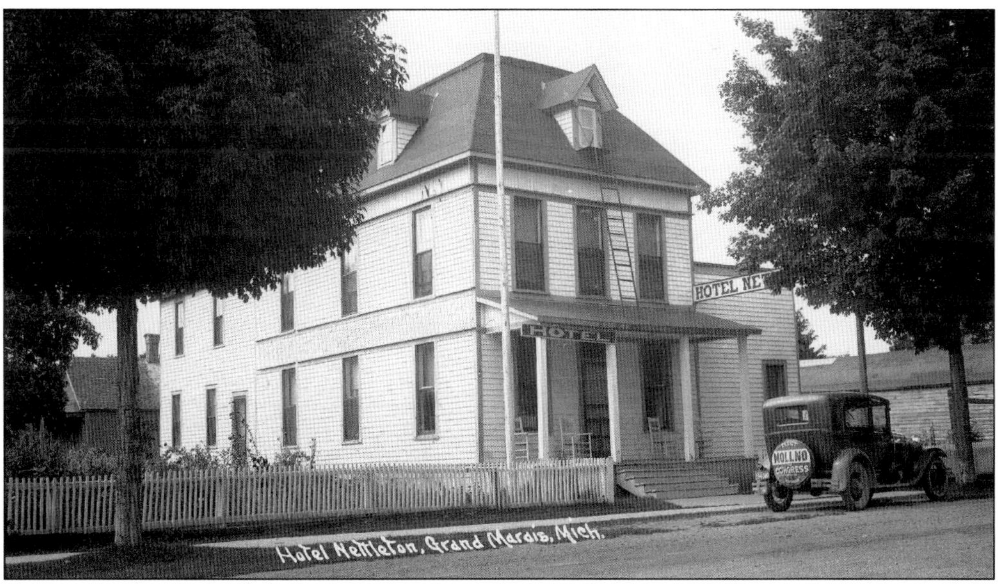

The 1930s brought an increase in visitors to the local hotels. One of the largest establishments in town was the Hotel Nettleton on Carlson Street, known for its good food. The addition at the right is a bathhouse. The car sports a campaign advertisement for George K. Mollno, who ran for U.S. Congress in 1932. The hotel is a private residence today. (GMHS.)

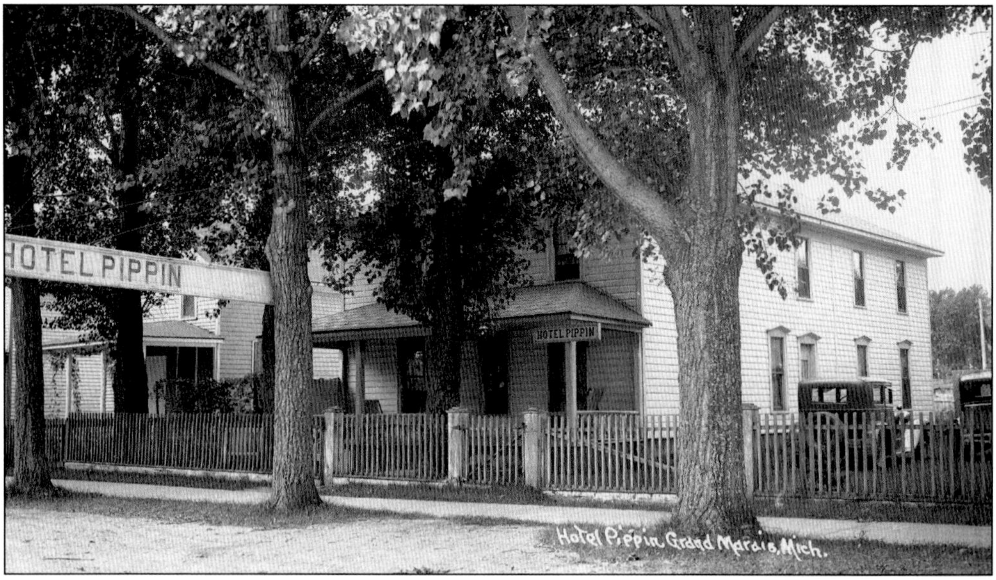

The Hotel Pippin, shown here in 1925, was located on Lake Avenue at the foot of the long hill coming into Grand Marais. In 1940, Alfred Lundquist purchased the hotel. He enlarged it and renamed it the Hotel Superior. A restaurant operated in the hotel until the mid-1940s. Now known as the Superior Hotel, it is still in business welcoming visitors to town. (Great Lakes Pilot.)

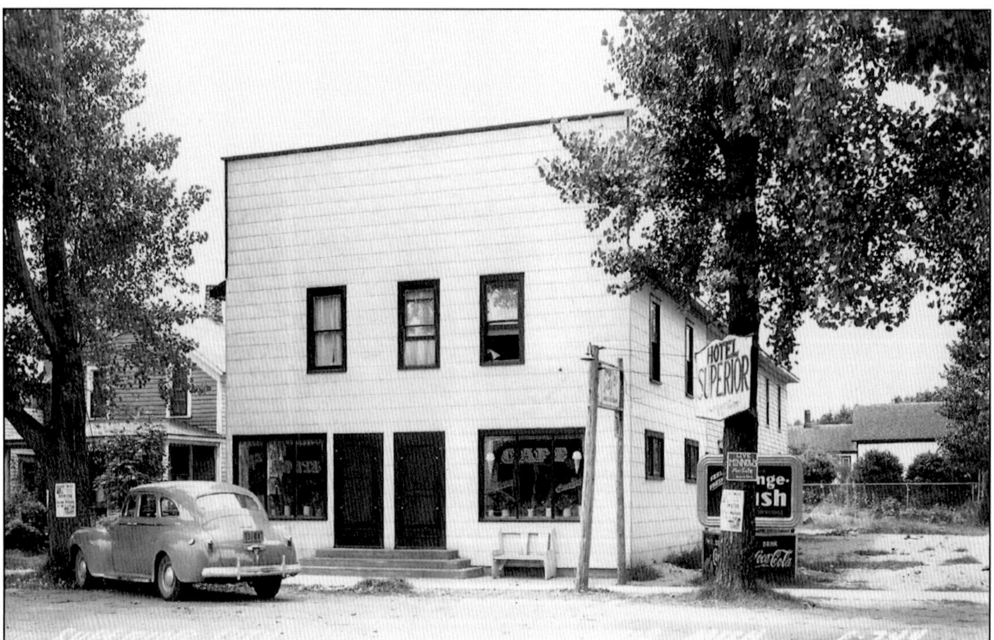

In the 1940s, the renovated Hotel Superior was a welcome stop for visitors. At one time, the hotel had the only public telephone in town. People would call, and Alfred "Grump" Lundquist would answer the telephone, go out and locate the person who was wanted, and bring that person back to the hotel for the call. There was even a telephone booth inside for the service. (DVTC.)

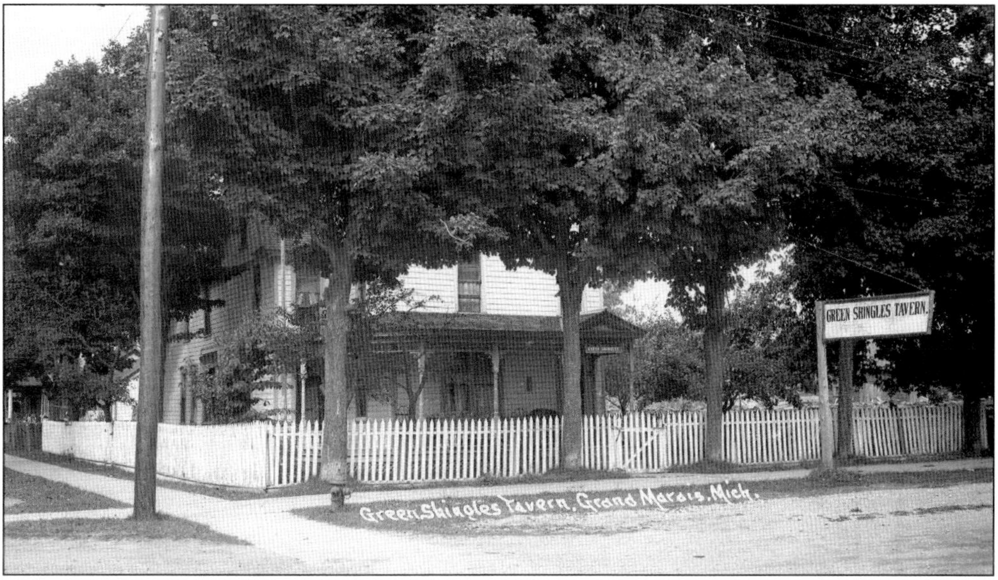

John F. Chisholm, an official with the Manistique Railway who was also the Grand Marais postmaster from 1898 to 1907, built this fine home as a private residence about 1895. In 1923, it was converted to a hotel and restaurant. Emma McDonald purchased the building in the 1940s and it then functioned as an adult rest home for many years. Today it is a private residence. (Great Lakes Pilot.)

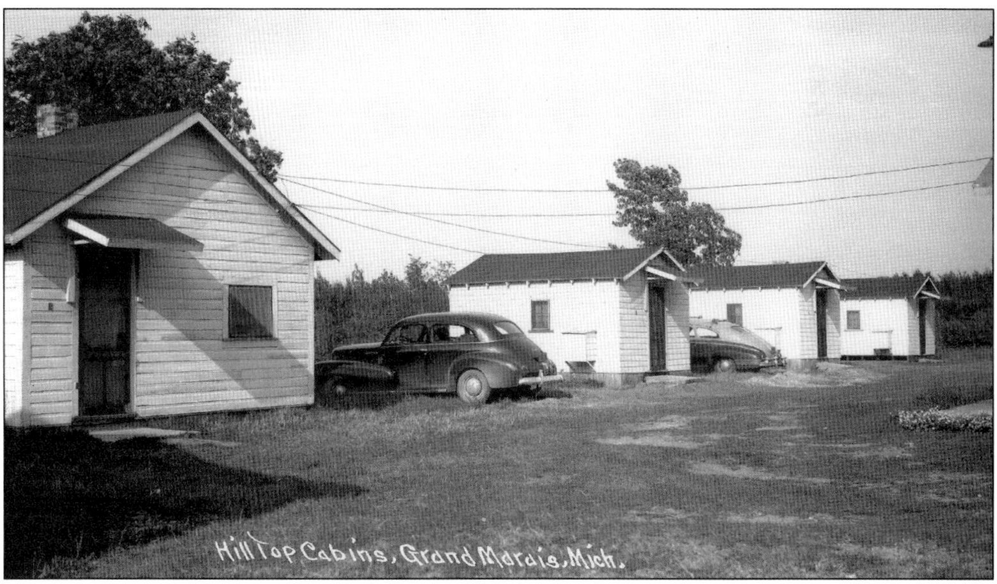

In addition to the local hotels, tourist cabins began to spring up around the bay in the 1930s and 1940s. A self-catering cabin offered a step up in comfort from camping. Fred Masse built Hill Top Cabins on Ellen Street, overlooking the bay, Coast Guard Point, and Lake Superior. The cabins are still operating today, welcoming visitors year-round. (Great Lakes Pilot.)

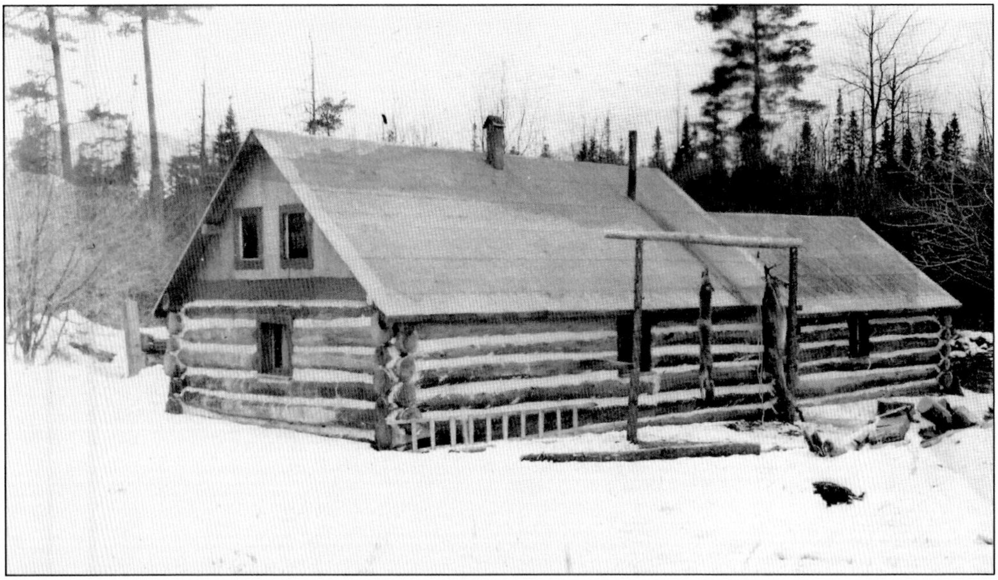

With the opening of the state trunk line road, a number of rustic, private hunting camps were established in the woods near Grand Marais. One of the earliest was Camp Newton, shown here in the 1920s. Hunters from Michigan's Lower Peninsula would make yearly trips up north to hunt deer. (Argie Thorrington.)

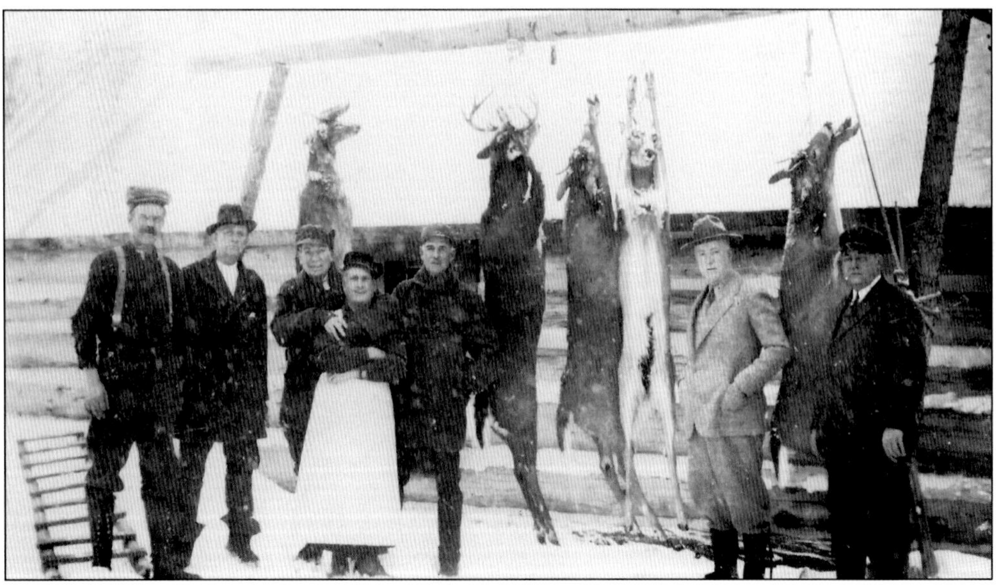

Men came from as far away as Detroit to hunt at Camp Newton. The camp would hire local townspeople to set up the camp prior to their arrival and also to cook during their stay. Peter Tellier was the camp cook at Camp Newton for many years. He is shown here during the 1920s with a group of successful hunters. (Argie Thorrington.)

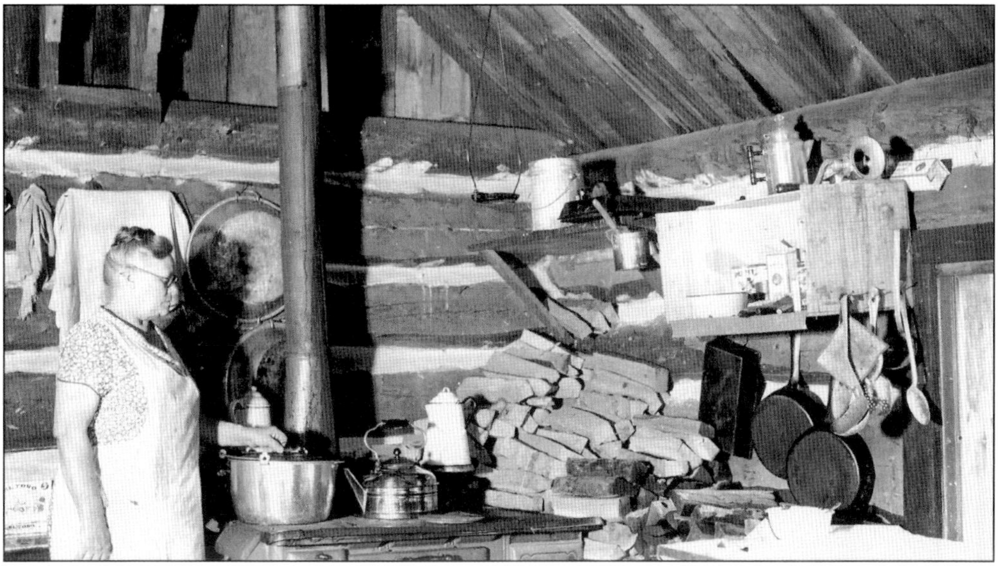

This photograph shows the inside of Camp Newton during the 1920s. Mary Tellier is shown cooking for the camp after her husband, Peter, became ill. Mary never stayed overnight at the camp, as it was not proper, but would spend the day cooking for the hunters. The big camp stove needed plenty of wood to keep it going, and the kettle was always on. (Argie Thorrington.)

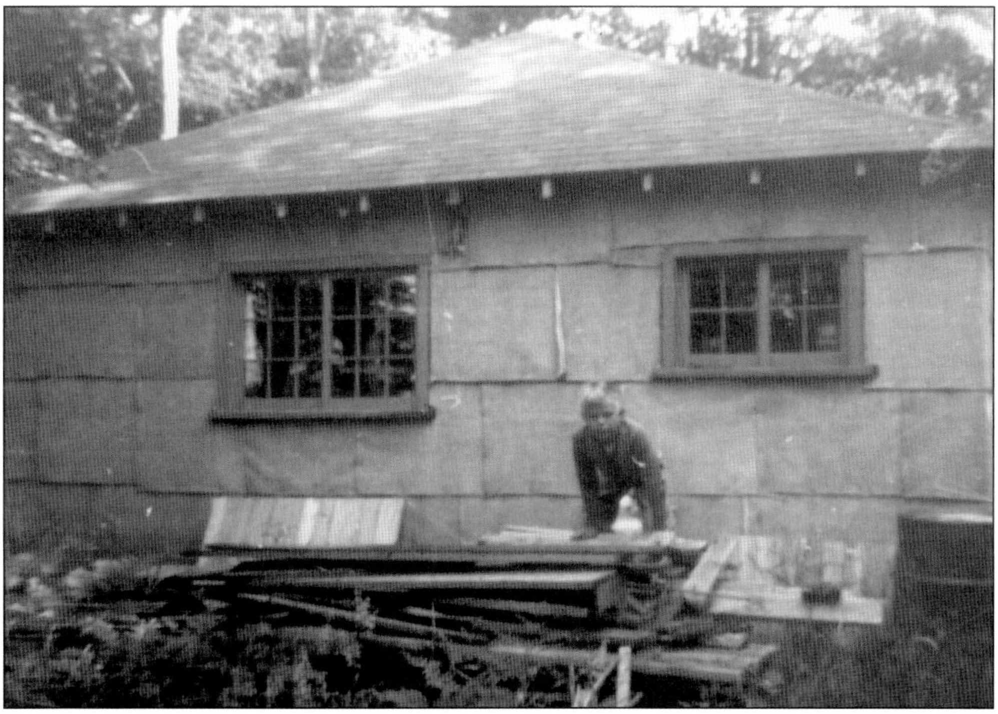

Small hunting and fishing clubs sprang up near Grand Marais throughout the 1930s and 1940s. The Sucker River Club is still a functioning club; its current owners are descended from the founders. Young Dan Miller, shown here at age nine in 1946, came with his family for vacations and helped around the camp. Kids especially enjoyed the time in the outdoors. (Sucker River Club.)

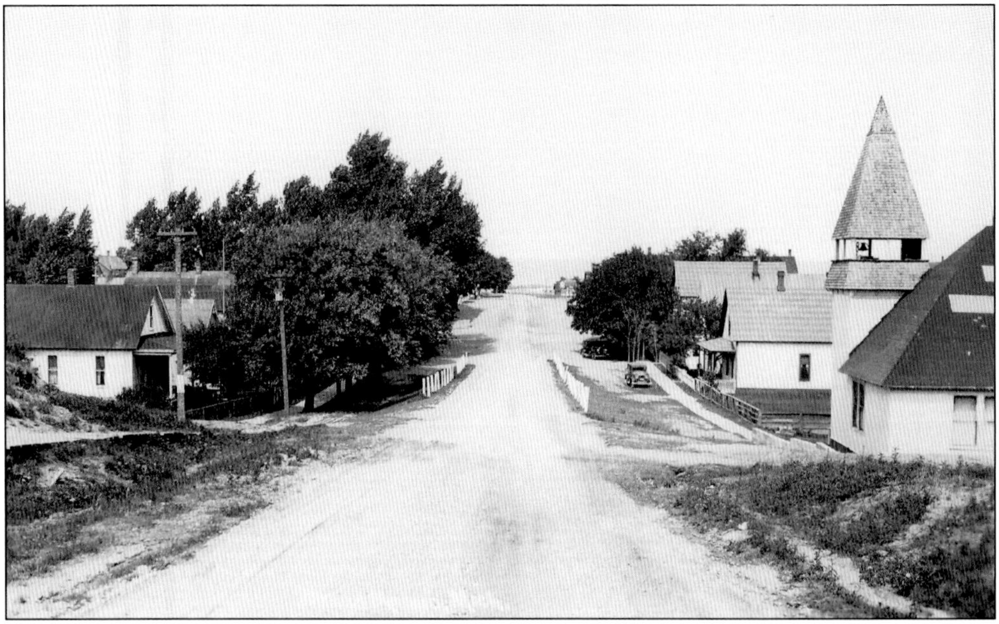

Although finished in 1925, the state road was not paved for many years. In the 1930s, Grand Marais was a peaceful destination that offered a welcome respite from the noise of city life. Children rode their bicycles around town, and summer visitors found the slower pace relaxing and refreshing. The Methodist church steeple, at right, was one of the first landmarks spotted by visitors upon their arrival. (GMHS.)

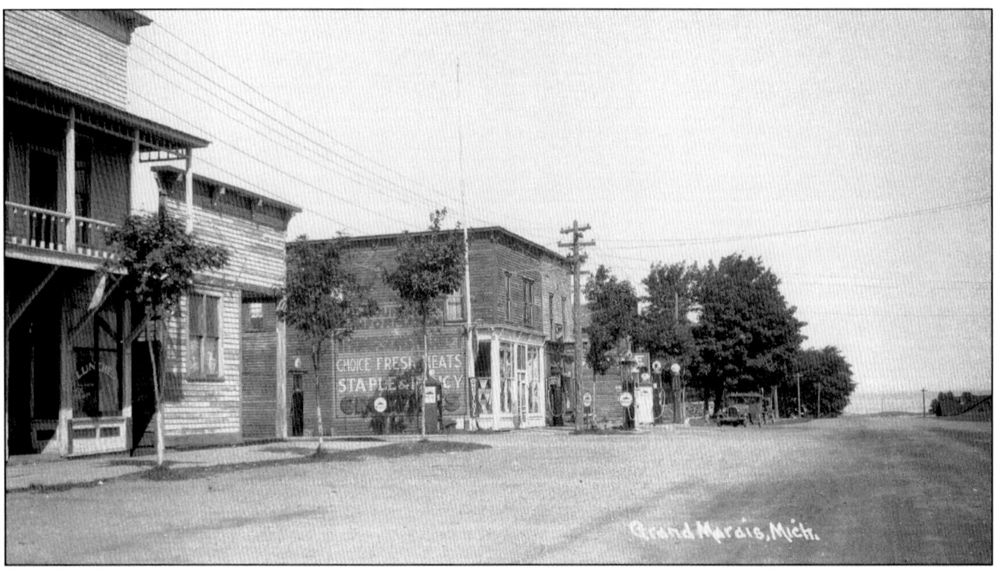

Lake Avenue in the 1930s still retains some of the original buildings from the 1890s. From left to right, the former Warren Kipp Saloon is a café, and Hugh Logan's Superior Sample Room has lost its second story and will soon become the Palace Theater. The original Duggan and Gamble Billiard Hall burned down in 1885, and the replacement structure is a grocery in this photograph. (Great Lakes Pilot.)

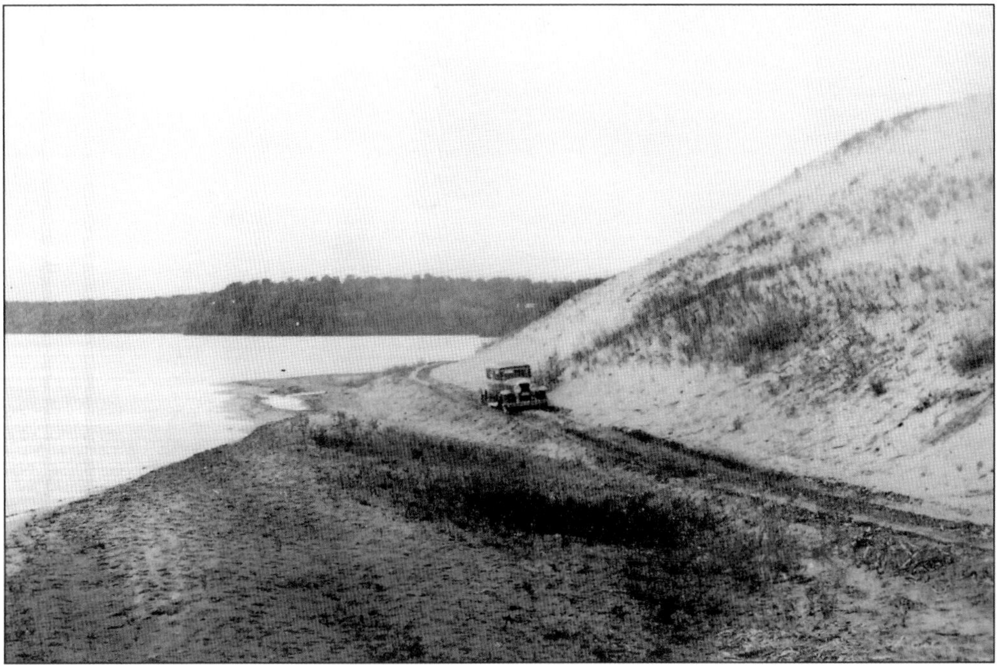

Just west of Grand Marais are the Grand Sable Dunes, stretching from Sable Lake north to Lake Superior. By the 1930s, a crude road ran along the north shore of the lake, but where the dunes came down to the lake, it was barely navigable in the spring. The sand had to be plowed back to make the road, as sand slides and wind constantly shifted the dunes. (Doris Krempa.)

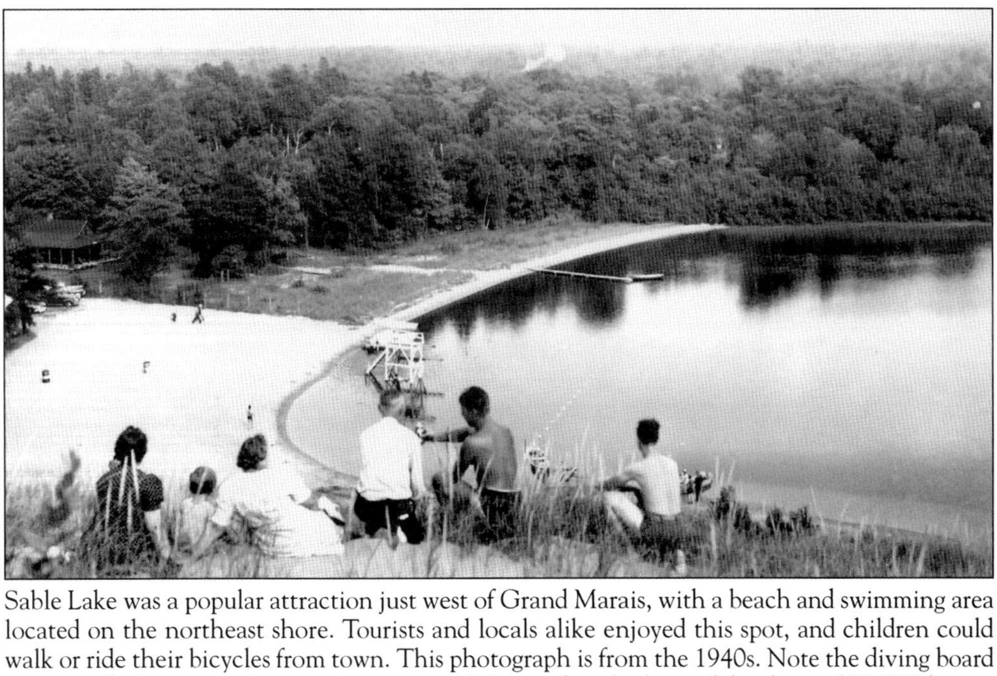

Sable Lake was a popular attraction just west of Grand Marais, with a beach and swimming area located on the northeast shore. Tourists and locals alike enjoyed this spot, and children could walk or ride their bicycles from town. This photograph is from the 1940s. Note the diving board and boat dock, the rowboat in the water, and the road at the base of the dunes. (GMHS.)

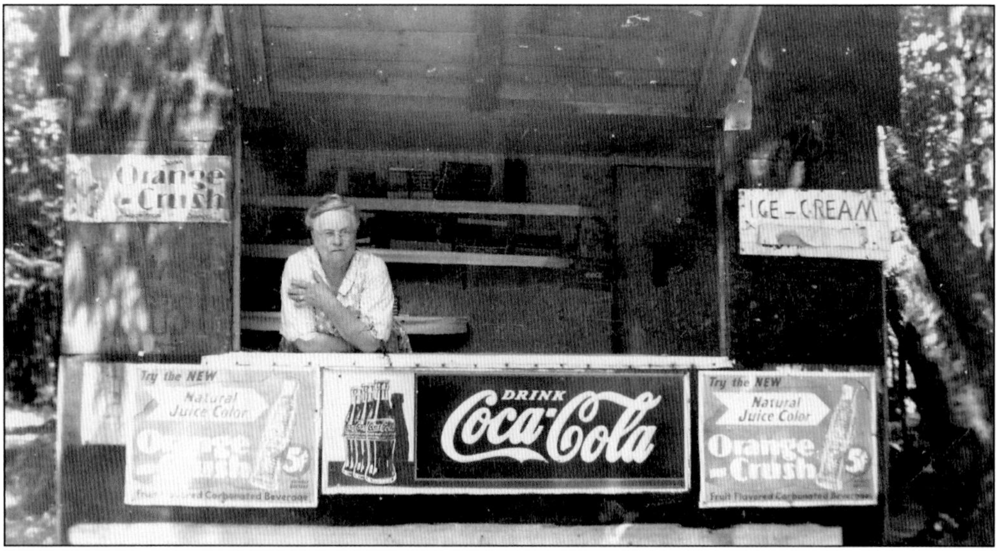

Every beach needs a refreshment stand, and Mary Tellier, shown here on a summer day, ran the concession stand at Sable Lake. Homemade ice cream and soda pop were available, along with candy bars and other snacks. Orange Crush and Coca-Cola cost a nickel, as did candy bars. Mary's husband, Peter Tellier, offered rowboats for rent to people who wanted to fish on Sable Lake. (Argie Thorrington.)

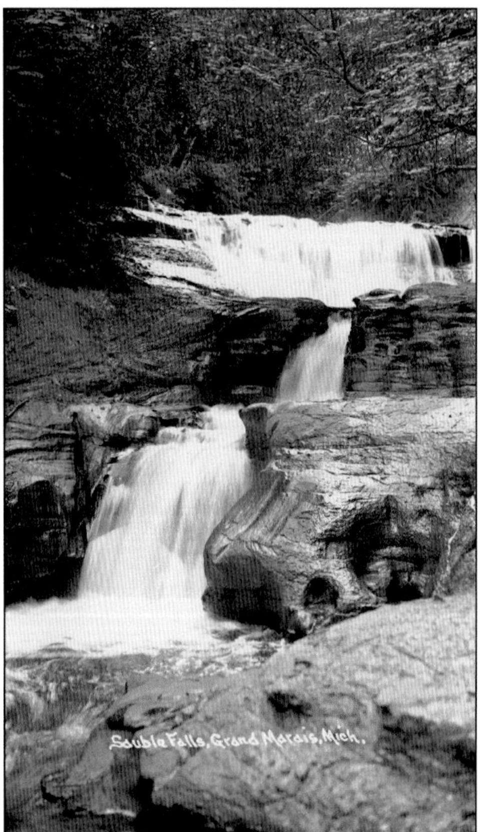

Sable Falls is located on the stream that drains Sable Lake into Lake Superior. The walk from the top of the falls down to the big lake was along a steep dirt path. With the creation of Pictured Rocks National Lakeshore in 1966, sturdy wooden steps and rails were built for safer access. Kids liked to sit on the rocks and let the water splash them. (Great Lakes Pilot.)

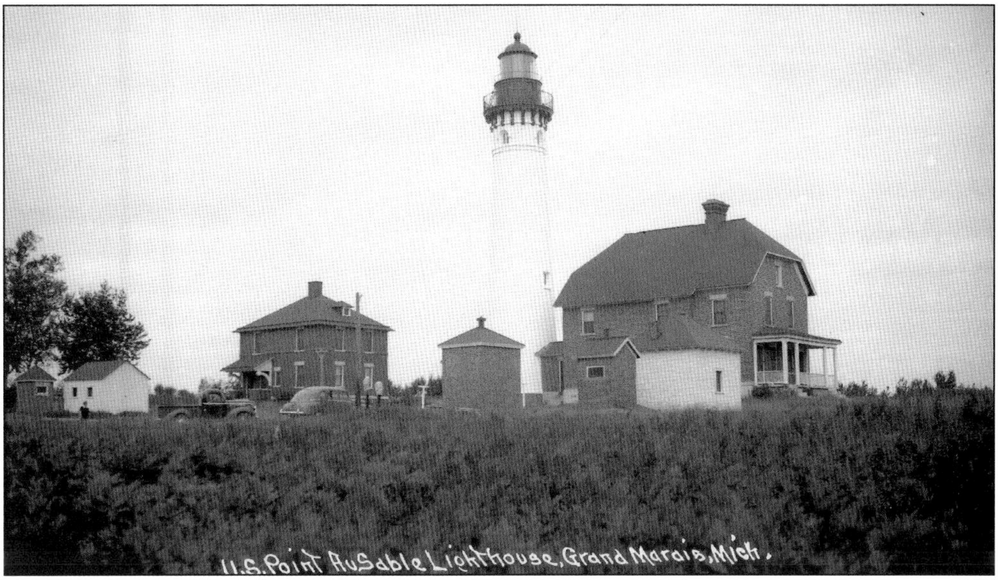

Au Sable Light, built in 1873, lies eight miles to the west of Grand Marais. Its beacon warns passing ships of a dangerous sandstone reef that extends out nearly a mile from shore. A road was built from Hurricane River in 1939, allowing tourists to access the light by car. The lighthouse is now part of Pictured Rocks National Lakeshore and is open to the public. (Great Lakes Pilot.)

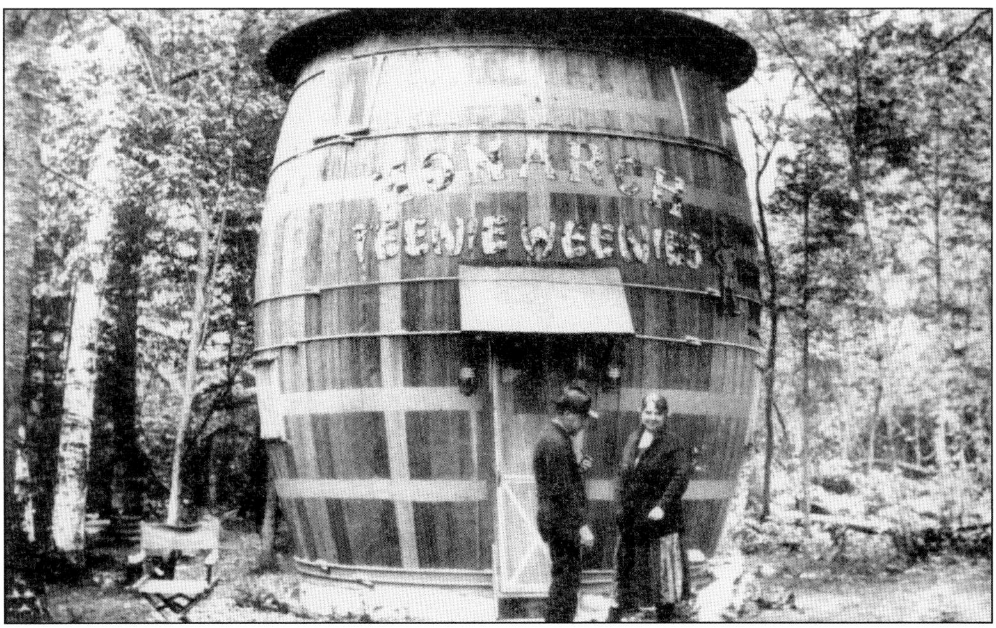

The Pickle Barrel House was the summer home of cartoonist William Donahey, creator of the famous *Teenie Weenies* cartoon characters, and his wife, Mary. The two-story barrel house stood on the shore of Sable Lake from 1926 to 1937. It was a gift to the Donaheys from Reid, Murdoch and Company of Chicago, whose Monarch Foods division sold a line of *Teenie Weenies* products aimed at children. (GMHS.)

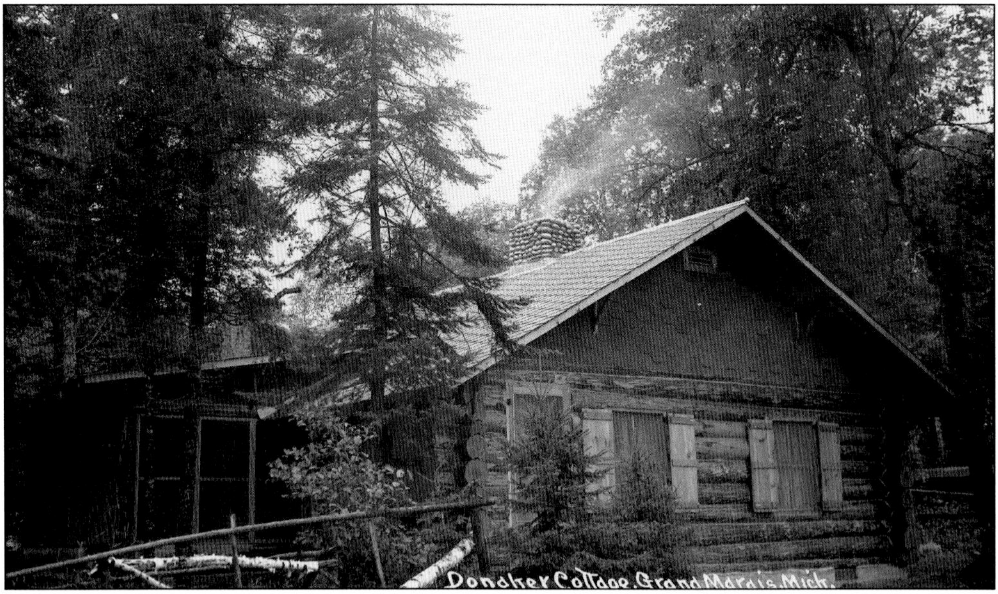

After 10 years of constant visits by curiosity seekers, William and Mary Donahey gave the Pickle Barrel House to a Grand Marais businessman, who moved it into town. The Donaheys built this rustic log cabin on the same spot, on the northwest side of Sable Lake. The Donaheys continued to spend their summers here while William worked on his *Teenie Weenies* illustrations. (GMHS.)

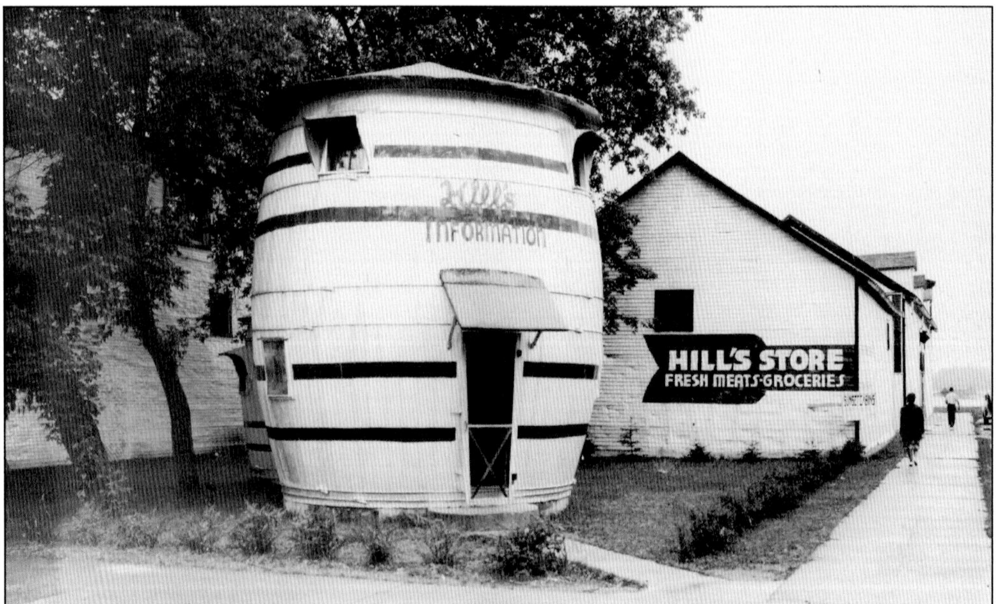

The Pickle Barrel House was moved into town in 1937, after William and Mary Donahey gave it to their friend, Irving Hill. Hill, who owned a general store, placed the barrel at the corner of Lake Avenue and Randolph Street. He opened an information booth in the barrel. Later it was an ice-cream stand and a gift shop. Today the barrel house is a museum open to the public. (GMHS.)

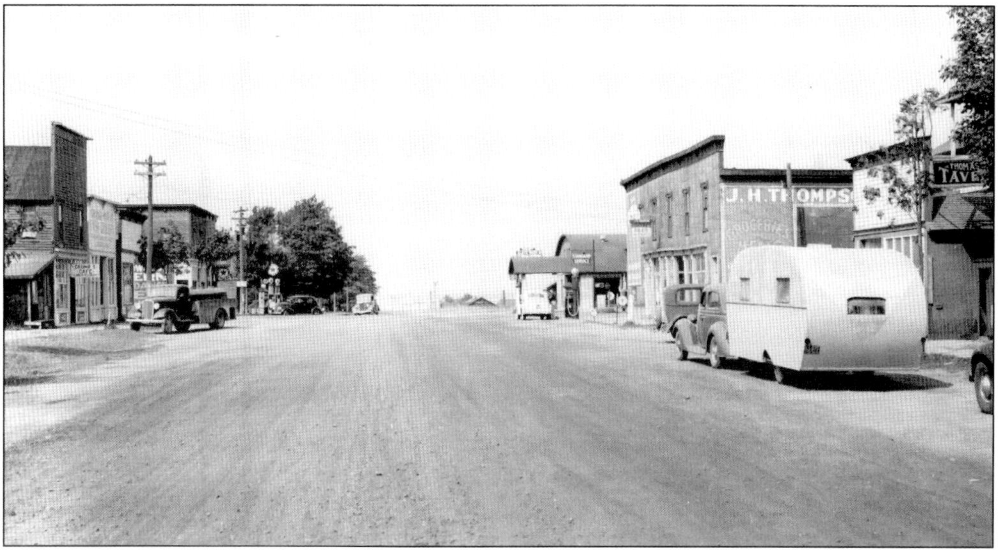

By the late 1930s, travel trailers were becoming a more popular alternative to tent camping. Their owners were sometimes referred to as "tin can tourists" in the 1920s, but the tow-behind units soon became known as "house trailers" because of their many amenities. This scene shows Lake Avenue around 1938. The abundance of sights around Grand Marais made it a perfect spot for camping. (GMHS.)

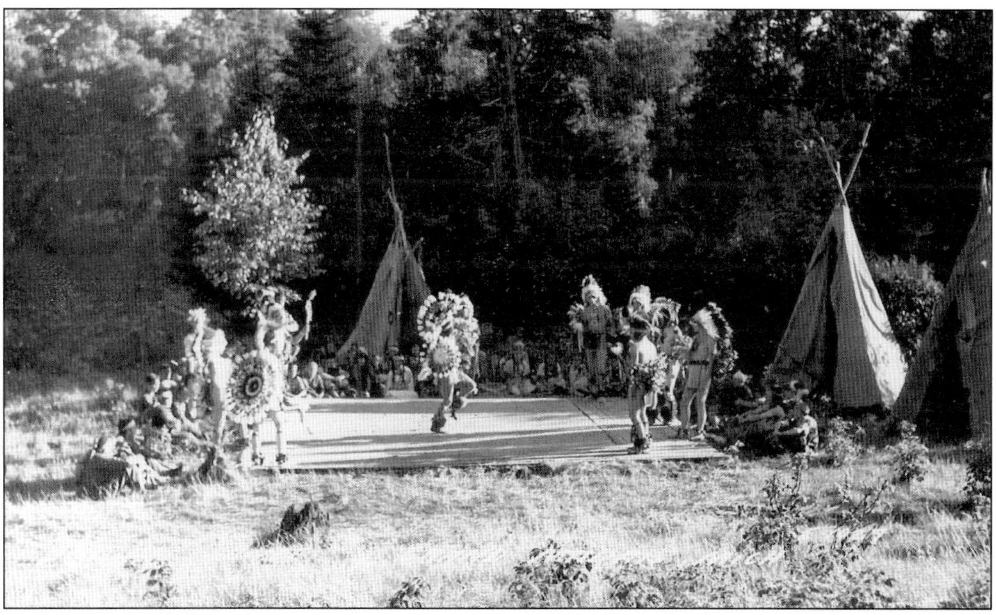

Grand Marais is linked to Henry Wadsworth Longfellow's epic poem *The Song of Hiawatha*. The word *gitchigumi* means "great water" in Ojibwa and refers to Lake Superior. In the 1940s, a summer pageant was performed on the shore of Sable Lake presenting the life of Hiawatha. Local folks and summer residents played the various roles in the pageant. (DVTC.)

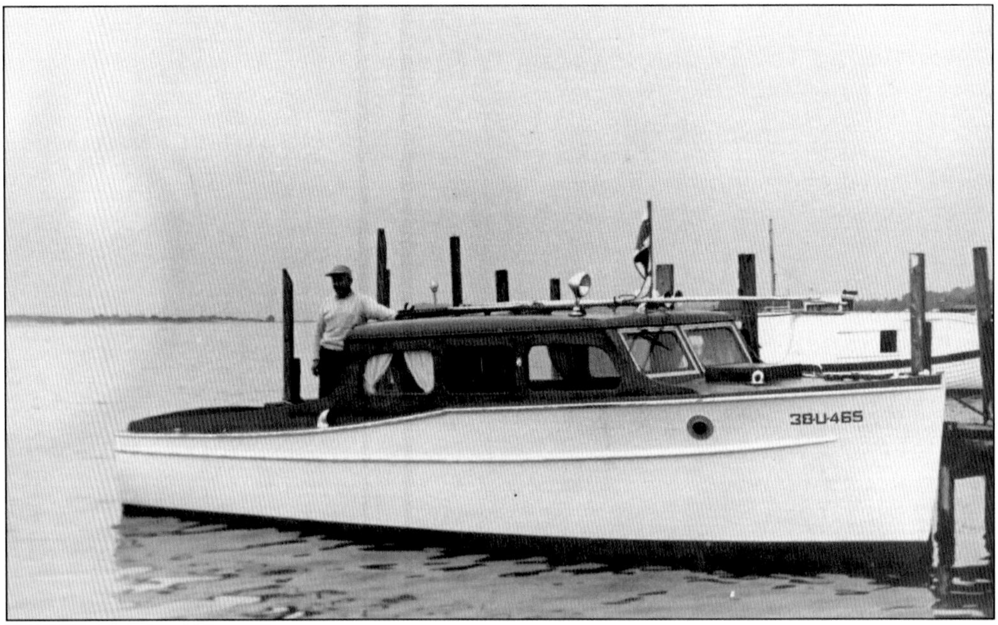

In the 1930s, sport trolling began to take hold in Grand Marais, and a number of charter boat operators began taking visitors on fishing expeditions. Capt. Francis Wood, shown here with his boat the *Evelyn*, came to Grand Marais after World War II. He brought his first boat through the Soo Locks using only a road map. Wood later started Wood's Resort, which is still in business. (Evelyn Wood.)

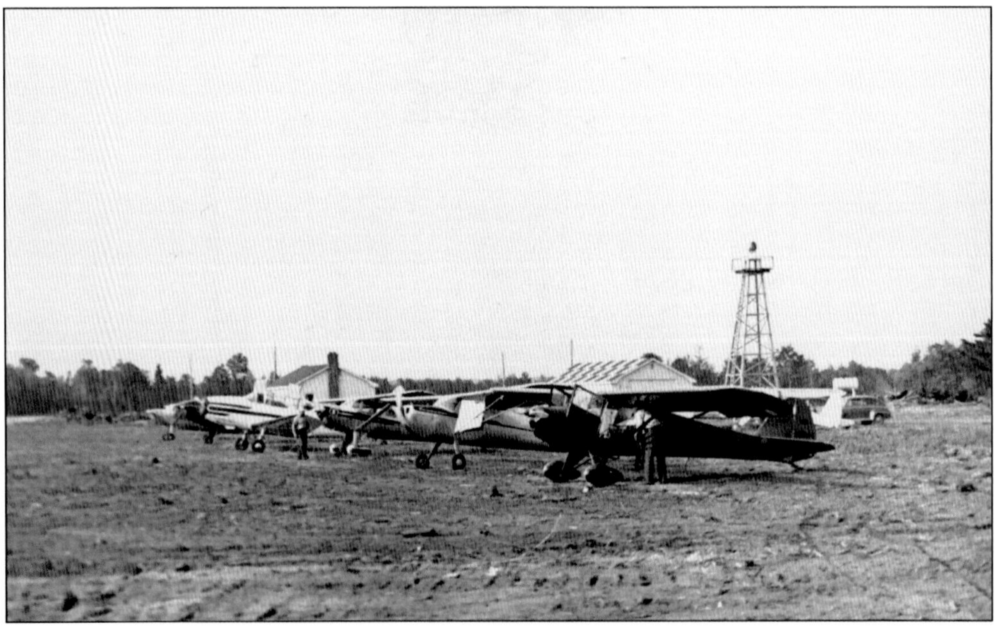

These airplanes landed at the small airstrip outside Grand Marais in the late 1940s, bringing a group of 30 Canadian fishermen to Wood's Resort for sport trolling. Trans-Canada Airways built an emergency airport with two mile-long landing strips outside Grand Marais in 1947. The facility soon became obsolete for landing large airplanes, and it was given to Burt Township in 1959. (Evelyn Wood.)

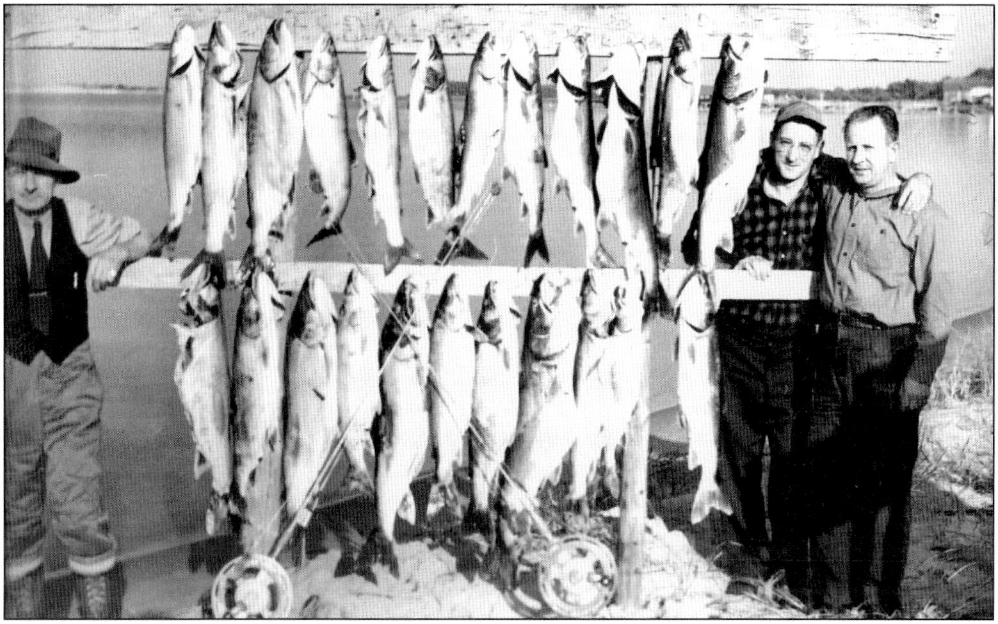

The Canadian fishermen had a great time in Grand Marais, going out six at a time on the local charter fishing boats. In two days, they caught 349 pounds of fish. When the boats came in, townspeople gathered to see the catch, and kids would watch the fish being cleaned. Many of the charter boat operators had a board where fishermen could display their catch and take photographs. (Evelyn Wood.)

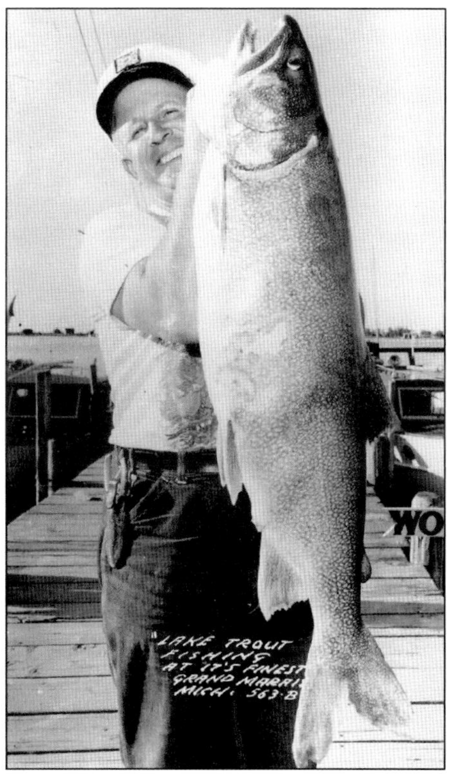

Capt. Francis Wood is shown here with a large lake trout in the mid-1950s. While the photograph is somewhat deceiving, as he is holding the trout closer to the camera, it was not unusual for fishermen to return from the lake with a giant fish or two. Trout fishing had been decimated by the sea lamprey in the 1940s, but lamprey treatment and restocking helped bring it back. (Evelyn Wood.)

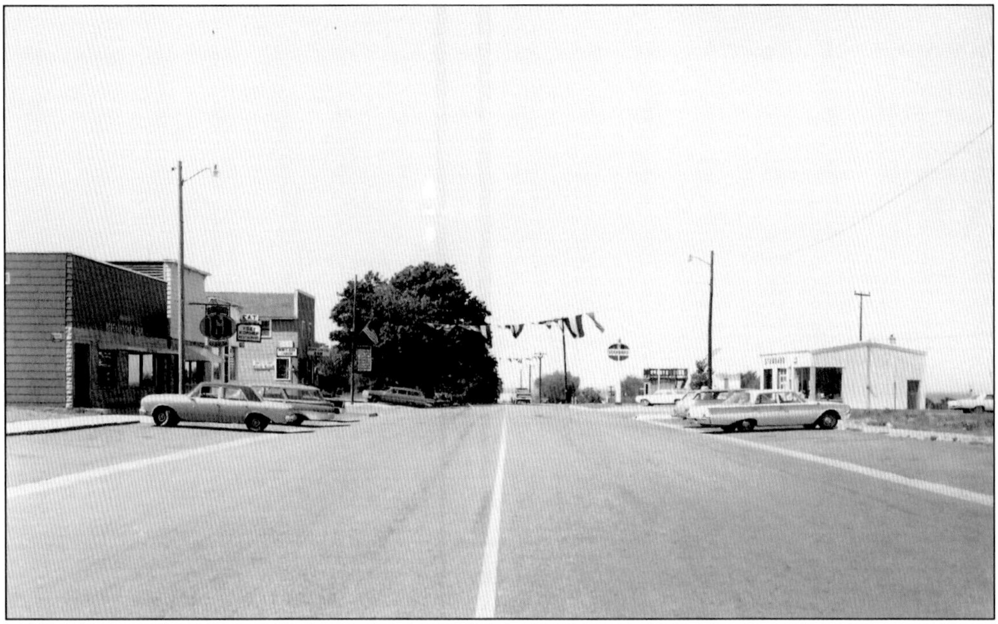

Tourism continued to thrive in Grand Marais, even as the look of the town changed over time. This photograph, taken in the late 1960s, shows Lake Avenue looking north. On the right is a new Standard station, built on the site where the former garage burned down in 1962. The lot next to it, where the same fire claimed the big department store, remains empty. (GMHS.)

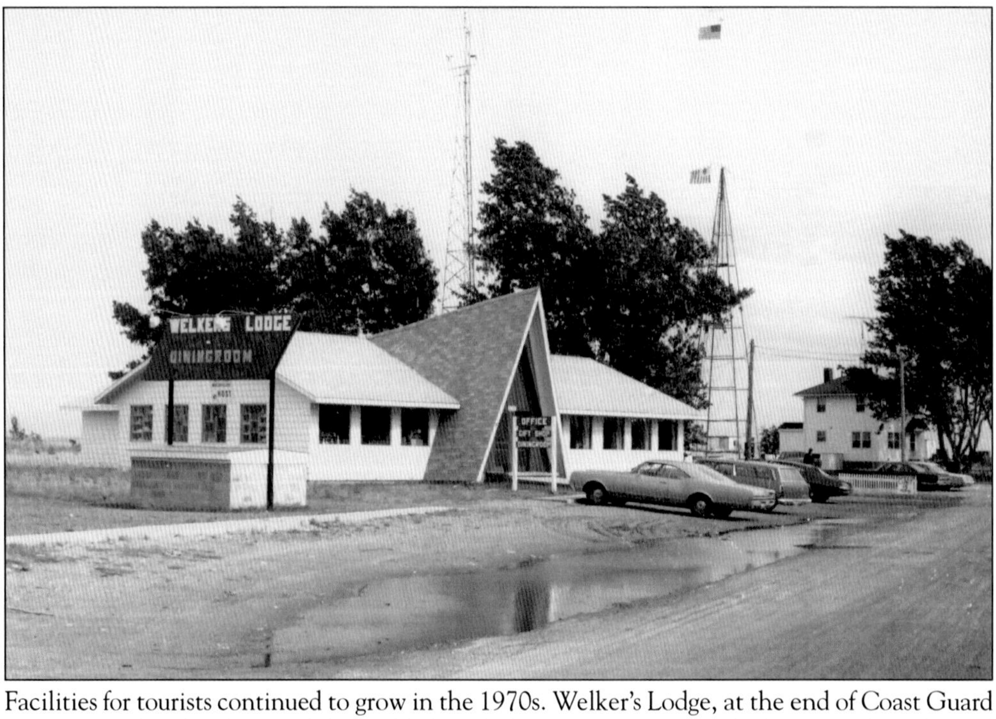

Facilities for tourists continued to grow in the 1970s. Welker's Lodge, at the end of Coast Guard Point, started with cabins and then added a gift shop, a restaurant, and a large number of motel units. The property reaches the bay on one side and Lake Superior on the other. Today it is the largest lodging establishment in Grand Marais. (Peoples State Bank.)

Nine

Grand Marais Today

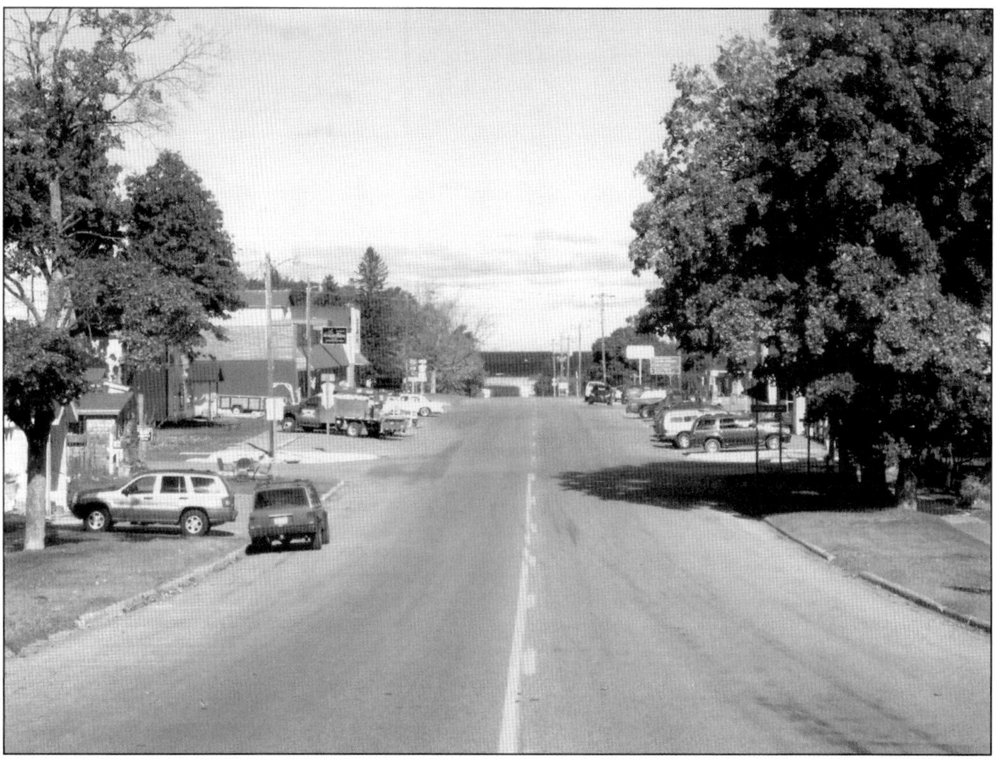

Today Grand Marais is a popular all-season destination point for tourists. Lake Avenue runs north to Lake Superior and businesses line the street. A 25-stop walking tour gives visitors a glimpse into the rich past of the town. Dozens of buildings dating back to the boom years of 1890–1910 still remain in the village and are occupied to this day. (GMHS.)

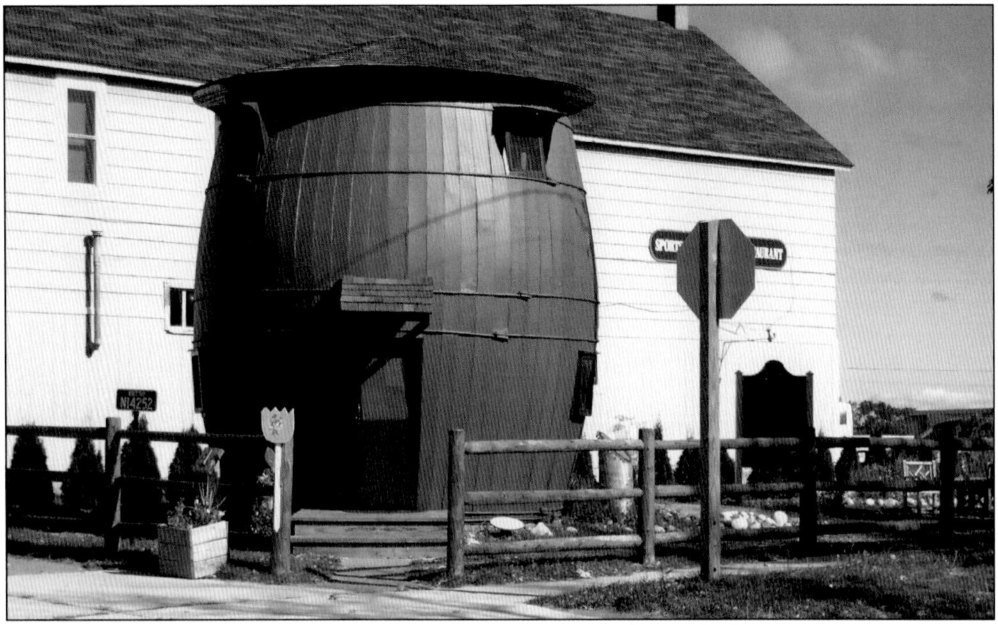

The famous Pickle Barrel House was built in 1926 by Reid, Murdoch and Company as a gift for cartoonist William Donahey, creator of the *Teenie Weenies* cartoons. Donahey and his wife, Mary, used the barrel as a summer home for 10 years. It was moved from its original location on Sable Lake to downtown Grand Marais in 1937. The house is now a museum open to the public. (GMHS.)

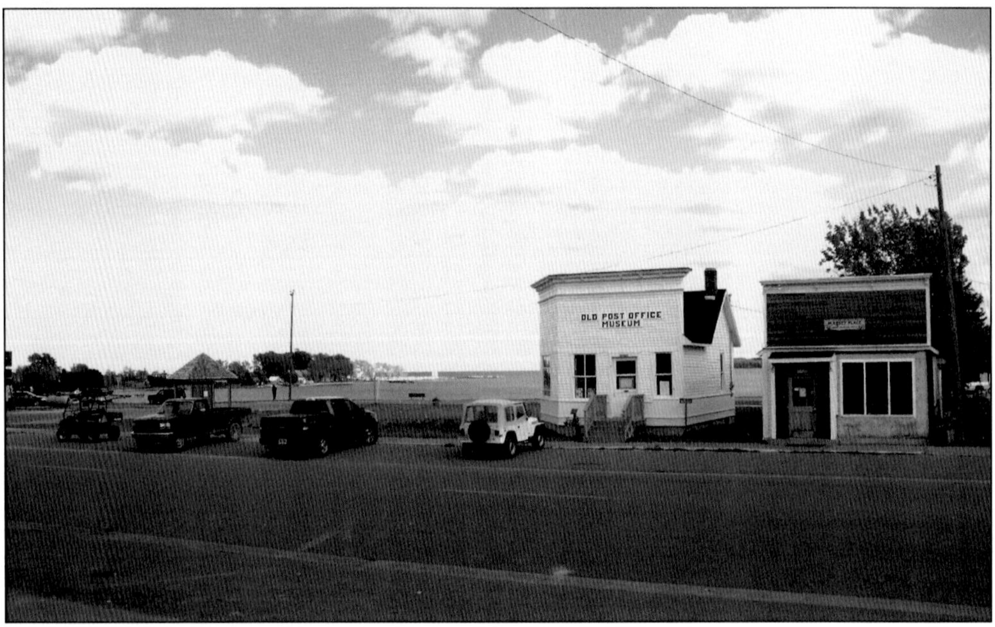

In recent years, the historical landscape of Grand Marais has transformed. The Pickle Barrel House Museum opened in 2005, the historical walking tour was renovated in 2006, and in 2007, the old post office was rescued from demolition and moved onto Lake Avenue. It is now a museum of local history. The harbor, beyond, is under threat from sand infill due to the deterioration of the old break wall. (GMHS.)

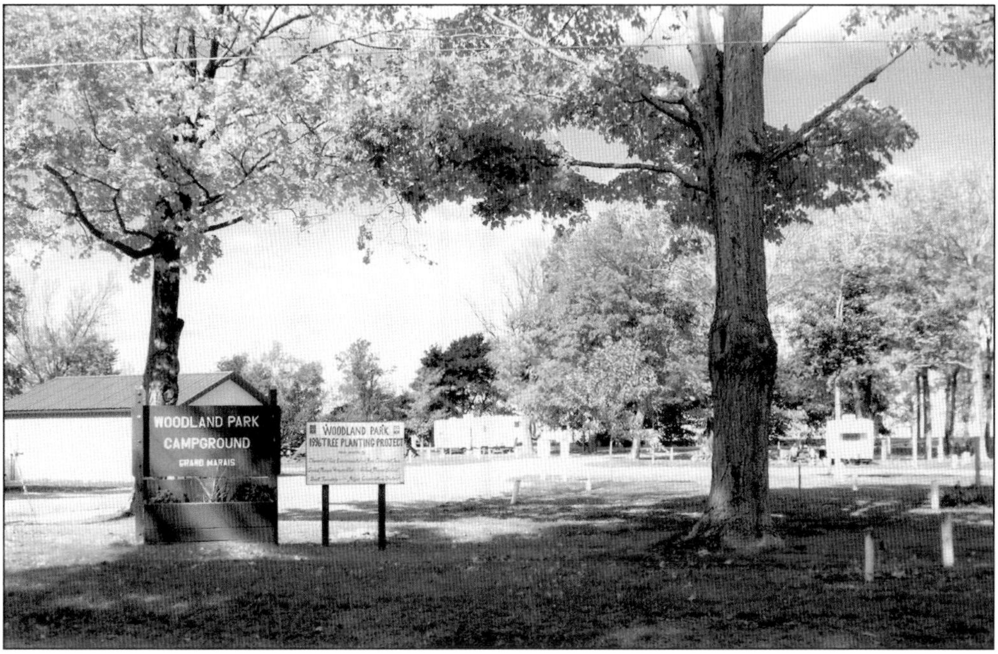

Woodland Park Campground, stretching nearly a half mile along Lake Superior two blocks from the main street, draws campers from all over the country to enjoy the pristine beach and modern amenities. The campground is owned by the township and has been in use since 1902, when it first opened on land donated by prominent area businessmen and lumbermen. (GMHS.)

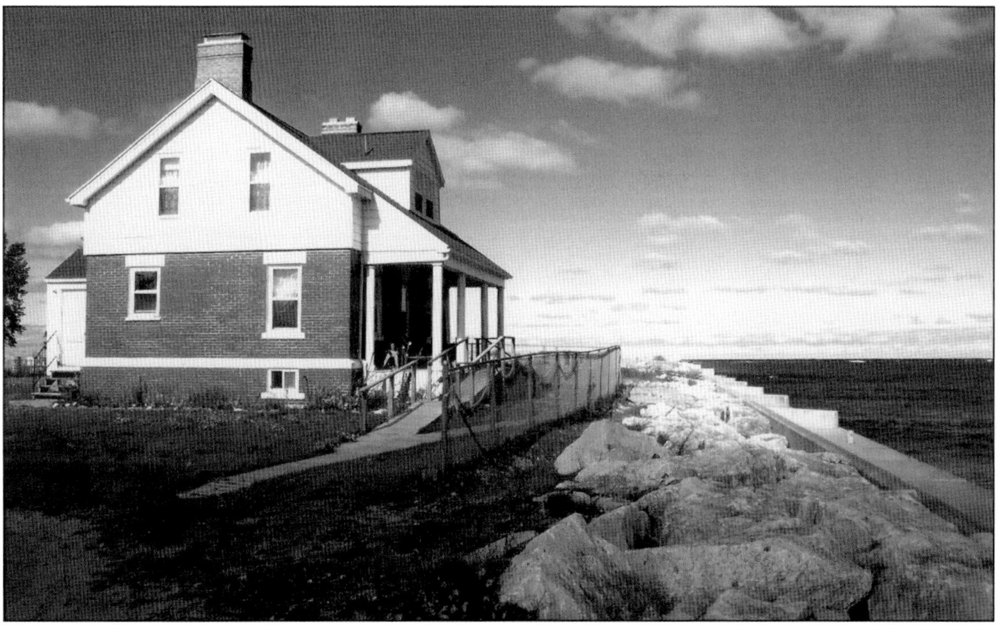

Today the original home of the Grand Marais lightkeeper is owned by the National Park Service. The Grand Marais Historical Society operates the building as the Lightkeeper's House Museum. The museum is open daily during the summer and offers visitors a glimpse into life in Grand Marais at the beginning of the 20th century. The long pier stretching beyond to the outer range light is a popular fishing spot. (GMHS.)

BIBLIOGRAPHY

Canfield, Edward J., and Thomas A. Allan. *Life on a Lonely Shore*. Sault Ste. Marie, MI: Lake Superior State University Press, 1991.

Carter, James. *Voyageur's Harbor*. Grand Marais, MI: Pilot Press, 1977.

Crowe, William S. *Lumberjack*. Skandia, MI: North Country Publishing, 2002.

Karamanski, Theodore J. *Deep Woods Frontier*. Detroit: Wayne State University Press, 1989.

Noble, Dennis L., and T. Michael O'Brien. *Sentinels of the Rocks*. Marquette, MI: Northern Michigan University Press, 1979.

Peters, Bernard C. *Lake Superior Journal: Bela Hubbard's Account of the 1840 Houghton Expedition*. Marquette, MI: Northern Michigan University Press, 1983.

———. *Lake Superior Place Names: From Bawating to the Montreal*. Marquette, MI: Northern Michigan University Press, 1996.

Pyle, Susan N., ed. *A Most Superior Land*. Lansing, MI: Two Peninsula Press, 1983.

Sivertson, Howard. *The Illustrated Voyageur: Paintings and Companion Stories*. Duluth, MN: Lake Superior Port Cities Press, 1999.

Stonehouse, Frederick. *Wreck Ashore: The United States Life-Saving Service on the Great Lakes*. Duluth, MN: Lake Superior Port Cities, Inc., 1994.

Wreck and Rescue Journal. *They Had to Go Out: True Stories of America's Coastal Lifesavers*. Gwinn, MI: Avery Color Studios, 2007.

www.boatnerd.com

www.terrypepper.com

About the Grand Marais Historical Society

The Grand Marais Historical Society was founded in 1982 to preserve and protect the historical features of the Grand Marais area. One of the goals of the society is to share local history through education, exhibits, and publications. Society volunteers staff three museums and a walking tour.

The Lightkeeper's House Museum, located on Coast Guard Point, showcases life in the early 1900s in the restored lightkeeper's residence, which has been furnished with period items. The museum is open on weekends in June and September and daily in July and August. Admission is free; donations are welcome.

The Pickle Barrel House Museum is a unique barrel home once used as a summer cottage by cartoonist William Donahey and his wife. Originally erected on the shore of Sable Lake west of town, it was moved into Grand Marais in 1937 and functioned as an information booth, ice-cream stand, and gift shop. The historical society acquired the empty building in 2004 and restored it to resemble the original cottage. The Pickle Barrel House is on the National Register of Historic Places and the Michigan Register of Historic Sites. The museum is open on weekends in June and September and daily in July and August. Admission is free; donations are welcome.

The Promenade through the Past historic tour is a 25-stop, self-guided walking/bicycling tour around Grand Marais. Historic buildings and sites of interest are highlighted. Guidebooks are available for a nominal fee at local businesses and museums.

The Old Post Office Museum showcases the history of the Grand Marais area. The building was constructed about 1895 and housed the Grand Marais post office from 1907 to 1978. It has a unique five-sided shape. The historical society acquired the building in 2007 and moved it one block to a new location on Lake Avenue.

More information about the Grand Marais Historical Society, including a membership form, can be found online at the historical society Web site, http://historicalsociety.grandmaraismichigan.com.

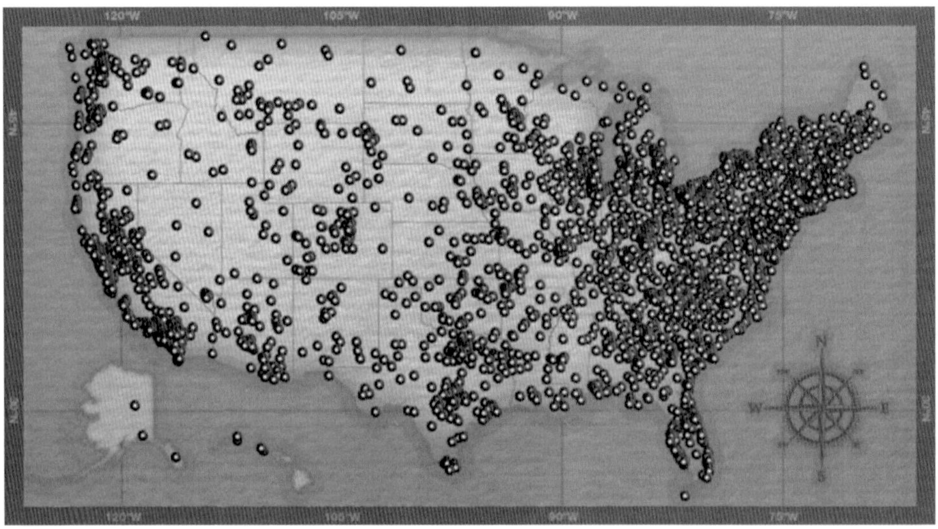

Consistent with our mission to preserve history on a local level, this book was printed in South Carolina on American-made paper and manufactured entirely in the United States. Products carrying the accredited Forest Stewardship Council (FSC) label are printed on 100 percent FSC-certified paper.

MADE IN THE USA